Postcolonial Representations

Reading
WOMEN
Writing

a series edited by
Shari Benstock and Celeste Schenck

Reading Women Writing is dedicated to furthering international feminist debate. The series publishes books on all aspects of feminist theory and textual practice. *Reading Women Writing* especially welcomes books that address cultures, histories, and experience beyond first-world academic boundaries. A complete list of titles in the series appears at the end of the book.

Postcolonial Representations

WOMEN, LITERATURE, IDENTITY

Françoise Lionnet

Cornell University Press

ITHACA AND LONDON

First published 1995 by Cornell University Press.

Printed in the United States of America

∞ The paper in this book meets the minimum requirements of
the American National Standard for Information Sciences—
Permanence of Paper for Printed Library Materials, ANSI Z39.48–1984.

Library of Congress Cataloging-in-Publication Data

Lionnet, Françoise.
  Postcolonial representations : women, literature, identity / Françoise Lionnet.
    p. cm.—(Reading women writing)
  Includes bibliographical references and index.
  ISBN 0-8014-2984-6.—ISBN 0-8014-8180-5 (paper)
    1. Women authors—20th century.   2. Women and literature.   3. Feminism and literature.   4. Literature, Modern—20th century—History and criticism.
  I. Title. II. Series.
PN471.L57 1995
809.3'99287—dc20   94-45471

for my families

Only in the fragments of ancient murmurings do I see how we must look for a restoration of the conversation between women . . . Only in the door open to the full sun . . . do I hope for a concrete and daily liberation of women.

—Assia Djebar, *Women of Algiers in Their Apartment*

Contents

viii   Contents

Preface

The reflections in this book have been largely informed by the kind of interdisciplinary work that feminist inquiry made possible since the 1980s. In the age of "cultural studies" interdisciplinarity has become the norm, but feminism continues to live up to its early promise. I believe that working across disciplines still means doing what feminism meant originally for Simone de Beauvoir in *The Second Sex*: questioning the ways in which a concept—be it "woman," "culture," or "difference"—comes to create a reality that is then ossified into an object of study urgently requiring reading and interpretation if it is to retain its usefulness as a category. To do this kind of interpretive reading, we must first of all immerse ourselves and our students in a broad concept of culture and literature, of literature as one aspect of culture among others, albeit an aspect that has a privileged relationship to the representation of subjectivity. The study of literature gives us insight into the mediated process of reading and decoding which is central to most of our cultural activities. Literature opens us up to a more complex understanding of difference and "marginality." My work attempts to question this notion of marginality itself, centering as it does on "noncanonical" women writers whose concerns intersect with two major issues of our time: identity and authenticity. These are issues that have to do with the vexed relationship between the particular and universal, the local and the global. As I see it, the challenge is, more than ever, to build bridges between the academy and the "real world" without replicating the divisions and the debilitating dogmas that can become cultural currency in both arenas.

Many people have helped me in many ways with this project. The writers themselves have given me invaluable encouragement, and I especially thank Maryse Condé and Nawal El Saadawi. Among the supportive colleagues I am very fortunate to have at Northwestern, I am grateful to Madhu Dubey for her generous and careful reading of the whole manuscript at a crucial stage of revision, and to the chair of French and Italian, William D. Paden, for flexible schedules and financial help for the color cover. My students have kept me grounded, and without their questions and objections the book would have been far less interesting than I hope to have made it. For their stimulating insights I owe a special debt to Traci Carroll, Mella Davis, Anne Donadey, Mara Dukats, Belinda Edmundson, Bishnu Ghosh, Russell Hopley, Jeanne Matthews, James McGuire, and Beth Willey. I am grateful to Joseph Heath for his help with translations of chapters previously published in French. Tomoko Kuribayashi and Chelsea Hardaway gave me much needed assistance with research and with technical aspects of word processing.

My research was supported by the American Philosophical Society, the American Council of Learned Societies, and Northwestern University's College of Arts and Sciences in the form of an AT&T faculty fellowship. The Rockefeller Foundation provided me with the opportunity to be humanist-in-residence at the Center for Advanced Feminist Studies of the University of Minnesota in Minneapolis. I thank the wonderful faculty and staff of the center—Shirley Garner, Naomi Scheman, and Karen Moon in particular—and my fellow Rockefeller Fellow during the 1991–92 year, Obioma Nnaemeka, whose critical acumen and contagious laughter were tremendously helpful. As a member of the "Minority Discourse Initiative," I benefited greatly from the stimulating discussions in our Tuesday seminars at the University of California Humanities Research Institute in Irvine. I am grateful to the institute for the residency fellowship it generously offered in the winter of 1992; to the convener, Abdul JanMohamed; and to the other fellows for rigorous and careful readings of my work. I thank Norma Alarcón, José Amaya, Vincent Cheng, King-Kok

Cheung, Anne Dannenberg, Emory Elliott, May Joseph, Haiming Liu, Lisa Lowe, Lilian Manzor-Coats, and Sterling Stuckey. I am grateful to James Clifford and Meyda Yegenoglu for inviting me to present my ideas at the Center for Cultural Studies at the University of California, Santa Cruz.

Various drafts of the chapters in this book were shared with academic audiences in this country and abroad. Their responses have always been stimulating and have forced me to clarify and develop many points. I am especially grateful for the interest that colleagues in many different institutions have shown over the past five years. Without them, this book would have taken much longer to write. I thank Valentin Y. Mudimbe for inviting me to participate in his session at the English Institute in 1990; Margaret Higonnet for asking me to discuss my research with the Study Group on Gender, Society, and Politics at the Center for European Studies, Harvard University; Elizabeth Mudimbe-Boyi for her comments on early drafts of several chapters; Ginette Adamson, Réda Bensmaïa, Vèvè Clark, Ava Collins, Jane Doering, Jean-François Fourny, Mary Jean Green, Ketu Katrak, Leslie Rabine, Claudine Raynaud, Sidonie Smith, Mireille Rosello, Julia Watson, Cathy West, and Winifred Woodhull for their questions, comments, and conversations; Salem Mekuria for her interest in my work on excision; and Bella Brodzki, Ronnie Scharfman, and Louise Yelin for their unflinching support. I am grateful to Nora Rodríguez Vallés for allowing me to use her art work for the cover, and to Agnes Lugo-Ortiz for putting us in touch.

Most of all I thank John McCumber for arguing me out of some of my obsessions, and Jonathan and Danielle for tolerating them with such good nature.

My editor at Cornell University Press, Bernhard Kendler, has been immensely patient and understanding and deserves special recognition. I thank Kay Scheuer, Patricia Sterling, and Barbara Salazar for their intelligent and careful editing.

The chapters in this book first appeared as journal articles. They have been revised and are reprinted here by permission:

—"*Logiques métisses:* Cultural Appropriation and Postcolonial Representations," *College Literature* 19 and 20 (1992/1993): 100–120.

—"Of Mangoes and Maroons: Language, History, and the Multicultural Subject of Michelle Cliff's *Abeng,*" *De/Colonizing the Subject:*

Gender and the Politics of Women's Autobiography, ed. Sidonie Smith and Julia Watson (Minneapolis: University of Minnesota Press, 1992), 321–45. Copyright 1992 by the Regents of the University of Minnesota.

—"Evading the Subject: Narration and the City in Ananda Devi's *Rue La Poudrière*," *L'Esprit Créateur* 32 (Summer 1993): 9–22.

—"*Traversée de la mangrove* de Maryse Condé: Vers un nouvel humanisme antillais?" *French Review* 66 (February 1993): 475–86.

—"Savoir du corps et écriture de l'exil: Les Romancières de la diaspora antillaise et le mythe de l'authenticité," *L'Express: Culture and Research* 1 (December 1991): 2–7, and in *L'Héritage de Caliban*, ed. Maryse Condé et al. (Paris: Editions Jasor, 1992): 111–21. It appeared in English as "Inscriptions of Exile: The Body's Knowledge and the Myth of Authenticity," *Callaloo* 15 (1992): 30–40.

—"Geographies of Pain: Captive Bodies and Violent Acts in the Fictions of Gayl Jones, Bessie Head, and Myriam Warner-Vieyra," *Callaloo* 16 (1993): 132–52.

—"Dissymmetry Embodied: Feminism, Universalism, and the Practice of Excision," *Passages: A Chronicle of the Humanities* 1 (1991): 2–4, and in *Borderwork: Feminist Engagements with Comparative Literature*, ed. Margaret Higonnet (Ithaca: Cornell University Press, 1994), 19–41. Copyright © 1994 by Cornell University. Used by permission of Cornell University Press.

—"Identity, Sexuality, and Criminality: The Legal Debate around the Issue of Female Excision in France," *Contemporary French Civilization* 16 (Summer–Fall 1992): 294–307.

—"Parcours narratif, Itinéraire culturel," in *Modernité, Fiction, Deconstruction, Etudes romanesques* 2 (Lettres Modernes-Minard, 1994): 137–58.

Chapters 3, 4, and 8 were translated by Joseph Heath. All other translations are mine unless specified otherwise.

Permission to quote from the following is also gratefully acknowledged:

—Louise Bogan, *The Blue Estuaries: Poems, 1923–1968* (New York: Farrar, Straus & Giroux, 1968).

—Gwendolyn Brooks, *Blacks* (Chicago: Third World Press, 1992).

—Michelle Cliff, *Abeng* (Trumansburg, N.Y.: Crossing Press, 1984); *Claiming an Identity They Taught Me to Despise* (Watertown, Mass.:

Persephone Press, 1980); *The Land of Look Behind* (Ithaca, N.Y.: Fire-brand Books, 1985).
—Maryse Condé, *Traversée de la mangrove* (Paris: Mercure de France, 1989).
—Tsitsi Dangaremba, *Nervous Conditions* (Seattle: Seal Press, 1989).
—Ananda Devi, *Rue La Poudrière* (Abidjan: Nouvelles Editions Africaines, 1988).
—Assia Djebar, *Women of Algiers in Their Apartment*, trans. Marjolijn de Jager (Charlottesville: University Press of Virginia, 1992). Used with permission of the University Press of Virginia.
—Suzanne Dracius-Pinalie, *L'Autre qui danse* (Paris: Seghers, 1989). © Seghers.
—Bessie Head, *The Collector of Treasures* (London: Heinemann, 1977). Published by Heinemann Educational Books Ltd. in the African Writers Series. Copyright © The Estate of Bessie Head, 1977.
—Gayl Jones, *Eva's Man* (Boston: Beacon Press, 1977).
—Audre Lorde, *The Black Unicorn* (New York: W. W. Norton & Co., 1978). Copyright © 1978 by Audre Lord.
—Nawal El Saadawi, *The Hidden Face of Eve: Women in the Arab World*, trans. Sherif Hetata (London: Zed Books, 1980); *Woman at Point Zero*, trans. Sherif Hetata (London: Zed Books, 1983).
—Leïla Sebbar, *Shérazade* (Paris: Stock, 1982); *Les Carnets de Shérazade* (Paris: Stock, 1985); *Lettres parisiennes: Autopsie de l'exil* (Paris: Bernard Barrault, 1986).
—Myriam Warner-Vieyra, *As the Sorcerer Said . . .* , trans. Dorothy S. Blair (Essex: Longman, 1982); *Juletane*, trans. Betty Wilson (London: Heinemann Publishers [Oxford], Ltd, 1987).

FRANÇOISE LIONNET
Evanston, Illinois

Abbreviations of Frequently Cited Works

A	Michelle Cliff, *Abeng* (Trumansburg, N.Y.: Crossing Press, 1984).
AV	Françoise Lionnet, *Autobiographical Voices: Race Gender, Self-Portraiture* (Ithaca: Cornell University Press, 1989).
CD	Edouard Glissant, *Caribbean Discourse: Selected Essays*, trans. J. Michael Dash (Charlottesville: University Press of Virginia, 1989).
CI	Michelle Cliff, *Claiming an Identity They Taught Me to Despise* (Watertown, Mass.: Persephone Press, 1980).
CS	Leïla Sebbar, *Les Carnets de Shérazade* (Paris: Stock, 1985).
CT	Bessie Head, *The Collector of Treasures* (London: Heinemann, 1977).
EM	Gayl Jones, *Eva's Man* (Boston: Beacon Press, 1977).
F	Myriam Warner-Vieyra, *Femmes échouées* (Paris: Présence Africaine, 1987).
H	Maryse Condé, *Heremakhonon* (Paris: UGE 10/18, 1976); *Heremakhonon*, trans. Richard Philcox (Washington, D.C.: Three Continents Press, 1982).
J	Myriam Warner-Vieyra, *Juletane* (Paris: Présence Africaine, 1982); *Juletane*, trans. Betty Wilson (London: Heinemann, 1987).
L'A	Suzanne Dracius-Pinalie, *L'Autre qui danse* (Paris: Seghers, 1989).
LLB	Michelle Cliff, *The Land of Look Behind* (Ithaca, N.Y.: Firebrand Books, 1985).
MP	Abdelkebir Khatibi, *Maghreb pluriel* (Paris: Denoël, 1983).
OK	Carole B. Davies and Elaine S. Fido, *Out of the Kumbla: Caribbean Women and Literature* (Trenton, N.J.: Africa World Press, 1990).
PR	Edouard Glissant, *Poétique de la relation* (Paris: Gallimard, 1990).
Q/S	Myriam Warner-Vieyra, *Le Quimboiseur l'avait dit . . .* (Paris: Présence Africaine, 1980), *As the Sorcerer Said . . .*, trans. Dorothy S. Blair (Essex: Longman, 1982).
RP	Ananda Devi, *Rue La Poudrière* (Abidjan: Nouvelles Editions Africaines, 1988).

Sh   Leïla Sebbar, *Shérazade, 17 ans, brune, frisée, les yeux verts* (Paris: Stock, 1982); *Shérazade. Missing: Aged 17, Dark Hair, Green Eyes,* trans. Dorothy S. Blair (London: Quartet Books, 1991).

W   Nawal el Saadawi, *Woman at Point Zero* (1975), trans. Sherif Hetata (London: Zed, 1983).

Postcolonial Representations

Introduction
Logiques métisses:
Cultural Appropriation and
Postcolonial Representations

Then, as before, I desperately dreamed of home ... As *I* remembered home, it was a battlefield, a boiling cauldron ...
If this weird, upside-down caricature of a country called America, if this land of refugees and former indentured servants, religious heretics and half-breeds, whoresons and fugitives—this cauldron of mongrels from all points on the compass—was all I could rightly call *home*, then aye: I was of it.
　　　　　　　　　—Charles Johnson, *Middle Passage*

However, there is no choice; it is necessary to learn, and with the tools at our disposal: a colonized body of knowledge and an adulterated language.
　　　　　　　　　—Claudine Herrmann, *The Tongue Snatchers*

The experience of academic feminist criticism since the 1970s has created almost insurmountable differences between "Western" modes of analysis of the concrete status of women in various non-Western cultures on the one hand, and non-Western women's subjective experience of their own position on the other. Whether it is conflict between "American" and "French" approaches, "essentialist" and "poststructuralist" epistemologies, or "first" and "third" world women, differences of ideology fuel disagreements that threaten to preclude dialogue. In such a climate, it has become imperative to reexamine the ground from which such conflicts develop and to try to modulate and nuance the conceptual frameworks that generate these oppositions. To do so, I propose a truly *comparative* feminist criticism, one performed on the border between those disciplinary categories. Such an approach aims not at conflict resolution but rather at reframing the issues in such a way that dialogue can remain open and productive, allowing critics to map out new articulations of cultural expressions.

Some critics have recently suggested that feminism should not be considered a "unitary entity . . . *in* which conflicts can or should be contained," and that feminist activism cannot be subsumed "under the illusion of unitary governing ideal," be it "woman" or "truth."[1] This argument implies that we might be ill advised to appeal to a set of "universal" (that is, Western humanist) values that would allow feminists to come to a consensus about the possibility of sharing certain beliefs or points of views regarding both the nature and function of feminism as a global process and the social construction of femininity within different cultural contexts. The point is well taken: ethnocentric value judgments have no place within a truly diverse, multicultural, and multiracial feminist inquiry. But does this necessarily mean that the only acceptable approach to a demystified multicultural feminist practice is the one based in cultural relativism? Is there a distinction to be made between *cultural* and *moral* relativism? What are the grounds upon which we might ask, as did Ralph Ellison's *Invisible Man*, "Who knows but that on the lower frequencies, I speak for you?"[2] Can feminist theory articulate common questions for a multicultural practice? What are the preconditions under which the formulations of identity and difference do not risk becoming static categories used to polarize and fragment intellectual and political communities?

The question of universalism comes back to haunt us if we do not carefully examine the consequences of a cultural relativism marked by ignorance of and indifference to everything non-Western, and thus exemplifying what Kathleen Barry has called a form of "Western liberal particularism that says 'hands off' to anything produced in Third-World nations or cultures." Antiethnocentrism can have the unfortunate consequence of undermining feminist political solidarity, and this kind of liberalism reinforces "Third World masculinist nationalism [that] . . . attempts to isolate women in their cultures and identify western women as their enemy."[3] It is therefore important to continue speaking of community

---

[1]Marianne Hirsch and Evleyn Fox Keller, eds., *Conflicts in Feminism* (New York: Routledge, Chapman & Hall, 1990), 2.

[2]Ralph Ellison, *Invisible Man* (New York: Vintage, 1972), 568.

[3]Kathleen Barry, Foreword to Evelyne Accad, *Sexuality and War: Literary Masks of the Middle East* (New York: New York University Press, 1990), ix. I am emphatically

and to attempt to find a common theoretical and ethical ground from which to argue for political solidarity without objectifying the "other" woman, or subsuming collective goals under the banner of sameness. As Gayatri Spivak stated in 1981: "However unfeasible and inefficient it may sound, I see no way to avoid insisting that there is a simultaneous other focus: not merely who am I? but who is the other woman? How am I naming her? How does she name me?"[4] And, I would add, *how does she name herself* in her own narratives? How does she find meaning in her own experiences, and how does she understand the role of language in her effort to name these experiences? How is she constructed by the paratextual apparatus that accompanies the marketing of her book and that may well contradict this self-naming? Finally, how does she articulate her relationship to a global system (of knowledge, of representation, of capital) within which her narratives are inevitably inscribed, yet not fully contained? Although these narratives exceed the power of such a system to circumscribe their meaning, they also reflect the dynamics engendered by the global system and its local manifestations. They are therefore an important site in which to study the personal, cultural, and political transformations that are the legacy both of the colonial encounter and of the postcolonial "arts of resistance" it produces.[5]

Throughout this book, I use the term "postcolonial;" it has acquired currency in critical academic circles and is unavoidable. I am nevertheless well aware that it can often be used imprecisely, generally connoting a utopian condition that seems to deny the facts of *neo*colonialism. What I want to suggest in my use of this

---

suggesting not that Hirsch and Keller are guilty of this kind of liberalism but that their theoretical positions might lead to such logical consequences.

[4] Gayatri Spivak, "French Feminism in an International Frame," *Yale French Studies* 62 (1981): 179. Feminist critics have used these lines to underscore the need for a "particularist" or "relativist" approach to the study of different cultures. See Elizabeth Abel, "Race, Class, Psychoanalysis? Opening Questions," in Hirsch and Keller, *Conflicts in Feminism*, 197–99; Jane Gallop, "The Monster in the Mirror: The Feminist Critic's Psychoanalysis," in *Feminism and Psychoanalysis*, ed. Richard Feldstein and Judith Roof (Ithaca: Cornell University Press, 1989), 13–24; and Helena Michie, "Not One of the Family: The Repression of the Other Woman in Feminist Theory," in *Discontented Discourses: Feminism/Textual Intervention/Psychoanalysis*, ed. Marleen S. Barr and Richard Feldstein (Urbana: University of Illinois Press, 1989), 15–28.

[5] See James C. Scott, *Domination and the Arts of Resistance* (New Haven: Yale University Press, 1990); Michel de Certeau, *The Practice of Everyday Life* (Berkeley: University of California Press, 1984).

word is that it refers to more than the static periodization that the "post-" implies. In fact, I find it useful to think of "postcoloniality" in terms of "postcontact": that is, as a condition that exists within, and thus contests and resists, the colonial moment itself with its ideology of domination. Within the tradition of Francophone writings, the one that has most strongly shaped my thinking about these issues, movements such as *négritude* and *indigénisme* were already "postcolonial," as were the writings of Frantz Fanon and Albert Memmi. To these thinkers who wrote during the colonial era, one can add the names of Edouard Glissant, Abdelkebir Khatibi, and Hélène Cixous, who are more properly *post*colonial, historically speaking. The women writers I discuss here form part of this tradition, which they in turn transform. It is by focusing on subjective elements and giving them broad relevance that these writers succeed in creating an intersubjective space where dialogue is possible.

My point is neither to suggest that the particular (that is, personal and local) experience of a given writer should be taken as an exemplar of the general (that is, sociopolitical and global) situation of a collectivity, nor to fold all the complex traditions and cultural practices of non-Western peoples into the discursive universes and narrative grammars available to Western-trained writers whose novels I examine. Nor am I suggesting that individual and personal voices are the only legitimate locus for analyzing global political issues or, to put it another way, that the personal is political in a static way.[6] My focus in on the *processes* that produce the personal and make it historically and politically unique; that is, I am interested in the different forms of métissage that exist in different geographical contexts. Understood as a dynamic model of relationality, I argue, métissage is "universal" even if, in each specific context, power relations produce widely varying configurations, hierarchies, dissymmetries, and contradictions. My purpose is to look at the interconnectedness of different traditions, to examine

[6]For a discussion of what is involved in the all too problematic leap between the merely personal and the broadly political, see Chandra T. Mohanty, "On Race and Voice: Challenges for Liberal Education in the 1990s," *Cultural Critique* 14 (Winter 1989–90): 179–208. See also Françoise Lionnet, *Autobiographical Voices: Race, Gender, Self-Portraiture* (Ithaca: Cornell University Press, 1989)—hereafter abbreviated *AV*—for an analysis of the way history and politics determine the "personal."

the approaches and insights of women writers, and to outline those writers' contributions to our understanding of complex identities and to the métissage of cultures. Teresa de Lauretis has analyzed the feminist subject as *"not unified* or *simply divided* between posi-tions of masculinity and femininity, but *multiply organized* across positionalities along several axes and across mutually contradictory discourses and practices."[7] Women writing in postcolonial contexts show us precisely how the subject is "multiply organized" across cultural boundaries, since this subject speaks several different lan-guages (male and female, colonial and indigenous, global and local, among others). The postcolonial subject thus becomes quite adept at braiding all the traditions at its disposal, using the fragments that constitute it in order to participate fully in a dynamic process of transformation.

The term "universalism" as I use it names the practice of the women who write in the interstices between domination and resis-tance. These authors refuse to be heard as merely idiosyncratic voices. They appropriate the concept of universality in order to give it a new valence and to define broader commonalities. They do not embed it in the context of Enlightenment philosophy. Rather, they attempt to distance it from the imperialist postures of the sovereign subject. Enlightenment claims about selfhood and individuality were underwritten by the simultaneous othering of those who had to be spoken *for* because they were said not to possess reason (slaves, women, children, the mad, the incarcerated, the disenfran-chised). Such "others" could not freely exercise the same rights as "the man of reason"—the only standard by which universality was to be measured and defined.[8] To the extent that postcolonial women writers wish to speak to a community of readers whose diverse experiences they address, their purpose is one of inclusion rather than exclusion. Their works de-exoticize the non-West, indicating the centrality of their concerns to the self-understanding of people everywhere. They insist on the relational nature of identity and difference, on the productive tensions between the two, and on the intricate and interdependent ways in which human agents func-

[7]Teresa de Lauretis, "Displacing Hegemonic Discourses: Reflections on Feminist Theory in the 1980s," *Inscriptions* 3/4 (1988): 136.

[8]See Genevieve Lloyd, *The Man of Reason: "Male" and "Female" in Western Philos-ophy* (Minneapolis: University of Minnesota Press, 1984).

tion.[9] In short, the universalism that is implied by such an approach is not the political ideology of consensus that universal suffrage upholds and that has been characterized as "the tyranny of the majority."[10] But it is grounded in the knowledge that "the West and the rest" share histories, modes of representation and of op-positionality, and that a study of such shared elements can only work against both provincialism and imperialism in "postcolonial" critical studies. It is in such a spirit of dialogue and exchange that these women writers create, and I take my critical cues from the cultural work that their narratives perform. This work, simply put, is engaged in the deconstruction of hierarchies, not in their reversal. The aim, in the end, is to reconstruct new imaginative spaces where power configurations, inevitable as they are, may be reorganized to allow for fewer dissymmetries in the production and circulation of knowledge.

Women writers living and writing in Africa and in the new worlds of the United States, the Caribbean, and the Indian Ocean, as well as those who emigrate to various European countries for personal, educational, professional, or economic reasons, have given us unique insights into what Renato Rosaldo has called the "border zones" of culture.[11] In those areas on the periphery of sta-ble metropolitan cultural discourses, Rosaldo explains, there is an incessant and playful heteroglossia, a bilingual speech or hybrid language that is a site of creative resistance to the dominant con-ceptual paradigms. In border zones, all our academic preconcep-tions about cultural, linguistic, or stylistic norms are constantly being put to the test by creative practices that make visible and set off the processes of adaptation, appropriation, and contestation governing the construction of identity in colonial and postcolonial contexts.

These processes are the ground upon which contemporary global

[9]For a classic approach to these questions, see Albert Memmi, *The Colonizer and the Colonized*, trans. Howard Greenfeld (Boston: Beacon Press, 1967), and *Dependence*, trans. Philip A. Facey (Boston: Beacon Press, 1984).

[10]See Lani Guinier, *The Tyranny of the Majority: Fundamental Fairness in Represen-tative Democracy* (New York: Free Press, 1994).

[11]Renato Rosaldo applies this term to areas of Hispanic influence in the United States. See his "Ideology, Place, and People without Culture," *Cultural Anthropology* 3 (February 1988): 85, and "Politics, Patriarchs, and Laughter," *Cultural Critique* 6 (Spring 1987): 67

culture can begin to be understood, defined, and represented, and postcolonial writers encode the everyday realities and subjective perceptions of a numerical majority whose cultural contributions are still considered to be the products of minority voices. By reproducing the changing cultural practices of this majority as it negotiates the conflicts between tradition and modernity, writers create a space for themselves within the dominant discourses while simultaneously articulating a problematic that is increasingly becoming accepted as a quasi-universal process. The global mongrelization or métissage of cultural forms creates complex identities and interrelated, if not overlapping, spaces. In those spaces, struggles for the control of means of representation and self-identification are mediated by a single and immensely powerful symbolic system: the colonial language and the variations to which it is subjected under the pen of writers who enrich, transform, and creolize it.

Writers such as Michelle Cliff from Jamaica, Ananda Devi from Mauritius, Maryse Condé and Myriam Warner-Vieyra from Guadeloupe, Suzanne Dracius-Pinalie from Martinique, Gayl Jones, an African American, Bessie Head from Botswana, Nawal El Saadawi from Egypt, and Leïla Sebbar, a Franco-Algerian, all share one important characteristic: they belong to an increasing number of astute interpreters of the postcolonial condition whose works, published in the 1970s and 1980s, have been redefining traditional conceptions of history and culture, literature and identity. They create new paradigms that represent, through innovative and self-reflexive literary techniques, both linguistic and geographic exile, displacements from the margins to a metropolitan center, and intercultural exchanges.

In order to understand the cultural and literary praxis of those writers, I want to make a brief incursion into the field of cultural anthropology, a field that has established some of the parameters within which we commonly understand negatively coded terms such as "acculturation" and "assimilation." My purpose is to develop, first of all, a theoretical argument about postcolonial culture. This argument is an eminently political one, and on one level it does address the current academic polemics about various forms of cultural fundamentalism. But my approach tends to be indirect. I want to raise some of these issues by way of the voices of postcolonial women *writers* whose perspectives on multiculturalism differ from those we are most familiar with in the United States. A term like "multiculturalism" takes on different valences in different linguistic and geopolitical contexts: that is, in countries where the relative power of hegemonic and subaltern groups shifts according to factors altogether different from the ones that obtain in this country. That is why the examples I choose are drawn from such diverse contexts. I thus suggest that the writers' concerns and perspectives make an important contribution to these debates, because they echo and often predate those of cultural anthropologists whose theoretical approaches are nonetheless very useful for analyzing the processes at work in the women's novels. My interest in using these novels to understand cultural configurations studied by social scientists is grounded in my belief that literature allows us to enter into the subjective processes of writers and their characters and thus to understand better the unique perspectives of subjects who are agents of transformation and hybridization in their own narratives—as opposed to being the objects of knowledge, as in the discourse of social science.

Let me start with some simple, commonsense definitions. "Acculturation," *Webster's New Twentieth-Century Dictionary* (Second Edition) tells us, is "the transfer of culture from one ethnic group to another," whereas "assimilation" is "the act of bringing or coming to a resemblance; . . . the merging of diverse cultural elements." Or, as the *Oxford English Dictionary* would have it, to assimilate is "to make like, to cause to resemble, to incorporate. . . . To become conformed to." Already, we can see some contradictions in the semantic fields of these terms: is "the transfer . . . from one ethnic group to another" only a one-way process that causes one culture to erase another? Or could we infer that transformation of both— or all—of the cultures in contact is extremely likely, if not inevitable, through this process of "acculturation" of one (or several) culture(s) to the other(s)? Is "the merging of diverse cultural elements" to be understood as the inevitable erasure of one element by another? Might it not also suggest that a more intricate phenomenon is in fact taking place, as in those "border zones" where a complex syncretic cultural system comes to replace two or more ostensibly simpler cultures? In such a case, acculturation would not be simply the means of making one element conform to another, assimilate to it, in order to become *like* that other; it would more truly be a process whereby all elements involved in the interaction would be changed by that encounter. Dominant systems are more likely to absorb and make like themselves numerically or culturally "weaker" elements. But even then, the "inferior" or subaltern elements contribute to the evolution and transformation of the hegemonic system by producing resistances and counterdiscourses.[12]

It has of course been ideologically and politically convenient for the dominant cultures to entertain the fiction of "assimilation" as a means of incorporating—"civilizing"—those cultures viewed as too different and "inferior" to be comfortably accepted and integrated into their norms.[13] But in the long run, the more powerful system does incorporate elements of the weaker one, often to the point where certain of its patterns and practices become indistinguishable from those of the imported or inferior culture. Kwame Anthony Appiah has recently said, "There is, of course, no American culture without African roots," but this fact is not—yet—a commonly accepted premise when couched in those terms.[14] It is commonly accepted that African Americans are "more or less" assimilated and acculturated to "white" American culture, but rarely do we hear the reciprocal formulation discussed in academic or popular circles.[15] As Toni Morrison forcefully puts it in an influential essay: "Afro-American culture exists and though it is clear (and becoming clearer) how it has responded to Western culture, the instances where and means by which it has shaped Western culture are poorly recognized or understood."[16] Similarly, South African anthropologists study the Westernization of blacks in

[12]I use "discourse" in the Foucauldian sense. See Michael Foucault, *The Archaeology of Knowledge and the Discourse on Language*, trans. Alan M. Sheridan Smith (New York: Pantheon, 1972).

[13]As Albert Memmi has indeed pointed out in *The Colonizer*, "it is the colonized who is the first to desire assimilation, and it is the colonizer who refuses it to him" (125), because to assume "that the colonizer could or should accept assimilation and, hence, the colonized's emancipation, means to topple the colonial relationship" (126). Assimilation is thus a fiction, uneasily perpetuated by a hegemonic system that fears what is—wrongly—perceived to be its inevitability.

[14]Kwame Anthony Appiah, "Is the Post- in Postmodernism the Post- in Postcolonial?" *Critical Inquiry* 17 (Winter 1991): 354.

[15]One notable recent exception is the work of historian Mechal Sobel. In *The World They Made Together: Black and White Values in Eighteenth Century Virginia* (Princeton: Princeton University Press, 1987), she analyses the contributions that African notions of time and space made to the slave owner's *Weltanschauung*, thus becoming part and parcel of the southerner's perception of reality.

[16]Toni Morrison, "Unspeakable Things Unspoken: The Afro-American Presence in America Literature," *Michigan Quarterly Review* 28 (Winter 1989): 3.

southern Africa, but not the Africanization of whites who adopt the culinary or musical tastes of blacks. Singer Johnny Clegg, the "White Zulu," and the white southern African youths who have assimilated (into) black culture have not yet, to my knowledge, become the object of the anthropologist's scrutiny.[17] Here in the United States, a white rap singer named Vanilla Ice has been called "the Elvis of rap," whereas the black rap singer named L.D. Shore rose to fame as "the Black Elvis." As Patricia J. Williams has pointed out, this is "divinely parodic: Elvis, the white black man of a generation ago, reborn in a black man imitating Elvis" (and, one might add, reborn in Vanilla Ice, a white man imitating the black rapper imitating Elvis: a dizzying thought).[18] What is interesting in all these cases, is that the point of reference remains "white culture," even if it is an already "mongrelized" white culture, to use Charles Johnson's formulation quoted in the epigraph above.

My quarrel, then, with terms such as "assimilation" and "acculturation" when used in the (post)colonial context is a quarrel with history: the terms have acquired through use a negative connotation because they underscore the relation of subjugation that exists between the colonized culture and the hegemonic system. Rosaldo points out that "metropolitan typifications suppress, exclude, even repress border zones"—those areas of shifting practices located in the orbits of established discourses—because, he suggests,

> the model for cross-cultural understanding that produces immigration as a site of cultural stripping away is the academic version of the melting pot: theories of acculturation and assimilation. In this view, immigrants, or at any rate their children and grandchildren, are ab-

[17]In a talk at the Program of African Studies at Northwestern University in 1990, Jean Comaroff gave a fascinating account of late nineteenth-century practices of South African blacks who were adopting Western clothing, including Victorian wedding gowns and suits. See Jean Comaroff and John Comaroff, *Of Revelation and Revolution: Christianity, Colonialism, and Consciousness in South Africa* (Chicago: University of Chicago Press, 1991), chap. 2.

[18]See James Bernard, "Why the World Is After Vanilla Ice," *New York Times*, February 3, 1991, sec. 2, pp. 1, 26; Patricia J. Williams, "Pre-Old Law, Post-New Man, and the Adventures of Everywoman," paper presented at Northwestern University, Cultural Studies Working Group, 5 February 1991.

sorbed into the national culture. Above all, the process involves the loss of one's past—autobiography, history, heritage, language, and all the rest of the so-called cultural baggage. . . . The theory of assimilation appears to have the inevitability of a law of history. If it doesn't catch up with you this generation, it will in the next.[19]

In this view, the "assimilated" are seen as existing passively, not as creative agents capable of transforming the practices that they come to adopt. The message proclaimed by contemporary art and literature from Africa and the Caribbean, however, is quite different. It is not assimilation that appears inevitable when Western technology and education are adopted by the colonized, or when migration to the metropole severs some of the migrants' ties to a particular birthplace. Rather, the move forces individuals to stand in relation to the past and the present at the same time, to look for creative means of incorporating useful "Western" tools, techniques, or strategies into their own cosmology or *Weltanschauung*.[20]

What is needed, then, is a new vocabulary for describing patterns of influence that are never unidirectional. Since the influence is usually mutual and reciprocal, however much that fact may have been occluded from the political consciousness and modes of self-representation of metropolitan cultures, a more appropriate term for describing this contact of cultures would be "transculturation." The Cuban poet Nancy Morejón has used this neologism (*transculturación*) to describe a process of cultural intercourse and exchange, a circulation of practices which creates a constant interweaving of symbolic forms and empirical activities among the different interacting cultures. As she puts it, "*reciprocal* influence is the determining factor here, for no single element superimposes itself on

[19]Rosaldo, "Ideology," 87, 82.

[20]One stunning example of such creative incorporation is the sculpture *Man with a Bicycle*, exhibited at the Center for African Art in New York in 1987 in the show "Perspectives: Angles on African Art." The piece was chosen by James Baldwin, a co-curator of the exhibit, and Appiah writes: "I am grateful to James Baldwin for his introduction to the *Man with a Bicycle*, a figure who is, as Baldwin so rightly saw, polyglot—speaking Yoruba and English, probably some Hausa and a little French for trips to Cotonou or Cameroon. . . . *Man with a Bicycle* is produced by someone who does not care that the bicycle is the white man's invention: it is not there to be Other to the Yoruba Self; it is there because someone cared for its solidity; it is there because it will take us further than our feet will take us; it is there because machines are now as African as novelists" ("The Post- in Postmodernism," 357).

another; on the contrary, each one changes into the other so that both can be transformed into a third."[21] Rejecting the binarism of self and other, nationalism and internationalism, Africa and Europe, women writers like Morejón point to a third way, to the métissage of forms and identities that is the result of cross-cultural encounters and that forms the basis for their self-portrayals and their representations of cultural diversity.

Cross- or transcultural exchange has always been "an absolute fact" of life everywhere, even if, as Edouard Glissant has pointed out, "the human imagination, in Western tradition, has always wished to deny or disguise" it.[22] The realization that the theory of the melting pot did not correspond to a reality but was a necessary myth, or perhaps an enabling metaphor in the construction of an American national identity, is opening the way for a more cautious understanding of the dialectical and complex phenomena of ethnic interactions that have existed in this country since the beginning of colonial times. Similarly, French theories of cultural assimilation aimed at turning colonized peoples—or, at any rate, the educated elites of the colonies—into acculturated évolués who could speak perfect French corresponds to only one aspect of a complex colonial picture: although the colonial linguistic enterprise is alive and well in the départements d'Outre-mer, it now coexists with a strong movement in favor of créolité, which aims not to reject French outright but to valorize the multilingual and multiethnic character of creole cultures.[23]

---

[21]Nancy Morejón, Nación y mestizaje en Nicolás Guillén (Havana: Union, 1982), 23 (my emphasis and my translation). See also my discussion of "transculturation" and its relationship to métissage in AV, 16. The concept of transculturation was first advanced by Fernando Ortiz, as Morejón explains; however, he implies the assimilation of Afro-Cuban culture into Hispanic culture. Morejón's view of transculturación is a more dialectic phenomenon, as is my use of the term "métissage." See also Diana Taylor, "Transculturating Transculturation," Interculturalism and Performance: Writings from PAJ, ed. Bonnie Maranca and Gautam Dasgupta (New York: PAJ Publications, 1991). I should add that this chapter was written before the publication of Mary Louise Pratt, "Arts of the Contact Zone" (In Profession 91 [New York: MLA, 1991]), an essay that forms part of her book Imperial Eyes: Travel Writing and Transculturation (New York: Routledge, 1992). Pratt's use of the term "autoethnography" is much the same as mine in my 1989 book (AV), although the corpus she studies and her approach are different from mine.

[22]See Edouard Glissant, Le Discours antillais (Paris: Seuil, 1980), trans. J. Michael Dash in Glissant, Caribbean Discourse: Selected Essays, hereafter CD (Charlottesville: University Press of Virginia, 1989), 251. See also my discussion in AV, 9.

[23]This is true both in the Caribbean—see Jean Bernabé, Raphaël Confiant, and

That is why the concept of transculturation proves so useful: the prefix "trans-" suggests the act of traversing, of going through existing cultural territories. Its specifically spatial connotations demarcate a pattern of movement across cultural arenas and physical topographies which corresponds to the notion of "appropriation," a concept more promising than those of acculturation and assimilation, and one that implies active intervention rather than passive victimization. It is easy to establish how useful this concept can be for our analysis. Abdelkebir Khatibi has shown—in his novel *Love in Two Languages* and his collected essays titled *Maghreb pluriel*—that for Francophone writers whose mother tongue may be Arabic, Berber, Wolof, or Creole, the use of French is a means of translating into the colonizer's language a different sensibility, a different vision of the world, a means therefore of transforming the dominant conceptions circulated by the more standard idiom.[24] To write in French is thus also to transform French into a language that becomes the writer's own: French is appropriated, made into a vehicle for expressing a hybrid, heteroglot universe. This creative act of "taking possession" of a language gives rise to the kind of linguistic métissage visible in many contemporary Francophone and Anglophone works.

Acts of appropriation will produce a greater degree of cultural complexity than the standard anthropological categories (metropolitan versus colonial, developed versus primitive, civilized versus aboriginal) tend to suggest. Indeed, the notion of culture has itself become quite controversial among some anthropologists. Rosaldo contextualizes and summarizes the issues:

Anthropologists hold contradictory notions of culture. The discipline's official view holds that all human conduct is culturally mediated. In other words, people act in relation, not to brute reality, but to culture-specific modes of perceiving and organizing the world. . . . No domain

Patrick Chamoiseau, *Eloge de la créolité* (Paris: Gallimard, 1989); "In Praise of Creoleness," trans. Mohamed B. Taleb Khyar, *Callaloo* (1990): 886–909—and in the Indian Ocean: see J. F. Sam-Long, "Créolie: Les premiers problèmes," *Expressions: Revue Culturelle Réunionaise* 1 (October 1988): 11–24; and Françoise Lionnet, "*Créolité* in the Indian Ocean: Two Models of Cultural Diversity," *Yale French Studies* 82 (1993): 101–12.

[24] Abdelkebir Khatibi, *Amour bilingue* (Paris: Fata Morgana, 1983), trans. Richard Howard as *Love in Two Languages* (Minneapolis: University of Minnesota Press, 1990); and Khatibi, *Maghreb pluriel* (Paris: Denoël, 1983).

of culture is more or less culturally mediated than any other. Indeed the quantitative notion of "more" or "less" culture appears to be a throwback to the days when "high culture" was (and, in certain sectors of the academy, still is) measured in terms of opera houses, museums, and literary salons.

If official [anthropological] view holds that all cultures are equal, an informal filing system, more often found in corridor talk than in published writings, classifies cultures in quantitative terms, from a lot to a little, from thick to thin, from elaborate to simple. . . .

Culture in this view is defined by difference. Difference . . . makes culture visible to observers.[25]

If "difference" is what makes culture visible to observers, then the emphasis on difference has the merit of underscoring specificities that would be muted and ignored otherwise. But an overemphasis on dissimilarities is likely to lead from racial and biographical determinism into an essentialist impasse. In this erroneous view of culture wherein difference is rigidly valorized for its own sake, or for the sake of identifying authentic and "pure products,"[26] any process of acculturation or transculturation (however real, inevitable, and reciprocal it may have been) is automatically labeled as merely assimilationist. Hence, assimilation is (mis)construed by the dominant system as the elusive means of retaining or creating a fictive purity and authenticity within which the colonized "people without culture" can be absorbed; in opposition to this tendency the subaltern group, on the other hand, will seek to retain a sense of its own cultural authenticity by advocating a return to precolonial traditions, thus contrasting the past to the present and mythifying its own original ethnic or cultural purity. Difference then becomes—on both sides of this binary system—the reason for exoticizing, "othering," groups that do not share in this mythic cultural purity.

The issue of defining identity in a colonial context has always been a highly charged one: the first thinkers of decolonization, represented by Aimé Césaire, Frantz Fanon, and Albert Memmi, examined with some anxiety the processes through which the

---

[25]Rosaldo, "Ideology," 78.
[26]See James Clifford, *The Predicament of Culture: Twentieth Century Ethnography, Literature, and Art* (Cambridge: Harvard University Press, 1988), 1–17.

colonized internalize a vision of themselves projected by the colonizer, a vision that promotes a form of mimetic idealization of and identification with the colonizer.[27] To a degree, these formulations remained dependent upon a Hegelian view of the master-slave dialectic and of the importance of recognition as the means of self-validation for both colonizer and colonized. Since the mid-1970s, by contrast, writers have largely engaged in a painstaking redefinition of the paradigms of decolonization, seeking to undermine any simplistic understanding of the process of assimilation and the concurrent presuppositions regarding the existence of authenticity in either the dominant or native cultures. As Rosaldo points out: "The view of an authentic culture as an autonomous internally coherent universe no longer seems tenable in a postcolonial world. Neither 'we' nor 'they' are as self-contained and homogeneous as we/they once appeared. All of us inhabit an interdependent late 20th century world, which is at once marked by borrowing and lending across porous cultural boundaries, and saturated with inequality, power, and domination."[28]

Hence, our task as critics, I suggest, is to describe the complex interweavings of traditions that the texts and voices of postcolonial women map out and interpret for us, and that philosophers and anthropologists theorize and propound in their own disciplines. As Appiah puts it, "If there is a lesson in the broad shape of this circulation of cultures, it is surely that we are already contaminated by each other, that there is no longer a fully autochthonous *echt*-African culture awaiting salvage by our artists."[29] He is echoed by the Swedish anthropologist Ulf Hannerz, who has pointed out that "the world system, rather than creating massive cultural homogeneity on a global scale, is replacing one diversity with another; and the new diversity is based relatively more on interrelations and less on autonomy."[30] Arjun Appadurai observes, "It takes only the merest acquaintance with the facts of the modern world to note that it

[27] Aimé Césaire, *Discourse on Colonialism*, trans. Joan Pinkham (New York: Monthly Review Press, 1972); Frantz Fanon, *Black Skin, White Masks* trans. Charles L. Markmann (London: Pluto Press, 1986); Memmi, *The Colonizer*; Glissant, *Le Discours antillais* and *CD*.

[28] Rosaldo, "Ideology," 87.

[29] Appiah, "The Post- in Postmodernism," 354.

[30] Quoted in Clifford, *Predicament of Culture*, 17.

is now an interactive system in a sense which is strikingly new," and he goes on to argue: "The past is now not a land to return to in a simple politics of memory. It has become a synchronic warehouse of cultural scenarios."[31] What these writers and thinkers— "from all points on the compass," as Charles Johnson puts it— increasingly underline is the dialectical tension that exists between local variations and a worldwide system of interdependent cultures, between diversity and resemblance, between relativism and universalism.

In his controversial book *Logiques métisses: Anthropologie de l'identité en Afrique et ailleurs*, the French anthropologist Jean-Loup Amselle echoes some of the statements made above and goes a step further in asserting that even before colonial times the interrelation of cultures was the norm, that it is the Western anthropologist who has "invented" separate ethnic groups as his objects of study. Arguing against ethnological reason and in favor of a form of originary indistinction or syncretism, he critiques the anthropological bias in favor of cultural relativism and attempts to define a universalist *logique métisse*:

> Given all the philosophies of history and other sagas of human progress, American culturalist anthropologists along with Lévi-Strauss were right to stress the particularist nature and the relative character of the values promoted by different societies. But the flip side of this generous attitude is the erection of impermeable cultural barriers that imprison each group in its own singularity.
>
> Doesn't the notion of multicultural society, the ambiguities of which have already been emphasized, follow directly from the concepts put forth by American cultural anthropology? Far from being an instrument of tolerance toward, and liberation of, minorities as its proponents like to claim, this notion reveals instead all the wrongs of ethnological reason, and that is why it has been claimed by the "new right" in France. To isolate a community by defining a set of characteristic "differences" can lead to the possibility of its territorial confinement, and its eventual expulsion. Ethnic labeling and the assignation of differences are self-fulfilling prophecies. They do not just correspond to the acceptance of cultural specificities, but are also correlative with the coercive affirmation of one identity, that of French

---

[31] Arjun Appadurai, "Disjuncture and Difference in the Global Cultural Economy," *Public Culture* 2 (Spring 1990): 1, 4.

ethnicity. This is why, if we are not mindful of it, the problematic of the multicultural society can lead straight into a state of separate development analogous to South African apartheid—itself a consequence of the misapplication of the notion of culture.

To this ethnic or cultural fundamentalism that some would like to assimilate to the "defeat of thought," one does not need to oppose the abstract notion of human rights, these principles that no one can truly define. Rather, one must support and articulate the idea of an originary mixing or métissage of the different groups which were formed all through human history.[32]

Amselle's remarks force us to rethink some of the fundamental notions that we are beginning to take for granted as literary and cultural critics: the respect for multiculturalism, the vexing questions of separatism and cultural autonomy, and the need for contemporary societies to respect difference without falling into a situation of apartheid. It is thus interesting to note that postcolonial women writers implicitly address identical issues in their recent essays and fictional works: they depict characters whose originality stems from the fact that the authors give them universal appeal, letting them live their métissage in the most original, ingenious, and beneficial ways. These characters exemplify the inevitability as well as the benefits and disadvantages of intercultural exchange. For, as Amselle goes on to add, "Cultures are not located next to one another, without doors or windows, like the monads of Leibnitz: they are situated in a fluctuating context which is *a structured field of relations.* . . . The definition of a given culture is in fact the resultant of a ratio of intercultural forces. . . . The modification of the ratio of forces . . . along with the appearance and disappearance of cultures explain the changes which occur in each subcultural system when one looks at them in isolation."[33]

To follow Amselle is to come to the conclusion that it is not the existence of *different* cultures which induces a comparative (ethnographical) approach; rather, it is the critic's (or anthropologist's) stance as comparatist which creates an arbitrary and singular object

---

[32]Jean-Loup Amselle, *Logiques métisses: Anthropologie de l'identité en Afrique et ailleurs* (Paris: Payot, 1990), 35. The phrase "defeat of thought" is a reference to Alain Finkielkraut, *La Défaite de la pensée: Essai* (Paris: Gallimard, 1987), against which Amselle argues.

[33]Ibid., p. 55.

(be it "Bambara culture," or "Francophone" or "postcolonial" studies") and thus imposes the constraints of a determinate set of
particularisms. Although Amselle does not deny the specificities
inherent in certain cultural manifestations, he is in fact arguing
against all theories of culture that would locate singularity within
a restrained space, an enclosed geographical area, a "nation," or a
"tradition."[34] Based on his extensive field research in Africa, *Logiques métisses* opposes Amselle's own theorizing of a sociological
and historical *espace métissé* to the traditional culturalist approach
of anthropology which, he says, is just another form of fundamentalism, itself the breeding ground for many contemporary forms of
fascism and essentialist tendencies: witness the pre–civil rights
southern ideology of "separate but equal" and the various other
forms of apartheid promoted in recent years by Enoch Powell in
Britain, Jean-Marie Le Pen in France, and David Duke in Louisiana.

The works of postcolonial women writers make concretely visible
the dialectical tensions present in Amselle's, Appadurai's, Appiah's, and Glissant's theorizing and shed new light on what previous generations of oppositional critics taught us to regard as an
"alienating" contact between cultures, one in which the dominant
group names and circumscribes the subjected one, instilling a colonized or victimized mentality into the latter. What these writers
illustrate instead is the dynamic and creative processes mobilized
by subgroups as means of resistance to the "victim" syndrome.
They use their transformative and performative energies on the language and narrative strategies they borrow from the cultures of the
West. To represent their regional cultural realities, they make use
of appropriative techniques that interweave traditions and languages. The way they portray characters transforms the way *they*
see the realities of their own worlds, as well as the way *we*—readers
who are outsiders to those regions or cultures—will in turn perceive them: that is, no longer as radically "other" realms, so dif-

---

[34]Amselle's work thus intersects with Benedict Anderson, *Imagined Communities*
(London: Verso, 1983); Eric Hobsbawm and Terence Ranger, *The Invention of Tradition* (Cambridge: Cambridge University Press, 1983); and Roy Wagner, *The Invention
of Culture* (Chicago: University of Chicago Press, 1975). For a different perspective
that emphasizes the importance of relativism as a mode of intercultural critique, see
Christopher Miller, *Theories of Africans: Francophone Literature and Anthropology in
Africa* (Chicago: University of Chicago Press, 1990), esp. chaps. 1–2.

ferent and alien that they could only alienate themselves more through contact with the West, but rather as microcosms of the globe. In other words, these recent works point the way back to a new and yet very old concept: humanism—a word that feminists of different stripes are beginning to revalorize—or, to borrow Evelyne Accad's more precise formulation, "femihumanism," a nonseparatist feminism committed to bringing about a pluralistic society based on the rejection of oppression and domination, whether globally or locally.[35] It is this ethical imperative that governs their search for new cultural forms and hybrid languages that better represent the particularisms of the communities about which they write, without locking them into idiosyncratic dead ends and narrow views of history.

Edouard Glissant has said that the "yearning for history is in the harking back to a history so often relived, the negation of history as encounter and transcendence, but the assumption of history as passion." He makes this comment in reference to the circularity of time in the works of Alejo Carpentier, Gabriel García Márquez, and William Faulkner, which he contrasts with the myth of the "everascending evolution of Mankind" as represented, for example, by the heroine of Joan Didion's *A Book of Common Prayer*. Implicitly referring to his own novels, and to the predicament of writers in what he calls "the Other America," he adds: "The difficulty of knowing history (*one's* history) provokes the deepest isolation. As opposed to the spiral *ascent* of the North American heroine, here we have a *return* down the spiral, infectiously tragic and decisively obscure, which not only a chosen hero but a people will want to use to repossess the beginning of their time."[36]

But what does it mean to try to "repossess the beginning of [one's] time"? What ideological presuppositions underlie the belief in a "beginning of time"? And how do *women* articulate their relationship to history in a postcolonial context that equates the notion of a "chosen hero" with the "people" itself? The novels of the women writers studied in this book are exemplary texts with and through which to address all these theoretical questions. These

---

[35] Accad, *Sexuality and War*, 25–26. For a brief philosophical and personal approach to the question of humanism and the Holocaust, see Sarah Kofman, *Paroles suffoquées* (Paris: Galilée, 1987).
[36] *CD*, 81, 82.

writers implicitly formulate responses to the metaphorical use of
the female body by male writers, articulating their own problematic
relationship to physical space (geography and travels) and to social
environments (nation, village, home, school, language, clothing,
photography) viewed as markers of cultural identity. Their narratives offer possible forms of involvement in and resistance to the
dominant ideology of their time and place, suggesting ways in
which a writer's commitment to change, her "essential gesture as
a human being," is an important form of cultural intervention.[37]

Chapter 1 focuses on Michelle Cliff's *Abeng*, a book that deals
with the "fictional" history of her native island, Jamaica. It is a
third-person autobiographical novel, striking in its narrative discontinuities, its complex interweavings of "official" and "forgotten" history. Corresponding to what Linda Hutcheon has called
"historiographic metafiction," it plays upon the truth and lies of
the historical record, foregrounding the liberating potential of coun-
ternarratives.[38]

Chapter 2, on Ananda Devi, addresses the questions of authenticity and universality in a specifically urban context. Devi's *Rue La
Poudrière* takes place in Port-Louis, capital of Mauritius. It stages
the experiences of a "universal" urban female subject, and the questions it raises include the identity of the literary text and the identity of the "subject." This novel shows that such categories, though
unavoidable, can be extremely limiting and confining.

In Chapter 3, on Maryse Condé's *Traversée de la mangrove*, I discuss this author's explicit rejection of all limiting categories of colonial and feminist literature. Condé's characters are multifaceted
and live in the present, going about their daily lives, self-possessed,
and speaking Creole. They do not live under the gaze of the colonizer; they are self-assured in their difference; and they do not
correspond to existing metropolitan stereotypes about the Antilles
or to any of the paradigms of exoticism.

The material weight of the body and the configurations of power
that inscribe meaning upon it are the central concerns of writers as

---

[37]I borrow the phrase "essential gesture" from Roland Barthes and Nadine Gordimer; see Gordimer, *The Essential Gesture: Writing, Politics, and Places*, ed. Stephen
Clingman (New York: Knopf, 1988), 286–87.

[38]Linda Hutcheon, *Narcissistic Narrative: The Metafictional Paradox* (London: Methuen, 1984), xiv.

diverse as Myriam Warner-Vieyra (*As the Sorcerer Said . . . , Juletane, Femmes échouées*), Suzanne Dracius-Pinalie (*L'Autre qui danse*), Gayl Jones (*Eva's Man*), Bessie Head (*The Collector of Treasures*), and Nawal El Saadawi (*Woman at Point Zero*). Chapters 4, 5, and 6 focus on the problems of exile and authenticity, subjectivity and physical pain, as these are constructed by writers who attempt to understand the specificities of feminine experience and women's relationship to the symbolic frameworks that define them as suffering subjects.

Examining the work of these writers leads me to a refutation of cultural relativism and to a much more nuanced view of the question of universalism: Chapter 7 addresses "the limits of universalism," taking a specific legal case as an example of the paradoxical problems that are raised when issues of authenticity and ethical considerations collide.

Finally, Chapter 8, on Leïla Sebbar's *Les Carnets de Shérazade*, shows how the intricacies of identity formation give insight into a form of universalism that does not overlook the discrete specificities of history. For Sebbar, the postcolonial condition is synonymous with exile, nomadism, and literary métissage. The theme of identity is central to her work, and her characters—from nowhere and everywhere—are emblematic of the societal shock resulting from the major upheavals of colonization. Sebbar's work allows me to conclude with what I take to be the difference between métissage and creolization, on the one hand, and postmodern fragmentation on the other.

What the writings of all these authors suggest is that the old dichotomies are no longer tenable, that the local and the global are increasingly interrelated, and that one cannot be fully understood without reference to the other. But at the same time it becomes clear that universality would be an empty proposition without the gendered specificities offered by particular writers representing different cultural configurations. Postcolonial women novelists offer us rich and varied means of understanding this contemporary dialectic—and the ways it reweaves the problematics of classical European humanism into a new tapestry in which there can be no room for the normative approaches of the past.

1

Of Mangoes and Maroons: Language, History, and the Multicultural Subject of Michelle Cliff's *Abeng*

To remain speechless or else to live in the third person. . . .
The past which can still split the person into the second and
third—has its hegemony been broken?
—Christa Wolf, *Patterns of Childhood*

In a well-known essay, "Conditions and Limits of Autobiography," Georges Gusdorf states that "the prerogative of autobiography consists in this: . . . that it reveals . . . the effort of a creator *to give the meaning of his own mythic tale.* . . . Artistic creation is a struggle with the angel, in which *the creator . . . wrestles with his shadow.*"[1] The invention of a personal (that is, private and individual) mythology is the project of many canonical authors whose writings constitute the basis of much theorizing about the nature of self-consciousness. This individualistic approach to the genre contrasts sharply with the one used by most postcolonial writers, male and female.[2] For them, the individual necessarily defines him- or herself with regard to a community, or an ethnic group, and their autobiographical mythologies of empowerment are usually mediated by a desire to revise and rewrite official, recorded history. Gusdorf's

[1] See Georges Gusdorf, "Conditions and Limits of Autobiobraphy," in *Autobiography: Essays Theoretical and Critical*, ed. James Olney (Princeton: Princeton University Press, 1980), 48 (my emphasis).

[2] And, I should add, with that of many women and non-Western writers since colonial times, as critics have indeed noted. See, e.g., William L. Andrews, *To Tell a Free Story: The First Century of Afro-American Autobriography, 1760–1865* (Urbana: University of Illinois Press, 1986); and the special issue on Afro-American autobiography which Andrews edited for *Black American Literature Forum* 24 (Summer 1990); Bella Brodzki and Celeste Schenck, eds., *Life/Lines: Theorizing Women's Autobiography* (Ithaca: Cornell University Press, 1989); Sidonie Smith, *A Poetics of Women's Autobiography: Marginality and the Fictions of Self-Representation* (Bloomington: Indiana University Press, 1987); and Joanne M. Braxton, *Black Women Writing Autobiography: A Tradition within a Tradition* (Philadelphia: Temple University Press, 1989).

belief that "autobiography . . . expresses a concern peculiar to Western man" is based on a rather reductive and narrow view of autobiography, since it does not take into account the culturally diverse forms of self-consciousness, or the necessarily devious and circuitous modes of self-expression that colonized peoples have always had to adopt in order to come to terms with their own subject positions. The colonized are marked, as Gusdorf rightly points out, by "a sort of intellectual colonizing to a mentality that was not their own" but *also*, it should be added, by ancient, often occluded traditions that need to be articulated through new discourses and new images. Postcolonial writers have had to invent mythologies of their own, stories and allegories of "self" and "other" that can translate this complex heritage and perhaps make a difference by helping to transform the mentality of the oppressed as well as their self-perception.[3]

Postcolonial autobiography, in all its myriad forms, is best defined by this transformative and visionary dimension: by the conviction that writing matters and that narrative has the power to transform the reader. Writers from a variety of colonial backgrounds are often moved by a sense of urgency and responsibility and by a need to take risks that help change the form of the genre as well as relations of power in society. In order to "wrestle with his shadow," a writer must be certain of casting one: women of color have yet to define the shape of the shadow that they are beginning to cast, and autobiography is helping them achieve self-definition in a multicultural context. Their acts of self-portraiture increasingly bear testimony to the diversity and richness of the traditions that subtend their innovative narrative projects.

Audre Lorde's "biomythography," *Zami* (1982), is a prominent example of the kind of revisionist mythmaking that a writer engages in when she does not feel legitimated and validated by a long tradition of self-conscious self-exploration. Because she breaks new ground, Lorde can "give meaning to [her] own mythic tale" and have it serve as testimony for others who have not yet had the opportunity to experience a life story whose shape could in some way compel, attract, or interest them. That is why I would argue

---

[3]Gusdorf, "Conditions," 29.

that *Zami* constitutes the condition of possibility for Michelle Cliff's *Abeng*, the novel that I deal with in the chapter.[4] By inventing a new way of narrating her experiences as a lesbian poet, Audre Lorde has made it possible for others like herself and Cliff, both immigrants from the Caribbean, to continue to shape and enrich their common cultural heritage.

Published in 1984 in the United States by a small feminist press, and written by a Jamaican-born author who focuses her narrative on the history, culture, and processes of gender and racial identity formation in the Caribbean, *Abeng* is at once fiction and autobiography in the third person. Written in English, it incorporates dialogue in Jamaican Creole. It appears, however, to be meant for a non-Caribbean audience as well, since it gives the reader the benefit of numerous cultural explanations and translations. The literal meaning of the word *abeng*, for example, is clarified on the title page: "*Abeng* is an African word meaning conch shell." Cliff adds that in the West Indies the *abeng* was used as an instrument of communication, the blowing of the conch serving either to call the slaves to work for the master in the canefields or to send messages that could be passed to Maroon armies.[5] The *abeng* is thus a culturally polysemic object, having both positive and negative connotations in the context of Caribbean slave societies. Because its main function is to facilitate communication, the *abeng* stands in an obvious parallel relationship to the novel we are reading: both are objects by means of which different messages can be passed on

[4]Michelle Cliff, *Abeng* (Trumansburg, N.Y.: Crossing Press, 1984), hereafter *A*. Page numbers are given in the the the text. For a reading of *Zami* as revisionist mythmaking, see Claudine Raynaud, "A Nutmeg Nestled inside Its Covering of Mace: Audre Lorde's *Zami*," in Brodzki and Schenck, *Life/Lines*.

[5]"Maroons" is a term applied to runaway slaves in many parts of the New World. In Jamaica they were able to hide in the central mountain to evade capture and started a "remarkable tradition of revolt . . . [which] as slave societies go, [was] an unusual, perhaps unique record," according to Orlando Patterson, "Slavery and Slave Revolts: A Sociohistorical Analysis of the First Maroon War, 1665–1740" in *Maroon Societies: Rebel Slave Communities in the Americas*, ed. Richard Price (New York: Anchor Books, 1973), 275. In 1739 a treaty was signed between the British and Maroon leaders, acknowledging a free and independent Maroon community with its own settlement. See Barbara K. Kopytoff, *The Maroons of Jamaica: An Ethnohistorical Study of Incomplete Polities, 1655–1905* (Ann Arbor, Mich.: University Microfilms, 1973).

(sometimes simultaneously) to different receivers; both are "double-voiced," duplicitous, and susceptible to ambiguous reception and interpretation.

I want to examine the way the multilingual context of Caribbean societies demarcates a specific set of cultural parameters that must be taken into consideration when one discusses subjectivity and self-conscious agency in relation to a postcolonial form of historical consciousness distinguished by the absence of "master narratives."[6] Not surprisingly, autobiographical practice reflects absence, and Michelle Cliff achieves a particularly successful rendering of the cultural discontinuities that form the basis of her protagonist's inquiry and motivation.

The Polyglot's Subjectivity

Michelle Cliff chooses the *abeng* as an emblem for her book because, like the conch, the book is an instrument of communication whose performative function seems to be valorized. The story she tells is meant to inform and educate Jamaicans and non-Jamaicans alike, and she goes to great lengths to demystify the past in order to imagine, invent, and rewrite a different collective and personal history for the protagonist. The narrative weaves the personal and the political together, allowing the protagonist, Clare Savage—who is a thinly disguised alter ego of the author—to negotiate the conflicting elements of her cultural and familial background. She thus succeeds in reclaiming the multifaceted identity that her family and society had "taught [her] to despise": namely, her mixed racial heritage, her femininity, and her homosexuality.[7]

The narrative sets up an uneasy and duplicitous relationship with its audience. It begins with the standard disclaimer, "This work is a work of fiction, and any resemblance to persons alive or dead is entirely coincidental," despite its clearly autobiographical

---

[6] I use this phrase in the sense made familiar by Jean-François Lyotard in *The Postmodern Condition: A Report on Knowledge*, trans. Geoff Bennington and Brian Massumi (Minneapolis: University of Minnesota Press, 1984).

[7] See Michelle Cliff, *Claiming and Identity They Taught Me to Despise* (Watertown, Mass.: Persephone Press, 1980), hereafter *CI*.

themes, which echo and repeat similar themes treated from a first-person perspective in Cliff's poetry and essays.[8] But *Abeng,* while engaging the reader in a dialogue that confronts the fictions of self-representation, discloses far more about the author than the poetry does. It would seem that for Cliff the third person is a self-protective device that creates sufficient distance and thus helps her deal with the burden of history. Acts of disclosure are always painful, and since Cliff admits that she has labored "under the ancient taboos of the assimilated" (*LLB,* 16), the "hegemony of the past" cannot easily be broken by a straightforward act of self-portraiture. Like the German writer Christa Wolf and the Chinese-American Maxine Hong Kingston, Cliff uses postmodern fictional techniques that, in the words of Sidonie Smith, "challenge the ideology of individualism and with it the ideology of gender."[9]

The use of Creole accentuates some of these structural ambiguities. Many instances of *patois* fragment the linguistic unity of the book and limit the range of textual understanding for the non-Jamaican reader. Cliff includes a glossary of Creole terms as a post-text without, however, giving any prior indication of that fact; this is tantamount to a gesture of inclusion/exclusion which forces readers to situate themselves with regard to their particular understanding of Jamaican Creole. Thus, American readers who approach this book for the first time may well remain unaware of the glossary and feel "excluded" unless they flip through to the last page.[10] The move from standard English to Creole speech is meant to underscore class and race differences among protagonists, but it also makes manifest the double-consciousness of the postcolonial, bilingual, and bicultural writer who lives and writes across the

[8]See in particular Michelle Cliff, *The Land of Look Behind* (Ithaca, N.Y.: Firebrand Books, 1985), hereafter *LLB.*

[9]See Christa Wolf, *Patterns of Childhood,* trans. Ursule Molinaro and Hedwig Rappolt (New York: Farrar, Straus & Giroux, 1985); Maxine Hong Kingston, *The Woman Warrior: Memoirs of a Girlhood among Ghosts* (New York: Random House, 1977); and Smith, *Poetics of Women's Autobiography,* 150. Smith's final chapter illuminates Kingston's work and postmodern self-representation.

[10]In my course on Caribbean women writers at Northwestern University, the nonlinear narrative and the unfamiliarity of Creole initially prevented some undergraduates from appreciating the book as much as they did, say, Jamaica Kincaid's *Annie John* or Miriam Warner-Vieyra's *Juletane,* which require less sustained attention and reader involvement.

margins of different traditions and cultural universes.[11] For Cliff, to attempt to define her own place is also to undermine all homogeneous and monolithic perspectives—especially those constructed by the official colonial historiography—and to situate her text within the prismatic field of contemporary feminist discourse.[12]

For these very reasons, Cliff's reception in Jamaica is quite problematic. It is in fact symptomatic of the alienated status of the feminist postcolonial writer: relatively unknown outside intellectual feminist circles, Cliff is blamed, like many other West Indian female intellectuals, for being an expatriate and for exhibiting a feminism colored by Euro-American ideology. Lloyd Brown, for example, in his introduction to a volume of selected conference papers (1981–83) titled *Critical Issues in West Indian Literature*, states that "one needs to be very sceptical about claims on behalf of 'radical' feminism and [the] 'revolutionary' women's movement in the Caribbean." Although ostensibly sympathetic to the feminist perspective, Brown sees the whole issue as still largely foreign to the culture of the region: "The need to address Caribbean literature and society through feminist and pro-feminist perspectives has been longstanding and embarrassingly neglected, but attributing some sort of mass 'radicalism' to a pervasively conservative, often reactionary, society is quite another thing. There is the possibility that the exercise can be little more than the smuggling in of so much foreign (North American) baggage rather than a demonstrated reality of West Indian life."[13] Although this tendency to discount feminism is bemoaned in the groundbreaking work of Carol Boyce Davies and Elaine Savory Fido, who have produced the first comprehensive anthology of feminist criticism of Caribbean literature, the im-

[11]This double-consciousness was first described by W. E. B. Du Bois, *The Souls of Black Folks: Essays and Sketches* (1903), intro. Saunders Redding (New York: Fawcett, 1961), 16, 17.

[12]On the question of feminist discourse in the context of the Caribbean, see "Talking it Over: Women, Writing and Feminism," preface to *Out of the Kumbla: Caribbean Women and Literature*, ed. Carole Boyce Davies and Elaine Savory Fido (Trenton, N.J.: Africa World Press, 1990), ix–xx; hereafter *OK*. Lemuel Johnson, "A-beng: (Re)Calling the Body (In)to Question," *OK*, 111–142, makes use of many different strands of contemporary feminist theory.

[13]Lloyd Brown, introduction to *Critical Issues in West Indian Literature*, ed. Erika Sollish Smilowitz and Roberta Quarles Knowles (Parkersburg, Iowa: Caribbean Books, 1984), 3.

pulse to regard Cliff's ideology as suspect remains strong among Caribbean critics.[14]

Cliff has been influenced by the American women's movement and the work of lesbian poets such as Audre Lorde and Adrienne Rich, whom she acknowledges at the beginning of *Abeng*. Like Audre Lorde, Cliff does not position herself as a "representative" of West Indian life, nor does she mean to be one. Certainly, her lesbianism is bound to be controversial in the Caribbean cultural context (where homosexuality, like feminism, is generally viewed as a "foreign import"). Unlike Lorde's *Afro*-Caribbeanness, however, which is never in question, Cliff's self-representation is problematic. And it is her position as a racially mixed Jamaican, who can "pass" for white but prefers to recover the African heritage of her matrilineal ancestry, that draws the interest of such critics as Pamela Mordecai and Betty Wilson:

> The only one of the recently published Caribbean writers who does not affirm at least aspects of being in the Caribbean place is Michelle Cliff, who along with [Jean] Rhys could be regarded as being more in the *alienated tradition* of a "francophone" than an anglophone consciousness. Personal history perhaps provides important clues: like Rhys, who felt isolated, Cliff is "white"—or as light skinned as makes, to the larger world, little difference. Also like Rhys, she went to the kind of school—quite comprehensively described in *No Telephone to Heaven*—which promoted the values of the metropole. Like Rhys, she left her island early and never really came home. One of the prices she has paid is a *compromised authenticity* in some aspects of her rendering of the creole.[15]

As an exile who has lived and studied in England and the United States, where she now lives, Cliff is clearly marginal to the Jamaican cultural mainstream. But what writer ever was truly part of a

---

[14]*OK*; see also note 12, above. I thank Belinda Edmondson for contributing to my understanding of the problematic reception of Cliff in Jamaica, esp. in her unpublished paper "Race, Audience, and the Use of Feminism in Two Contemporary West Indian Works," which compares Cliff's *Abeng* with the Sistren's Collective, *Lionheart Gal* (London: Women's Press, 1986).

[15]Pamela Mordecai and Betty Wilson, eds., *Her True-True Name: An Anthology of Women's Writing from the Caribbean* (Portsmouth, N.H.: Heinemann, 1989), xvii; my emphasis.

"mainstream"? Indeed, exile and marginality are perhaps the necessary preconditions and, on the eve of the twenty-first century, the increasingly ordinary experience that allows for what Myra Jehlen calls "the extraordinary possibility of our seeing the old world from a genuinely new perspective."[16] To blame Cliff for belonging to an "alienated tradition" of Caribbean writers is to misunderstand the point of her representational strategies for reclaiming a lost heritage, for affirming what has been devalued while simultaneously re-presenting and narrating the processes and experiences that obscured and obfuscated those traditions in the first place. Indoctrination into the culture of the metropole was an integral part of the "elite" private school system, and Cliff painstakingly shows how middle-class Jamaicans were assimilated by that system. It is true that her project is comparable to those of Francophone authors such as Maryse Condé *(Heremakhonon)* and Myriam Warner-Vieyra *(As the Sorcerer said . . . and Juletane)*, whose heroines are ambiguously passive.[17] But the theme of alienation has been central to women's literature in the Caribbean and in the United States, whether it is alienation because of what Mary Helen Washington has called the "intimidation of color"—the values used to breed conformity to white culture's expectations and standards of behavior and beauty—or the self-hatred generated by "passing" and self-denial.[18] The right pigmentation and "good" hair were always overvalued in the colonial context. Having both light skin and straight hair, Clare Savage in *Abeng* embodies the physical ideal of

[16]Myra Jehlen, "Archimedes and the Paradox of Feminist Criticism," in *The Signs Reader: Women, Gender, and Scholarship,* ed. Elizabeth Abel and Emily K. Abel, (Chicago: University of Chicago Press, 1983), 94.

[17]For a discussion of Maryse Condé, *Heremakhonon,* trans. Richard Philcox (Washington, D.C.: Three Continents Press, 1982; hereafter *H*), see *AV,* chap. 5. For a brief discussion of Myriam Warner-Vieyra's *As the Sorcerer Said . . . ,* trans. Dorothy S. Blair (Essex: Longman, 1982; hereafter *S*), and *Juletane,* trans. Betty Wilson (London: Heinemann, 1987; hereafter *J*), see Françoise Lionnet, "Myriam Warner-Vieyra," in *Fifty African and Caribbean Women Writers,* ed. Anne Adams (Greenwood Press, forthcoming). Also useful are Audre Londe, "The Transformation of Silence into Action," in her *Sister Outsider* (Trumansburg, N.Y.: Crossing Press, 1984), 40–44; and Adrienne Rich, "Resisting Amnesia: History and Personal Life," in *Blood, Bread, and Poetry: Selected Prose 1979–1985* (New York: Norton, 1986), 136–155.

[18]See Mary Helen Washington, "Teaching Black-Eyed Susans: An Approach to the Study of Black Women Writers," in *All the Women Are White, All the Blacks Are Men, But Some of Us Are Brave: Black Women's Studies* ed. Gloria T. Hull, Patricia Bell Scott, and Barbara Smith (Old Westbury, N.Y.: Feminist Press, 1982), 210.

the assimilated—a situation that estranges her from her darker sister and mother and thus isolates her from that part of her own heritage. Alienation is therefore a given that must be dealt with before the narrator can begin to make sense of the past. As Cliff's prose poem puts it, to face the past becomes a matter of personal survival:

> In the family I was called "fair"—a hard term. My sister was darker, younger. We were split: along lines of color and order of birth.

> That family surface: treacherous—always the threat the heritage would out: that blackness would rise like slick oil and coat the white feathers of seabirds. Lies were devised. Truth was reserved for dreams. . . .

> This kind of splitting breeds insanity. (CI, 11)

It is this split subjectivity of the narrator that is mirrored accurately in the self-conscious move from English to Creole, since the appropriation of the vernacular sets off the discontinuous and fragmented nature of the postcolonial subject. Indeed, as Daryl Dance has observed, "there are many language forms available" to the Caribbean writer, so that the question of "*which* word" to use becomes inseparable from the way subjectivity is defined. Because "language and identity are inseparable," poets have always known that in order to liberate the world one must start by liberating the word.[19] Aimé Césaire and Derek Walcott have made extensive use of neologisms in attempting to capture the uniquely hybrid, *métis*, and heteroglot world of the Caribbean.[20] Since it is in the nature of oral languages not to have a fixed and codified system of orthography, it is not entirely fair to state, as Mordecai and Wilson do, that Cliff's rendering of Creole is "compromised" by a lack of "authenticity." For Cliff, the use of written Creole becomes essential to the project of "retracing the African part of ourselves, reclaiming

[19]Daryl Cumber Dance, introduction to *Fifty Caribbean Writers: A Bio-Bibliographical Critical Sourcebook* (New York: Greenwood Press, 1986), 4–5.

[20]See Aimé Césaire, "Notebook of a Return to the Native Land," in *The Collected Poetry*, trans. Clayton Eshleman and Annette Smith (Berkeley: University of California Press, 1983); and Derek Walcott, *The Castaway* (London: Cape, 1965).

as our own, and as our subject, *a history sunk under the sea, or scat-tered as potash in the canefields,* or gone to bush, or trapped in a class system notable for its rigidity and absolute dependence on color stratification. On a past bleached from our minds. It means finding the artforms of these of our ancestors and speaking the *patois* for-bidden us" *(LLB,* 14; my emphasis). That is why Evelyn O'Cal-laghan can write of Cliff that "this deliberate counterbalancing is crucial for a 'writer coming from the culture of colonialism' . . . and has politically influenced the direction her writing has taken. . . . In consolidating *the literary potential of the Jamaican Creole continuum,* . . . writers are challenging the hegemony not only of the 'Queen's English,' but of any outward-looking value system."[21]

The cultural nationalism at work in the Caribbean has encour-aged writers to develop a new hybrid language, based on the oral traditions of the area and capable of capturing the elusive—and often subversive—subtext of those ancient and noncanonical tra-ditions. Maryse Condé also uses images, turns of phrase, and sounds that give her *Traversée de la mangrove* a particular flavor. The use of everyday "Antillean" language and speech patterns lend this novel a singular beauty (see Chapter 3). Linguists increasingly agree that the language situation no longer fits the binary model of "bilingualism" or "diglossia" that used to be applied to the region. There is in fact a linguistic "continuum" that allows speakers to vary their speech along the spectrum from Standard English at one pole to what is known as "Broad Creole" at the other—even though, as Pauline Christie points out, it is still true that

> for most people in the community, the roles of Creole and English seem to be clearly demarcated, as are the individuals and groups they associate with each. The fact is, that the roles are not always easily definable and what is usually considered English more often than not includes a number of features which characterize it as distinctly Ja-maican or West Indian, while the so-called Creole reveals the contin-ued influence of English. . . .
>
> On the one hand, increasing social and cultural interaction within the society has led to *greater acceptance of Creole forms in formal usage.* . . . On the other hand, the physical and psychological distancing from

[21]Evelyn O'Callaghan, "Feminist Consciousness: European/American Theory, Ja-maican Stories," *Journal of Caribbean Studies* 6 (Spring 1988): 157, 158 (my emphasis).

expatriate models . . . has given rise to innovations in formal speech and writing which can be seen as *developments from English structure*.[22]

Caribbean languages are shaped by an all-encompassing syncretism that generates new forms of social and national identities for speakers and writers. Hence, any attempt at establishing rigid demarcations between users of one or the other form of speech reveals itself to be an artificial gesture favoring a view of identity and subjectivity which perpetuates a false ideal of purity—an ideal that is, however, the aim of all assimilationist ideologies.

As Cliff discusses it in her essay "A Journey into Speech," the West Indian writer's relationship to language has been extremely problematic because of what O'Callaghan terms "the outward looking value system" and Christie, the "expatriate models." These have strongly influenced the educational system, creating an Anglocentric cultural mold that some contemporary writers have been unable to resist, mimicking in their work the canonical models of British literature:

> One of the effects of assimilation, indoctrination, passing into the anglocentrism of British West Indian culture is that you believe absolutely in the hegemony of the King's English and in the form in which it is meant to be expressed. Or else your writing is not literature; it is folklore, and folklore can never be art. Read some poetry by West Indian writers—some, not all—and you will see what I mean. You have to dissect stanza after extraordinarily anglican stanza for Afro-Caribbean truth; you may never find the latter. But this has been our education. The anglican ideal—Milton, Wordsworth, Keats—was held before us with an assurance that we were unable, and would never be enabled, to compose a work of similar correctness. No reggae spoken here. (*LLB*, 13)

[22]Pauline Christie, "Language and Social Change in Jamaica," *Journal of Caribbean Studies* 3 (Winter 1983): 207, 226 (my emphasis). As she points out, the linguistic situation is by no means simple: "The continuum designation, however, not only obscures the fact that a range is not equally or at all observable in all parts of the 'system,' it also fails to take into account local stereotypes. In the mind of most members of the speech community, the situation involves English on the one hand and Creole on the other. In other words, they tend to ignore the marked variation in what they actually include under each label and the practical impossibility of drawing a dividing line between the two codes" (206).

Elsewhere in the Caribbean, the Francophone writer Maryse Condé has acknowledged that the "lullabies that rocked [her] to sleep were sung in metropolitan French . . . while [her] neck was strait-jacketed by French verbal conjugations." But in the same essay she adds: "Today, we can summon to memory the languages of our ancestors. . . . French and English together with Creole and indigenous Caribbean languages, Bambara and other African tongues form a matrix for the breaking of new linguistic ground and unexplored derivatives."[23] Cliff's project is to explore this hybrid dimension of vernacular speech, and to dig beneath the linguistic surface so as to comprehend the power of individual words to recall and connote a forgotten cultural matrix. She is involved in an "archaeological" enterprise, not unlike that of Michel Foucault in his *Archaeology of Knowledge*. Digging underneath the colonial process of subject formation, Cliff examines the various cultural strands that make up Creole culture: the European and the African influences, braided together; the experience of dispossession, which is characteristic of slave societies; and the concomitant need to question the tenets of Western humanism. When history is recognized to be full of gaps, it is impossible to subscribe to a traditional notion of the subject as theorized by Western humanism. That system of thought has created the illusion that memory and history can define the self and give meaning and authority to each utterance. By contrast, Cliff's strategy is to let the narrative show that authority is a construction of language and that the multicultural subject is always the site of contradictions.[24]

The Martinican critic Roger Toumson has cautioned that we must approach the issue of identity with a full understanding of the role that Western philosophy has played in the rationalization of inequality, in the subjugation of an "other" defined and coded negatively vis-à-vis a master who is the only "proper" person and full subject of history. Thus, Toumson adds, "humanism was able to

[23]Maryse Condé, "Beyond Languages and Colors," *Discourse* 11 (Spring–Summer 1989): 110, 111–12.

[24]Cliff's protagonist is adept at manipulating codes, switching from *patois* to *backra* whenever she needs to reassert her class superiority. *Backra* or *buckra* is a Creole term meaning white person and, by extension, "white" language. See *A* 100–101, 122–23, 133–34, for episodes in which Clare reveals her problematic relationship to Zoe and her ability to manipulate the social dissymmetry between them in order to maintain power and control.

legitimize a praxis of barbariousness [*sic*]." A system of thought that represents the "other" as a variation of the "same" cannot do justice to the multicultural environment of the Caribbean, and for Toumson the questions that must now be asked are these: "What philosophy of the subject, what concept of difference can bear witness to the Caribbean cultural particularity without the experienced difference being neither put as difference in relationship to the European or African model nor brought back to a repetition of one or the other of these models? How else can we conceive ourselves *otherwise?*"[25] Echoing Frantz Fanon's formulation in *Toward the African Revolution,* Toumson goes on to say: "The Caribbean logic of experience no longer authorizes the transfer of the biological to the anthropological. . . . [We must] try to put an end to the binary theory of identity as soon as possible by preventing the morbid resurgence of the discourse of absolute otherness. When, for example, the White illusion is followed by the Black illusion there is passage only from the same to the same."[26]

"To conceive ourselves otherwise" means to scrutinize the assumptions that buttress our systems of ideology, including the ones that tend to essentialize language as an entity that is not permeable to its "other" or that can be judged authentic or inauthentic, depending on the subject position adopted or evinced by the speaker. Because linguistic innovations tend to undermine the separation between standard language and vernacular speech, this highly creative process of cultural creolization also forms the basis for a praxis of self-invention through and in language that is the virtual project of many writers who are the products of colonial encounters and whose works experiment with the emancipatory potential of language.

[25]Roger Toumson, "The Question of Identity in Caribbean Literature," *Journal of Caribbean Studies* 5 (Fall 1986): 134.

[26]Ibid., 141. See Frantz Fanon, "West Indians and Africans," in his *Toward the African Revolution,* trans. Haakon Chevalier (New York: Grove Press, 1969), 17–27; Fanon states: "Then, with his eyes on Africa, the West Indian was to hail it. He discovered himself to be the transplanted son of slaves; he felt the vibration of Africa in the very depth of his body and aspired only to one thing: to plunge into the great 'black hole.' It thus seems that the West Indian, after the great white error, is now living the great black mirage" (27).

The "Noises" of History

How can we theorize this possibility of thinking "otherwise"? In scrutinizing the role played by the vernacular in the constitution of a postcolonial subjectivity that truly reflects the discontinuities of Caribbean history, a brief discussion of communication theory will help me show how Creole can function as "noise" in the alienated discourse of the assimilated subject. Cliff's book, like the *abeng*, is a polysemic means of communication that addresses different audiences simultaneously; what is "message" for a Creolophone audience may simply be construed as "noise" by an Anglophone reader. What does this self-conscious articulation of "noise" and "message" tell us about the discourse of the postcolonial writer?

It has become a truism—at least since Claude Shannon and Warren Weaver published their pathbreaking research on the mathematical theory of communication in the 1940s—that there is no message without "noise," that any channel of communication contains some form of interference that impedes, to a greater or lesser degree, the reception of a message.[27] It has also been a tenet of poststructuralist theory to argue against the binary sterility and linearity of subject-object and sender-receiver models of analysis, precisely because this linear formal approach evacuates the "noise": that is, the contextual and connotative dimensions of the message being communicated. By contextual dimensions, I mean the heterogeneities and pluralities that subtend any act of language, any act of representation, and that we have to take as *givens* in any culture.

Thus, also, the French mathematician and philosopher Michel Serres, in his book *Le Parasite*, relates noise in the communicative context to biological parasitism: the French word *parasite* means "interference" or "static," as on the sound waves of telecommunication systems, as well as an organism that thrives on a host's body. Serres's point about "noise" is that what may be perceived as interference is perhaps simply another message trying to get through, trying to be heard against the background of existing discourses. He gives in particular the example of the ringing telephone that interrupts a dinner conversation: on one level it is random,

[27]Claude Shannon and Warren Weaver, *The Mathematical Theory of Communication* (Urbana: University of Illinois Press, 1949).

unwelcome noise; but by answering the phone, I receive a message in its own right, a message with which the dinnertable conversation interferes because *it* will now function as noise.[28]

Viewed from this perspective, any message can become the noise or static that disrupts the orderly proceedings of another communicative act; the more obvious the disturbance, the easier the task of containing, ignoring, or neutralizing the disruptive factors. The point, though, is this: if the discourse of an author is outside the acceptable norms of common linguistic practice, and if he wants to use it to disrupt or resist those dominant norms, one way to proceed is to undermine from within in order to avoid being too easily neutralized. Of course, the author might also run the risk of having her message mistaken for meaningless noise, if she communicates it in a language that is not a part of the general frame of reference of that dominant discourse.

The predicament I have just outlined is that of all so-called "marginal" writers who belong to several hierarchized cultural universes and who generally express themselves in a "dominant" language. Such is the case with African American writers, who have the choice between Standard English and vernacular traditions, and with postcolonial writers whose mother tongue may be *patois*, Creole, Joual, Wolof, Bambara, Berber, or Arabic, but who write in French or in English. The vernacular mother tongue will produce interferences in the text, interferences that only a reader trained to recognize the—sometimes duplicitous, sometimes obvious—use of the vernacular, and receptive to its message, will not dismiss as "noise."

In his essay "Bilinguisme et Littérature," Abdelkebir Khatibi discusses this "translation" problem as it relates to North African literature:

> Tant que la théorie de la traduction, de la bi-langue et de la pluri-langue n'aura pas avancé, certains textes . . . resteront imprenables selon une approche formelle et fonctionnelle. La langue "maternelle" est à l'oeuvre dans la langue étrangère. De l'une à l'autre se déroulent une traduction permanente et un entretien en abyme, extrêmement difficile à mettre au jour. . . . Où se dessine la violence du texte, sinon

---

[28]Michel Serres, *Le Parasite* (Paris: Grasset, 1980), 93.

dans ce chiasme, cette intersection, à vrai dire, irréconciliable? Encore faut-il en prendre acte, dans le texte même: assumer la langue française, oui *pour y nommer cette faille et cette jouissance de l'étranger* qui doit continuellement travailler à la marge. [As long as a theory of translation, of this double- and multi-language has not progressed, some texts . . . will remain beyond appropriation by a formalist or functionalist approach. The "mother" tongue is at work within the other tongue. There is a permanent movement of translation from one to the other, a dialogue as with a mirror, extremely hard to elucidate. . . . The violence of the text takes shape precisely in this chiasmus, this intersection, this irreconcilable difference. We must however take note of it within the text itself: we need to assume the French language, but in order *to name this divide, this fault, and this joyful use of what is foreign*, with its process of undoing the margin continually.][29]

It is important to note that the term *jouissance* is not used here simply in the sense made familiar by psychoanalysis and contemporary French theory (Lacan, Kristeva, Barthes, and others). What is also implied in the text is the *legal* aspect of the term, as in the legal phrase *jouissance d'un bien*, which means to have the use and possession of a piece of property (the usufruct). Khatibi relates meaning to the use and possession of a language, to the process of "making a language one's own" as Mikhail Bakhtin also understands it: that is, the way an individual appropriates a language or a cultural code, transforms it, and makes it his or her own, despite the fact that that code may continue, on a certain level, to resist appropriation.[30]

But what is most important for Khatibi is that the fact of recognizing and naming the proliferation of textual gaps between different levels of discourse effaces territorial boundaries and continually undoes the margin. This, for him, is the function of the vernacular in the text when it operates as message in its own right and not as noise: it undoes and undermines the binary relation

[29] Abdelkebir Khatibi, *Maghreb pluriel* (Paris: Denoël, 1983), 179 (my emphasis); hereafter *MP*.

[30] Jacques Lacan, *Le Séminaire*, (Paris: Seuil, 1975) bk. 20, "Encore"; Julia Kristeva, *Desire in Language: A Semiotic Approach to Literature and Art*, trans. Tom Gora, Alice Jardine, and Léon Roudiez (New York: Columbia University Press, 1980); Roland Barthes, *Le Plaisir du texte* (Paris: Seuil, 1973), and Mikhail Bakhtin, "Discourse in the Novel," in *The Dialogic Imagination* (Austin: University of Texas Press, 1981), 258–422.

between center and periphery, message and noise, history and fiction, language and "dialect." In other words, the vernacular offers a continual play of resistance. Although it may clearly be marked as "other"—thus leaving itself open to the possibility of co-optation—it can also create tensions and contradictions within the dominant discourse, setting in motion the dynamics of dissent, intervention, and change which can ultimately allow a "minority" position to resist integration and assimilation and even to become its own exclusionary system (which might eventually exist in a symbiotic relationship with the dominant ideology, just as a parasite sometimes does in the host's body). When viewed from this perspective, the vernacular can help us understand particular configurations of power at a given historical moment.

When Michelle Cliff strives to reinvent the past, she is guided by its traces as they exist and show up in the everyday world. More often than not, these traces are present in language in the form of words whose etymology is "foreign" and often unknown to the majority of the people using them. In such cases, the vernacular is "parasitic," its existence dependent upon the relative unrecognizability of its origins. That is why Cliff takes on the role of cultural translator: "The people . . . did not know that their name for papaya—*pawpaw*—was the name of one of the languages of Dahomey. Or that the *cotta*, the circle of cloth women wound tightly to make a cushion to balance baskets on their heads, was an African device, and African word" (*A*, 20). Interestingly, words such as *pawpaw* and *cotta* function as "noise" in *both* Standard English and Jamaican Creole. Although commonly used in everyday speech and assimilated into the language, they retain a radical difference that can point to their submerged origins on the palimpsest of history. In Anglocentric "literary language," of course, *pawpaw* and *cotta* could be recuperated as "folkloric" cultural detail, but for Cliff they become polyvalent signifiers, lifelines to a different past, the means by which a different artform—one closer to an oral tradition of storytelling and self-representation—can begin to take shape.

This linguistic practice confirms Trinh T. Minh-ha's view that "vernacular speech . . . is not acquired through institutions—schools, churches, professions etc.—and therefore not repressed by either grammatical rules, technical terms, or key words." Its intent and purpose, she goes on to explain, are outside the realm of persuasion. Vernacular speech does not aim at clarity, for "clarity as a purely rhetorical attribute serves the purpose of a classical feature in language, namely, its instrumentality." Echoing Khatibi, she adds: "Clarity is a means of subjection, a quality both of official, taught language and of correct writing, two old mates of power: together they flow, together they flower, vertically, to impose an order."[31] The presence of Creole creates for the non-Jamaican reader an opacity that places Cliff's text beyond appropriation, demarcating it as radically "other" for an English speaker and preventing any simplistic understanding based on its purely referential value. Hence, that opacity has a doubly subversive function: its aim is not simply to suggest (*pace* Mordecai and Wilson) a specific link to a more or less "authentic" cultural past; *and* it prevents the ideological adoption of a static form of humanism because it stresses the distance between narrator and reader, between insiders and outsiders, Creole speakers and their others, while undermining the reader's belief in the value of "clarity."

Not unlike Zora Neale Hurston, who has been a major influence on her work and her thinking, Cliff is what I have called an *auto-ethnographer*, because her narratives belong in a new genre of contemporary autobiographical texts by writers whose interest and focus are not so much the retrieval of a repressed dimension of the *private* self but the rewriting of their ethnic history, the re-creation of a *collective* identity through the performance of language.[32] Thanks to the appropriation of the oral tradition, the written text becomes a patchwork of discontinuous influences; Cliff points out that her experience as a writer, her "struggle to get wholeness from fragmentation while working within fragmentation, producing work which may find its strength in its depiction of fragmentation, through form as well as content," is similar to the experience of many other writers coming from colonial backgrounds (*LLB*, 14–15).

That is why the reconstruction of her fictive ancestors' past is translated through what Eduoard Glissant has called an *economie parcellaire*.[33] She has recourse to a textual economy of "small plots"

---

[31]Trinh T. Minh-ha, *Woman, Native, Other: Writing, Postcoloniality, and Feminism* (Bloomington: Indiana University Press, 1989), 16–17.

[32]See *AV*, chap. 3.

[33]Edouard Glissant, *Le Discours antillais* (Paris: Seuil, 1984), 69.

that seems to correspond to the economy of "small plot farming" that Maroon slaves used to engage in. Because she wants to claim the cultural heritage of the Maroons who survived in large numbers in Jamaica, Cliff uses a narrative fragmentation that is but the mimesis of another form of cultural and economic dispersion and segmentation. In order to survive in the high mountain regions of the island, the Maroons—always on the move to avoid being captured by their former masters—would cultivate small plots of land that could be cleared out and left fallow. Whereas the totalizing discourse of colonial historiography appears to correspond to the economy of large, self-sustaining plantations, the small "portions" of texts, episodes, and plots in Cliff's narrative seem rather to reapportion and reassign authority and agency to a different set of elusive actors, always on the move and present on both the public and private stages of history. The narrative discontinuities and the polyphonic tone of *Abeng*, as well as the shifts among different linguistic registers, all suggest a form of subjectivity bound to the fluid configurations of memory, language, and landscape and representable only in nonlinear forms.

Cliff's search for a means of cultural representation that can do justice to the heterogeneities of the present and to the absent categories of the past is echoed throughout the Caribbean in the work of male or female, Francophone or Anglophone, writers (C. L. R. James, Edward Kamau Brathwaite, Aimé Césaire, Daniel Maximin, Simone Schwarz-Bart, Maryse Condé, to name just a few). This is how Edouard Glissant formulates it:

> The past, to which we were subjected, which has not yet emerged as history for us, is, however, obsessively present. The duty of the writer is to explore this obsession, to show its relevance in a continuous fashion to the immediate present. This exploration is therefore related neither to a schematic chronology nor to a nostalgic lament. It leads to the identification of a painful notion of time and its full projection forward into the future, without the help of those plateaus in time from which the West has benefited, without the help of that collective density that is the primary value of an ancestral cultural heartland. That is what I call *a prophetic vision of the past*. (CD, 63–64)

Contemporary Caribbean writers address and reject the Hegelian view of history as a single hierarchical and linear process that

would run its unique—European—course, bypassing the Caribbean as it did Africa.[34] But this intolerable absence in the realm of
self-conscious representations can in fact allow the postcolonial
writer to invent and re-create a sense of continuity and community
rooted in this absent temporal landscape. It is by becoming an agent
in this shared process of cultural mutation that writers such as Cliff
and Condé free themselves from the straitjacket of a Eurocentered
vocabulary.

Unlike the previous generation of Caribbean writers, from Césaire to George Lamming, whose discourse on *exile* established the
parameters within which much of negritude was to become understood, Cliff's effort rejoins the patient reconstructions of history and
physical landscape already attempted by Glissant:

> Landscape is more powerful in our literature than the physical size of
> countries would lead us to believe. The fact is that it is not saturated
> with a single History but effervescent with intermingled histories,
> spread around, rushing to fuse without destroying or reducing each
> other....
>
> We are finished with the fight against exile. Our task today is
> reintegration. Not the generalized power of the scream, but the pains-
> taking survey of the land.... [We have] the difficult duty of consid-
> ering the function of language and the texture of self-expression. In
> particular, [we must be careful] not to use Creole in a mindless fash-
> ion, but to ask in all possible ways, *our* question: How do we adapt
> to the techniques of writing an oral language that rejects the written?
> How do we put together, in the dimension of self-expression, the use
> of several languages that must be "mastered"? (*CD*, 154)

By situating herself on the postmodern side of the ideological fence
separating different generations of Caribbean writers, Cliff sets the
stage for the kind of "historiographic metafiction" that locates post-

---

[34]See G. W. F. Hegel, *Vorlesungen über die Philosophie der Geschichte, Werke* 12
(Frankfurt: Suhrkamp Verlag, 1970), 120: "Jenes eigentliche Afrika ist, soweit die
Geschichte zurückgeht, für den Zusammenhang mit der übrigen Welt verschlossen
geblieben; es ist das in sich gedrungene Goldland, das Kinderland, das jenseits des
Tages der selbsbewußten Geschichte in die schwarze Farbe der Nacht gehüllt ist.
[As far back as history goes, the true Africa has remained cut off from all contact
with the rest of the world; it is the golden land pressed in upon itself, and the land
of childhood removed from the daylight of self-conscious history, wrapped in the
dark mantle of night]" (my translation).

colonial subjectivity within the interstices of heteroglossia[35] and in the "lived rhythms" (*CD*, 154) of orality. But she also belongs in the tradition that begins with Césaire's "Notebook," a work James Clifford has described as "a tropological landscape in which syntactic, semantic, and ideological transformations occur."[36] Like Césaire, Cliff undermines the colonial language and transforms reality by her use of tropes,[37] which function as subversive or "deviant" historical categories that allow her to redefine the private and public genealogies of the Savage family.[38]

Wild Mangoes and Windward Maroons

Two of the tropes that Cliff uses quite consistently in *Abeng* are "mangoes" and "Maroons." Both connote the "wild," the uncultivated, the free, and both imply radical resistance to any form of hegemonic control: "Some of the mystery and wonder of mango-time may have been in the fact that this was a wild fruit. Jamaicans did not cultivate it for export to America or England—like citrus,

[35]I borrow the phrase "historiographic metafiction" from Linda Hutcheon, *Narcissistic Narrative: The Metafictional Paradox* (New York: Methuen, 1984), xiv: "Historiographic metafiction . . . works to situate itself in history and in discourse, as well as to insist on its autonomous fictional and linguistic nature." In *The Politics of Postmodernism* (London: Routledge, 1989), Hutcheon adds: "Subjectivity is represented as something in process, never as fixed and never as autonomous, outside history. It is always a gendered subjectivity" (39); and: "Postmodern texts consistently use and abuse actual historical documents in such a way as to stress both the discursive nature of those representations of the past and the narrativized form in which we read them" (87). Chapter 8 discusses what I take to be the difference between the "postmodern" so understood and the postcolonial condition as manifested in the creolized or *métis* texts of the women writers examined here. For the term "heteroglossia," see Bakhtin, "Discourse in the Novel."

[36]James Clifford, *The Predicament of Culture: Twentieth Century Ethnography, Literature, and Art* (Cambridge: Harvard University Press, 1988), 175.

[37]This clearly suggests that the oversimplification of traditions in terms of periodization or colonial languages (i.e., Francophone vs. Anglophone) becomes inappropriate in the Caribbean. The lines of literary filiation and affiliation are as complex as the bloodlines of slave cultures.

[38]I use the word "deviant" here in the sense made familiar by Michel Foucault in *Discipline and Punish: The Birth of the Prison*, trans. Alan Sheridan (New York: Vintage Books, 1979); I return to it in the chapter's conclusion. His concept of "heterotopia" can also clarify my point. See Foucault, "Of Other Spaces," trans. Jan Miskowiec, *Diacritics* 16 (Spring 1986): 22–27. The tropes used by Cliff contribute to the delineation of new spaces within the old landscapes.

cane, bananas. . . . For them the mango was to be kept an island secret" (*A*, 4); "The Windward Maroons . . . held out against the forces of the white men longer than any rebel troops. . . . Nanny was the magician of this revolution—she used her skill to unite her people and to consecrate their battles" (14).

In Cliff's mythmaking the mango becomes a heterogeneous signifier, which can be readily opposed on the symbolic level to the rigid classificatory practices of the colonial system. An example of schoolyard gossip amply demonstrates the systematic stratification of social classes according to the color line and the divisive impact on children of this rigid classification: "The shadows of color permeated the relationships of the students, one to one. When the girls found out that Victoria Carter, whom everyone thought was the most beautiful girl in school, was the daughter of a Black man who worked as a gardener and an Englishwoman who had settled in Jamaica, her position in their eyes was transformed, and girls who had been quite intimidated by her, now spoke about her behind her back" (100). On the first page of the book, in order to create her own counterdiscourse to this disabling situation, Cliff establishes the mango as emblem of the hybrid, mixed-race people of the island:

> It was a Sunday morning at the height of the mango season. . . . There was a splendid profusion of fruit. The slender cylinders of St. Juliennes hung from a grafted branch of a common mango tree in a backyard in town. Round and pink Bombays seemed to be everywhere. . . . Small and orange number elevens filled the market baskets at Crossroads. . . . Green and spotted Black mangoes dotted the ground at bus stops, schoolyards, country stores—these were only to be gathered not sold. The fruit was all over and each variety was unto itself —with its own taste, its own distinction of shade and highlight, its own occasion and use. In the yards around town and on the hills in the country, spots of yellow, pink, red, orange, black, and green appeared between the almost-blue elongated leaves of the fat and laden trees. (3)

The use of food imagery as a marker of cultural identity is common to several African American women writers: Maya Angelou, for example, also refers to the variety of skin colors among blacks by means of tropes and metaphors.[39] By consciously using the mango, Cliff alludes to the nineteenth-century discourse of scientific racism. Her poem "Passing" echoes and repeats these pages of *Abeng*, but there the emphasis is on the ideological constructions of racial ambiguity in terms of *animal* referents:

> In Jamaica we are as common as ticks.
> We graft the Bombay onto the common mango. The Valencia onto the Seville. We mix tangerines and oranges. We create *mules*.
>
> (*CI*, 6; my emphasis)

I will not dwell on the question of institutionalized scientific racism. As Nancy Stepan has argued, the discourse of "races and proper places" was grounded in the monogenists' and polygenists' belief in the necessity of keeping races "pure" and "apart" for fear that interracial breeding would create subhumans akin to the mule: that is, infertile mulattoes who would cause the white race's degeneracy and its eventual extinction.[40] What interests me here is the fact that this discourse is turned on its head: images of abundance and fertility, generated by the height of the mango season, are linked to the idea of variety and diversity. Cliff constantly stresses that this diversity is a source of strength. Furthermore, she makes an explicit rapprochement between Clare's mother's light skin color and the fruit: "She was in fact quite light-skinned, the shade of her younger daughter, like the inside of a Bombay mango when the outside covering is cut away" (*A*, 127). The mango represents femininity and fertility, and it is as central to the islanders' experience as the sea ("The smell of the sea and the smell of mangoes mixed with each other" [20]) and the cool tropical nights (in which "the scent of ripe mangoes was present and heavy" [22]), which are also ambiguous maternal symbols.

Abeng underlines the matrilineal filiation, which, under the laws governing slave societies, would have been the only permissible

---

[39]See, e.g., Maya Angelou, *Gather Together in My Name* (New York: Random House, 1974), 14; and My discussion in *AV*, 156.

[40]See Nancy Stepan, "Biological Degeneration: Races and Proper Places," in *Degeneration: The Dark Side of Progress*, ed. J. Edward Chamberlin and Sander Gilman (New York: Columbia University Press, 1985); and my discussion in *AV*, 9.

filiation, the only acknowledged genealogy, hence the only possible means of retracing memory and charting the contours of a historical past which, in the Caribbean, is both submarine and subterranean: "sunk under the sea, or scattered as potash in the canefields" (*LLB*, 14). This re-presentation of the mother serves the double purpose of establishing both filiation and affiliation. Described as a strong and passionate woman who suffers from the absence of the kind of historical legitimacy that the narrative simultaneously creates for her daughter, Kitty is a virtual descendant of the famous Maroons. But locked in a negative image of the past (128), she clings to her people's condition of "victim," ignoring the existence of strong female Maroon figures such as Nanny, and initially passing on to her daughter the belief that "speaking well" and reading English books would be her passport to freedom and integration into the white world. Although Kitty is "more comfortable speaking patois and walking through the bush" (99), she remains the "phallic mother," the one who helps buttress the patriarchal foundations of language and who deprives her daughter of that Creole dimension of her own subjectivity because it is a dimension trapped in silence.[41] Wishing to grant Clare an "easier" life than her own, she tries to prevent the development of a double vision and a double consciousness in the child. As Clarisse Zimra argues, the patriarchy hides "the silent presence of a Mother not yet fully understood."[42]

But Cliff can use the broken threads of the colonial diaspora to weave a different narrative of belonging, inclusion, and kinship. *Abeng* becomes the performative rewriting of the web of multicultural influences that her mother could not—and would not—pass on to her. It is in the reconstructions of Kitty's (fictive) childhood memories that the narrative most explicitly reveals the narrator's desire for a past that can transform her view of the present and be the antidote for the Anglocentric obsessions of the father. In naming their daughter Clare, Kitty allows her husband to believe that the choice signals her acceptance of a patriarchal legacy of learning, since Clare is the name of the college his grandfather attended at

[41]On the term "phallic mother" as used here, see Kristeva, *Desire in Language*, esp. 190–208.

[42]Clarisse Zimra, "Righting the Calabash: Writing History in the Female Francophone Narrative," in *OK*, 157.

Cambridge University. But this naming is a stunning act of "sig-nifying",[43] a gesture of dissimulation on the part of the mother who thus also honors and recalls a devoted young black woman named Clary, who had played the role of surrogate mother to Kitty when she was seven. By creating such a mythical link between her own name and her mother's past, Cliff's protagonist situates Kitty within a long tradition of female resistance and invents a new iden-tity for herself, in accordance with her desire for a different per-sonal history. This history begins with the life of the legendary slave and Maroon women whose presence in the text allows for the development of a counternarrative that challenges established historical practices and compels reinterpretation of the past through a different, Afrocentric lens.

The conventions of the dominant historical and anthropological discourses are used to express Cliff's own subversive perspective, just as slaves used the *abeng* to "signify." Combining descriptions of geography and religion, of social and familial arrangements, Cliff does linguistic archaeology (such as her comments on the word *pawpaw*) while giving "folk" details: for example, "They did not know . . . that Brer Anancy, the spider who inspired tricks and tales, was a West African invention" (20). She directly relates Jamaican popular culture to African *practices*, establishing the links in the necessary process of cultural resistance to the theoretical and mythic adherence to European models of culture. This retrieval of the collective, and of the collectively repressed dimension of the cultural self, is mediated by the recognition that writing is an act of language which refigures the real. Cliff's apparently discon-nected narrative moves generate interruptions and suspensions that allow her to take possession of all the threads in her multicultural background and to articulate a form of multivalent subjectivity ca-pable of resisting shifting networks of power. By appropriating the repressed otherness of *patois*, she writes across the margins, at the same time questioning the very notion of marginality, since her position demonstrates that marks of difference and otherness are ambiguous and shifting. Much like the fading wallpaper in the

---

[43]On the term "signifying" and its role in the cultures of the African diaspora, see Henry Louis Gates, Jr., *The Signifying Monkey: A Theory of Afro-American Literary Criticism* (New York: Oxford University Press, 1988).

mansion that used to belong to the slave owners, her father's ancestors (25), the English language is shown to be but a thin veneer barely hiding a creolized, *métis* culture where the woman as native and the native as other merge with and emerge from the blind spots of official historiography.

It is by means of linguistic *practices* embedded within the apparently hegemonic function of the colonizer's language that *Abeng* enacts this transformation of culture. This clearly illustrates, as Foucault has pointed out, that "a change in the order of discourse does not presuppose 'new ideas,' a little invention and creativity, a different mentality, *but* transformations in a practice, perhaps also in neighboring practices, and in their common articulation."[44] This suggests that one way of accounting for the transformation of discursive apparatuses within a postcolonial context may be to identify and highlight those categories (such as "dialect" or "noise" in language, and "Maroons" in historical narrative) which, in Foucault's terminology, would be termed "deviant" and to focus on the way they function in the larger culture. To the extent that new practices can provide means of resistance, they enable us to understand the conditions of possibility for a true paradigm shift in postcolonial culture.

Abeng accomplishes just such a modification in autobiographical discursive practice, bearing testimony to the pluralities of postcolonial existence and thus challenging us, its readers, to become multicultural subjects as well, capable of recognizing the different shapes that a postcolonial artist's shadow might cast on the conventions of genre (as outlined by Gusdorf) and on the ideology of authenticity (as romanticized by some critics). Only then will we be able to understand fully the "conditions and limits" of autobiographical practice outside a narrowly defined idea of self-writing or of community.

[44]Michel Foucault, *The Archaeology of Knowledge and the Discourse on Language*, trans. Alan M. Sheridan Smith (New York: Pantheon, 1972), 209.

2

Evading The Subject: Narration and the City in Ananda Devi's *Rue La Poudrière*

Rue de la Poudrière, its worm-eaten bridge, its old, patched, and huddled shacks transformed, on this Sunday morning, into temples of the sun.
— Robert-Edward Hart, "Métamorphose,"
Cycle de Pierre Flandre

Seek and learn to recognize who and what, in the midst of the inferno, are not inferno, then make them endure, give them space.
— Italo Calvino, *Invisible Cities*

Childhood is the divining rod of melancholy, and to know the mourning of such radiant, glorious cities one must have been a child in them.
— Walter Benjamin, "Marseilles"

Ananda Devi, an Indo-Mauritian writer, has consistently addressed issues of authenticity and universality in her short stories as well as in her first novel, *Rue La Poudrière*, which is the focus of this chapter.[1] Devi's first-person narrative explicitly stages and narrates "deviancy." Her female narrator, Paule, becomes an urban prostitute, the deviant character par excellence of the European novelistic tradition since *Manon Lescaut* or *Moll Flanders*. Devi does not use the same kind of "double-voiced" narrative devices that we saw in *Abeng*. Her technique is to rely instead on the instabilities and ambiguities of the narrative process in order to question the conventions that assign a particular role as "deviant character" to the urban prostitute. She destabilizes the traditional Western categories of female subjectivity, such as the whore/madonna dichotomy, by showing the constructed nature of identity. She also refuses to confine her characters to an externally defined view of

---

[1] Ananda Devi, *Rue La Poudrière* (Abidjan: Nouvelles Editions Africaines, 1988); hereafter *RP*. Page references are given in the text.

what an "authentic Mauritian" identity might be: "My short stories tend toward universality rather than being the descriptive observation of groups that constitute our society. . . . my novels are anchored in Mauritian reality. . . . *Rue La Poudrière* takes place in a Creole milieu, the poorest and most disadvantaged of Port-Louis, . . . but my purpose is to extract from [this description of society] the universal aspects common to the whole of humanity; to explode the geographical confines of the island."[2]

In distinguishing between descriptive observation and universality, Devi alludes to the traditional distinction between anthropology and literature, two disciplines with which she is familiar, for she is a trained anthropologist as well as a writer of fiction. Though now considered arbitrary by such anthropologists as Stephen Tyler and Michael M. J. Fischer, the distinction is an enabling one for this writer, since it allows her to demarcate a space in which she can freely create new fictional scenarios. Within this space she allows herself to test her concept of universality by bringing into focus issues central to contemporary global culture.

By the year 2005, it has been estimated, 50.1 percent of the world's population will be living in urbanized areas, negotiating their survival in an environment that increasingly gives shape to a "modern" subject, evolving from that of more rural or traditional surroundings.[3] Urban spaces are becoming central features of the narratives of postcolonial writers, just as they are in Western literary traditions. Indeed, Western political, fictional, and imaginary landscapes—from the Greek *polis* to Baudelaire's Paris and Sartre's or Baudrillard's New York—have been shaped by many writers' conflicted relationships to a given cityscape. Images of cities and images of women have often been linked, their conspicuous beauty of hidden charms idealized by the nostalgic myths and sentimental geographies of a writer's recollections, his travel, and his autobiographical impulses.[4] Because opportunities for casual sex or anonymous eroticism are widely available in the city, this aspect of the

---

[2] Ananda Devi to Danielle Chavy Cooper, 16 January 1989. I thank Professor Cooper for sharing this information.

[3] UN Secretariat, Population Division, "The World Urbanization Prospect, 1992," microfiche (Summer 1993). I thank Tom Cook for directing me to this source.

[4] I purposely use the masculine pronoun here, as I am outlining a particularly male view of the world.

urban experience has been used to conflate the part and the whole, to describe the city in terms of unrestrained sexuality or deviant femininity. Such images feed dangerous fantasies; they engender allegories of perversity and atavistic evil, desire, and depersonalized longing; they provoke expressions of pleasure or disgust, inspire tales of love or abjection, or represent both extremes simultaneously—what Baudelaire called *l'azur et la boue* [the azure skies and the filthy mud]. Used as emblems, symbols, and correlatives for a wide range of emotions and feelings, from the noblest to the most perverse, the metaphysical to the sexual, cities have been read as both utopian and dystopian.[5]

In a state of constant change and perpetual motion because of population migrations, changing topographies, and evolving skylines, cities can signify either dynamic transformation or decomposition, progress or decay, abundance or violence. In our own postcolonial fin-de-siècle, such dichotomies have become commonplace from Singapore to Kinshasa, London to Los Angeles. The growing urban proletariat and the destabilization of familiar forms of social arrangement create situations that reproduce age-old conflicts between the archaic and the modern, the refined and the corrupt. The city has thus become a figurative as well as a literal crossroads, a visual and linguistic site that functions, in the words of V. Y. Mudimbe, as a "locus of paradoxes that [call] into question the modalities and implications of modernization." This locus is often identified with a narrative of loss, despair, and marginality, especially for the female subject who must negotiate the perils of urban life and the demeaning roles in which it casts her. As Mudimbe also notes in *The Invention of Africa*: "Marginality designates the intermediate space between the so-called African tradition and the projected modernity of colonialism. It is apparently an urbanized space . . . [that] reveals not so much that new imperatives could achieve a jump into modernity, as the fact that despair gives this intermediate space its precarious pertinence and, simultaneously, its dangerous importance."[6]

---

[5] Among many studies on this topic, see esp. Bram Dijkstra, *Idols of Perversity: Fantasies of Feminine Evil in Fin-de-Siècle Culture* (New York: Oxford University Press, 1986); and Charles Bernheimer, *Figures of Ill Repute: Representing Prostitution in Nineteenth-Century France* (Cambridge: Harvard University Press, 1989).

[6] V. Y. Mudimbe, *The Invention of Africa: Gnosis, Philosophy, and the Order of Knowledge* (Bloomington: Indiana University Press, 1988), 5.

One of the obvious dangers of that space is that it can fix meaning, assign roles, and imprison the female subject in a web of significations that severely limit her narrative functions, confining her to conventional and stale plots. The female protagonist who is linked to a narrative of urban decline finds herself, ipso facto, associated with the idea of the fall, of a loss of innocence that inexorably leads to ruin and perdition; novelistic closure is conveniently provided through her demise. This trajectory from luminous madonna to shadowy whore, with its numerous intermediate possibilities, is frequent in literature from Antiquity to the Romantic and modern periods.[7]

What can the postcolonial woman writer do with these *lieux communs* of literary practice? How does she use and transform these conventions inherited from the nineteenth century and European modernity? How does she deal with these urban images and the subjective spaces that are supposed to conform and correlate to the images? How does she define and shape those spaces in her writings, and how are her writing strategies shaped by the urban phenomenon?

To attempt an answer, I focus on Devi's character Paule. She is a child of the city of Port-Louis, the capital of Mauritius; it is there that "la vertigineuse trappe de la féminité [the dizzying trap of femininity]" (72) relentlessly closes in on her. Using Paule as a dark alter ego, Devi scrutinizes the tragic aspects of the female condition in a style that blends social realism with the surreal and the eerie. She writes of the most marginalized postcolonial subjects, the urban female underclass, obsessively exploring the social construction of femininity and its dark recesses.

Port-Louis, with its natural harbor and sweeping backdrop of hills and mountains encircling the bay, has often been represented in a way that emphasizes its serene, luminous, and radiant qualities. In the poetry of Robert-Edward Hart, for example (see this chapter's epigraph), the city shimmers with possibilities. Artists and writers, native to the island or visiting from afar, have fre-

---

[7]For discussion of the ways in which femininity and death are linked, see Nicole Loraux, *Façons tragiques de tuer une femme* (Paris: Hachette, 1985), trans. Anthony Forster as *Tragic Ways of Killing a Woman* (Cambridge: Harvard University Press, 1987); and Margaret Higonnet, "Speaking Silences: Women's Suicide," in *The Female Body in Western Culture*, ed. Susan R. Suleiman (Cambridge: Harvard University Press, 1986).

quently exoticized its solar qualities. But like all tropical colonial cities, Port-Louis is also an inferno, teeming with sordid lives and unresolved conflicts. Devi's book, which features urban life and prostitution as twin sites of conflict, marginality, and danger, points toward this darker reality. The novel is set in the changing landscape of mid-twentieth century Port-Louis, where the declining sugar-based colonial economy, urban renewal, projected free-trade zones, and old-fashioned squalor generate an apocalyptic narrative of prostitution and monstrosity. For the first time in the literature of Mauritius, the city and its infernal elements are revealed, brought to light. But this is not the flattering luminosity that transmutes poverty, "les maisons rapiécées tassées par l'âge [its old, patched, huddled shacks]," into those shining temples dear to Hart; it is rather the dim glow of mourning and melancholy, fueled by a writer's feelings of grief and bereavement before the wretched spectacle of ruined childhoods. In Devi's work, the city of Port-Louis loses its romantic aura to become a more troubling, problematic, and ambiguously engaging site.[8]

Packaging the Book, Situating the Story

Rue La Poudrière escapes all critical attempts to domesticate, label, or immobilize it within an unambiguous literary or cultural framework. In order to situate this Francophone writer, to make her novel "readable" within the shifting sands of "Francophone literature," I begin nonetheless by establishing some historical parameters and interpretive contexts that can give depth to my reading. In this particular case, though, it is equally important to stress that the packaging of Devi's book, as well as its self-reflexive narrative strategies, seem calculated to undermine any such conventional framing by critical discourse. To grasp the full impact of the novel, it becomes necessary to articulate the contradictory meanings generated not only by the language of the text but also by the book itself as material object and primary frame of a reader's first encounter with it.

[8]For many other contemporary Mauritian writers and artists, the city's sentimental appeal is as strong as ever; see G. André Decotter, *Port-Louis: Visions d'artistes* (Ile Maurice: Océan Indien, 1991), and *Guirlande pour une capitale* (Port-Louis: Municipalité de Port-Louis, 1966).

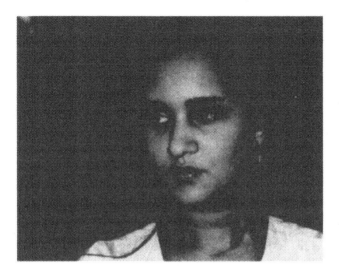

Figure 1. Ananda Devi as she appears on jacket of *Rue La Poudrière.* By permission of Nouvelles Editions Ivoirennes.

Nothing about the outer appearance of the book permits us to identify clearly the national origin of the author or the actual geographic location to which the title refers. On the back of the book (Figure 1), a photograph of the author features a pensive and somewhat melancholic young Indian woman with a beautiful and sad face. Under the picture a short biography indicates her date of birth, 1957; her real name, Ananda Devi Nirsimloo-Anenden; but not her place of residence—although the topic of her doctoral dissertation, "L'Identité ethnique du groupe Telegu de l'île Maurice," is indeed mentioned.[9] We might surmise that she belongs to the Telegu-speaking ethnic group, one of several ethnic groups from the Indian subcontinent which have been in Mauritius since the nineteenth century. The blurb claims that she has written another novel, *Le Rêve carnassier,* which I have not been able to locate. The twelve-line summary of the novel that follows does not clarify the writer's or the book's identity; it indicates that Paule is a protagonist who "lutte avec sa propre identité de femme [struggles with her own female identity]" and that the principal elements of the story consist

[9] Ananda Devi holds a doctorate from the School of African and Oriental Studies, University of London. Her dissertation was published as *The Primordial Link: Telegu Ethnic Identity in Mauritius* (Moka, Mauritius: Mahatma Gandhi Institute Press, 1990).

in her difficult relationship with her parents and with the pimp Mallacre, who initiates her into his nightmare world of prostitution.

The front cover of the book, however, steers the reader toward a different cultural and geographic context (Figure 2). The color photograph of a slum clearly appears to have been taken in an African city. Since the novel was published by the Nouvelles Editions Africaines, in Abidjan, one might infer that this tropical slum is to be found on the outskirts of that city. Three people are in the picture: two African women, looking tired, are seated on the ground between two entrances to a row of corrugated iron shacks, and a young man is standing in front of them with his back to the camera, one hand in his pocket, the other folded behind him and holding what appears to be a wallet. His posture suggests that he may well be the *proxénète* (pimp) mentioned on the back cover.

The author's name, Ananda Devi, is at the top of the front cover, in dark blue letters that stretch across the tropical sky (*l'azur?*) above the lush green palm and mango trees that serve as backdrop to the shacks. The title of the novel is printed at the bottom, across the dirt road or alley (*la boue?*), as though literally naming it "rue la poudrière," and next to the title is added the word *roman*. Because of the acoustic similarity between the French words *la poudrière* (powder mill) and *la poussière* (dust, dirt), it seems highly probable that both meanings unconsciously inhere in any first reading of the cover. Furthermore, slippage between the masculine (*le poudrier*: face-powder compact) and feminine meanings is also possible, simultaneously suggesting makeup and adornment (the tools of seduction, which connote dissemblance, dissimulation, and feigning) as well as armaments and gunpowder (the tools of war and violence, which can also connote the relentless war between the sexes). These indeterminacies and ambiguities are echoed and reinforced by various narrative strategies deployed in the situation of the telling, at the scene of narration.

For a Francophone reader unfamiliar with Mauritius, this book cover creates a fictional world that is at least partially determined by the external reality of postcolonial urban Africa, with its marginal inhabitants who eke out a meager living on the outskirts of the commercial areas of large cities. The book is very carefully designed to suggest as much. The combination of extratextual elements creates an imaginary Africa by means of visual details that

Figure 2. Front of jacket for *Rue La Poudrière*. By permission of Nouvelles Editions Ivoirennes.

Figure 3. "Rue de la Poudrière," ink drawing by Hervé de Cotter. Used by permission of the artist.

anchor the narrative in a very specific though unknown locale. The book thus appears to belong to the symbolic context of international *francophonie* and to the material reality of contemporary urban Africa. But even if this cover seems to be calculated to produce a particular impression, a specific *effet de réel* (reality effect), as Barthes would say, to judge the book by its cover may constitute a serious cultural and geographic misreading.

In fact, for a Mauritian reader, "rue de la Poudrière" (written with the "de" that local Creole colloquial speech eliminates) refers to a very real street in an old neighborhood of the capital city of Port-Louis (Figure 3). Until the 1950s this street was frequented by prostitutes and lined with *maisons closes* (houses of prostitution) well known to visiting sailors, tourists, and local bourgeois. It is not exactly a "slum," such as the one depicted on the cover, but one of the oldest streets in the colonial city. Located in the western part of town, it leads from the old harbor to an eighteenth-century powder mill or *magasin à poudre*, built on a hill by the French and transformed into an Anglican church by the British conquerors after 1810. The historian Auguste Toussaint recounts that in the early part of this century there were two main areas of the city where prostitutes worked. One was called "La Plaine Verte," a mostly Muslim quarter on the eastern edge of the harbor where Muslim women plied their trade. Among the prostitutes on the other side of the city, Toussaint states, there were "many Africans, ranging in skin color from black to brown, as well as Indo-Africans. They work[ed] in the Western quarter and especially on Poudrière and Entrecasteaux streets."[10] (This particular "business" moved from the city to a beachfront resort area when urban renewal and the spread of modern office buildings forced its practitioners out during the 1950s and 1960s.) That is the real geographic context of the novel, the referent of the title, which is deliberately left out of the visual frame of the book.

The contradictions between the concrete visual packaging and the historico-cultural connotations of the title are bound to affect the reception of the book; the average Francophone reader who comes across it in a bookstore or library will be justified in assuming that he or she has picked up an African novel, since such a reader is unlikely to have any extensive knowledge of Mauritius. The native Mauritian, on the other hand, may recognize the name of the writer, and certainly that of the infamous street, but may find it difficult to place the text within a familiar tradition of Mauritian writing. This is because Devi's style is unique and because she is uninterested in describing the tropical landscape, the sea, the island, or the cultural diversity that have been celebrated by generations of writers before her. She approaches her material with a certain deliberateness and marks it with her combined French and Hindu sensitivity, making multiple allusions to European narrative and poetic traditions as well as to metamorphosis, reincarnation, predestination, and the karma of Hindu orthodoxy. As Danielle

[10] Auguste Toussaint, *Port-Louis: Deux siècles d'histoire (1735–1935)* (Port-Louis: La Typographie Moderne, 1936), 443.

Chavy Cooper puts it: "Themes common to Hindu mysticism recur: . . . destiny, reincarnation, spirituality, the cosmos. Aerial images, light, stars, and flight replace the marine images so dear to other Mauritian writers. . . . It is karma, the belief that every action, every intention is inscribed in the destiny of all living beings, which constitutes the background of all of Ananda Devi's characters."[11] Devi combines the Hindu belief in fate with another credo: that biology is destiny. Paule is a victim of these ideologies, but as narrator she also exposes them for what they are: fictional constructs that govern our actions in the world. Whereas the thematic focus of the tale remains sharp and clear (the plight of the female subject, the material conditions of her existence, and the apparent atavism of her sexuality), the self-reflexive nature of the writing underscores the instabilities and ambiguities of the narrative process.

The novel has the same lyrical qualities that Egyptian writer Nawal el Saadawi brings to her fictional autobiography of Firdaus, a Cairo prostitute and murderer, in *Woman at Point Zero*. Like Saadawi, Devi was educated in the West and does not share in the condition of the characters she creates. She has lived and studied in England, as well as Africa and Mauritius. She is well aware of her lived relation to processes of Westernization and rejects all nativist ideologies or facile legitimation in the guise of "authenticity" and "national identity." She exemplifies in her narrative practice Teresa de Lauretis's theoretical articulation of the *multiple* positionalities that are those of the female subject.[12] For Devi and for Saadawi (Chapter 6), this multiplicity of subject-positions produces an elusive subject who must be represented in relational terms, not as an autonomous and determinate category. Hence the indeterminacies that set their narratives in motion.

Still relatively unknown in the Francophone world, Devi's work has not been anthologized, although she has received critical acclaim since 1972. In his *Histoire de la littérature mauricienne de langue française* (1978), Jean-Georges Prosper hailed her as "une adolescente prodige, . . . [un] écrivain précoce [a teenage prodigy, a pre-

[11]Danielle Chavy Cooper, "Ananda Devi et le poids des êtres," paper read at the Ninth Annual International Conference on Foreign Literature, Wichita State University, 1992.

[12]See Teresa de Lauretis, "Displacing Hegemonic Discourses: Reflections on Feminist Theory in the 1980s," *Inscriptions* 3/4 (1988): 136; and this book's Introduction.

cocious writer]."[13] She received early recognition in the form of various awards, including the 1972 "Prix de la meilleure nouvelle de langue française" (award for the best short story in French) for "La Cité Atlee," a story entered in a competition organized by the French Agence de Coopération Culturelle et Technique and the state-owned radio and television station ORTF. She has since published two volumes of short stories, *Solstices* (1977) and *Le Poids des êtres* (1987),[14] as well as *Rue La Poudrière* (1988) which has been acclaimed by Cooper as "a gripping, powerful, relentless novel, a mystical poetic epic—one of a kind."[15] The novellas have a very distinctive descriptive style, with strong dramatic and narrative control. Some, such as "La Petite de Ganvié" in *Le Poids des êtres*, inspired by the years Devi lived in Brazzaville, are actually set in Africa. This may explain the African photograph on the cover of her novel. She has been in a position to observe the seamy side of life in African cities and may well be suggesting that the conditions under which poor women live are tragically similar from city to city.

Devi crosses cultural, geographic, and aesthetic boundaries, and her contribution consists precisely in making the kinds of connections between distant sites that her novel makes, revealing links and suggesting similarities. As Foucault has shown, our experience of the world today "is less that of a long life developing through time than that of a network that connects points and intersects with its own skeins."[16] The network of images created by Devi links those "intermediate spaces" defined by Mudimbe, those sites where despair underscores the dangers and the corruptions of modernization.[17] She is familiar with the urban problems which are increasingly the same in the "first" and "third" world. *Rue La Pou-*

---

[13]Jean-Georges Prosper, *Histoire de la littérature mauricienne de langue française* (Ile Maurice: Océan Indien, 1978), 294, 295.

[14]Ananda Devi, *Solstices* (Port-Louis: Editions Patrick Mackay, 1976), and *Le Poids des êtres* (Ile Maurice: Editions de l'Océan Indien, 1987).

[15]Danielle Chavy Cooper, review of *Rue La Poudrière*, *World Literature* 64 (Summer 1990): 515.

[16]Michel Foucault, "Of Other Spaces," trans. Jan Miskowiec, *Diacritics* 16 (1986): 22.

[17]Mudimbe addresses these issues in his fictional practice as well as in *The Invention of Africa*; see *Le Bel Immonde* (Paris: Présence Africaine, 1976), trans. Marjolijn de Jager as *Before the Birth of the Moon* (New York: Simon & Schuster, 1989).

drière is her very elusive, allusive, and disquieting narrative response to these experiences.

The Scene of Narration

The elusive quality of Devi's style surfaces in the first sentence: "Je cours; très vite, le monde déferle à mes côtés, gris, informe" [I am running very fast, the world, gray and shapeless, unfurls alongside my path]" (*RP*, 3). The narrator's, and the narrative's, double flight from meaning and reality, from fixed location and stable identity, are stressed by this voice and thematized in her mobility, her desire to escape from a circumscribed existence. This flight suggests ways of evading the patriarchal order and the institutional conventions that impose meaning on the lives of poor women, confining them to preestablished roles. The voice warns: "Ne cherchez plus à concevoir dans votre esprit ma forme charnelle. Il n'est nécessaire que d'entendre une voix, sortant de l'ombre [Do not try to imagine my bodily shape. You need only to hear a voice coming out of shadows]" (6). This disembodied voice addresses the reader directly and refuses to be stifled or contained by the usual labels or maps for reading (such as the ones I have nonetheless given) which we tend to activate when approaching a text. The flow of words propels the narrator through disconnected images, visions of body parts, the sense organs of those who happen to be in her path: "ici, un oeil surpris de ma course, là, une bouche ouverte sur une question amputée, autre part, une main tendue vers moi [here, a look of surprise at my running, a mouth open with an aborted question, there, a hand stretched in my direction]" (3). These blurred images then merge into one massive vision of hostility: "Des stalagmites de haine croissent aux quatre coins de moi, . . . les êtres s'agglomèrent pour n'être qu'un grand cri [I am growing stalagmites of hatred from all sides of my body, . . . masses of people are nothing but a loud scream]". They elicit contradictory sensations that cannot be contained, expanding beyond the body of the narrator, swelling up and taking on unforeseen proportions, "s'enflent jusqu'à déborder de l'espace étroit qui les encastre [inflated to the point of bursting out of the narrow space that surrounds it]." The young female narrator, "précoce, prête pour la vie,

faite pour être pétrie et moulue, . . . prête pour être forme et cour-
bure [precocious, ready for life, ready to be kneaded and molded,
. . . to be shaped into curves]," ambiguously describes herself in
terms of the formless matter of life to which events, encounters,
and narrative attempt to give shape, to make into an object of pleasure, but which will always exceed all framing and controlling
mechanisms.

If this evasive self-positioning of the subject of the enunciation is
meant to evoke an elusively "universal" female protagonist, what
are the means by which the narrator strives to escape the aesthetic,
ideological, and material determinations that are usually associated
with the subject of prostitution? How does she succeed in opening
up new interpretive frames around this subject?[18] What kind of
fictional world does the narrative create in its rigorous attempt to
distance itself from the material realities (outlined above) which it
nonetheless represents?

Wolfgang Iser has shown how acts of fictionalizing depend upon
three distinct but interdependent operations that all involve the
crossing of boundaries, the stepping beyond limits, and the blurring
of categories for the purposes of endowing the imaginary with
what he calls "an articulate gestalt" capable of transforming the
diffuseness of its fantasies into more determinate images, while also
exceeding, going beyond, the determinacies of reality. These operations are selection, combination, and self-disclosure. The extratextual elements selected (the real world of urban life, the images of
Africa, the name of a real street, colonial experiences, and the like)
are combined by means of syntactic and semantic relations that
"give rise to intratextual fields of reference" (the denotative and
figural functions of "rue la poudrière," for example), which reveal
in turn the self-referential, self-disclosing attributes of literary fictions: their ability to convey the appearance of reality while brack-
eting that reality and representing the activity of fictionalization
itself, the feigning and dissembling that are constitutive of that activity. Moreover, Iser adds, "in self-disclosure, it is the reader's ha-
bitual attitudes towards the represented world of the fictional

---

[18]See, e.g., Amanda S. Anderson, "D. G. Rossetti's 'Jenny': Agency, Intersubjec-
tivity, and the Prostitute," *Genders* 4 (Spring 1989); and Anderson, "Prostitution's
Artful Guise" (review of Bernheimer's *Figures of Ill Repute*), *Diacritics* 21 (Summer–
Fall 1991).

'as-if' " that become marked by "a continual, however distinctly graded, process of transformation." By revealing its status as fiction, a narrative is thus able to engage the reader in a sensemaking activity that will produce a new gestalt and wrest new insights about a fairly conventional topic (here, prostitution, fatalism, and the city).[19] Rather than reinforcing old representations and simply adding new facets to them, self-referentiality transforms traditional functions (for example, the female heroine's role in the narrative development of her fall) by exposing the constructed nature of all representations.

That is why the narrative voice in *Rue La Poudrière* is self-consciously concerned with the act of fictionalizing, with the telling of the tale. The city street that names the novel clearly functions as a metaphor for the narrative process, laying bare the teleological and linear movement through time and space that has been constitutive of the genre: the child Paule becomes the fallen woman on the road to perdition, repeating—albeit differently—her mother Marie's secret and monstrous activities, her father Edouard's failed existence, "cet étrange jeu de conjugalité qui était aussi un jeu de destruction et de torture [this strange game of conjugal life which was also a game of destruction and torture]" (18). As Steven Winspur puts it, "The street on which a fictional character walks leads in a certain direction and points to a certain end, . . . towards the disclosure of certain problems of human action, . . . towards their eventual dissolution or closure."[20]

Here, Paule's self-reflexive comments on the linear movement of storytelling have an unsettling and destabilizing effect. The novel's beginning undermines the interpretive moves of the reader-critic before these can begin to be mapped out. But the opening sentence also generates a dark journey that will end in stasis, thus reproducing the conventional moves of the genre. Closure is reached as the narrator finally stops running and succumbs to sleep and inertia: "Ma tête est emplie d'une somnolence, je suis figée dans un état embryonnaire, je ne peux plus agir [My head is full of sleep, I

---

[19]Wolfgang Iser, "Feigning in Fiction," in *Identity of the Literary Text*, ed. Mario Valdès and Owen Miller (Toronto: University of Toronto Press, 1985), 205, 212, 224.

[20]Steven Winspur, "On City Streets and Narrative Logic," in *City Images: Perspectives from Literature, Philosophy, and Film*, ed. Mary Ann Caws (New York: Gordon & Breach, 1991), 60.

am frozen at the embryonic stage, I cannot act]" (196). She lets herself be tempted by the lure of death and awaits her fate in the old wooden house, "la maison-fantôme, la maison-viscère de la Butte [the phantom-house, the visceral house of La Butte]" (186), slated for demolition in order to make way for the "façades de béton et de ciment [walls of concrete and cement]" (197). Her fate exemplifies the disposable quality of individual lives, "l'incohérence de notre misère [the incoherence of our needfulness]" (35), plowed under the wheels of capitalist expansion and economic progress, with as much value as those "éléments transitoires de l'existence [transitory elements of life]" that are left to disappear without trace, "sans rien déranger, s'éteignant souplement [disturbing nothing, quietly snuffed out]" (197). Nor does her death underwrite the rebirth and renewal of another subject, another space open to modernity. Port-Louis is burning, consuming itself under the "soleil-forge qui cogne sur les choses rougies à vif. Le soleil-glaive qui fouille et s'enfonce dans votre tête, consumant l'esprit [anvil of the sun which turns everything red; the sword of the sun which penetrates deep into your head, burning your mind]" (196). Life goes on "au jour le jour, de seconde en seconde, dans une terrible ritualité sans signification [from day to day, second to second, in a terrible and meaningless ritual]" (195).

The narrative oscillates between developing a conventional framework and evading the meanings that such a framework would prescribe. The text conflates the narrator's fate and the city's: "C'est moi qui incarne le plus étroitement son amertume de cité vendue à toutes les convoitises. . . . ils ont tous morcelé la cité à leur désir. . . . Combien de temps faudra-t-il à la cité pour vivre son désintègrement? [I am the perfect incarnation of the sadness that envelops this city sold to all who covet it. . . . They have partitioned the city in accordance with their own desires. . . . How long will it take for the city to live out its disintegration?]" (74); and later on: "A l'intérieur de moi, tout brûle. . . . Et hier ou aujourd'hui, je me suis consumée. . . . je me suis brûlée à petit feu [Inside of me, everything burns. . . . Yesterday or today I have been consumed. . . . I have been burned in a slow fire]" (193). But the narrative goes on to denaturalize these connections, to make clear that these are ritualized scenes that allegorize the activity of reading: "Mes paroles se sont déroulées en lianes souples et fortes, à la sève brûlante, elles forment une chevelure folle autour du visage anonyme du lecteur [My words have been unfurling like a lithe and strong creeper, with burning sap, that surrounds the reader's anonymous face like a head of wild hair]" (195). An implicit analogy is drawn here between the reader and Medusa. The activity of reading seems to imprison the reader in the persona of Medusa, whose interpretive gaze turns the text to stone, fixing its meaning, containing its development. It is interesting to note that conventional gender codes are broken: the text, like the body of the nubile narrator, is transformed by the look of a reader who is coded both as male (the prostitute's client who uses and transforms her body) and as the traditionally castrating female, Medusa. Rather than being co-creators of the meaning of the text, narrator and reader seem to be locked in a deadly game, just like the city and its rapacious developers.

The intensity and urgency that emerge from the first pages are sustained throughout this narrative development. The voice continually engages the reader while keeping him or her at a distance, always a few steps behind the *je* who is in flight through the streets. This distance prevents the possibility of identification between narrator and reader, voice and follower. The *je* demands that the *vous* embark with her on an itinerary into the depths of a fictional world poised on the edge of a crisis of meaning and understanding: "Vous me suivez, n'est-ce pas? Maintenant que j'ai pris l'habitude de votre présence sur mes pas, suivant ma pensée comme un mirage . . . je ne voudrais pas vous perdre. . . . Vous suivez mes repères? . . . Il faut savoir les reconnaître et leur donner une cohérence [You follow me, don't you? Now that I am used to your presence behind me, to your following my thoughts like a mirage . . . I would not want to lose you. . . . Do you get my clues? . . . You have to know how to recognize them and how to make sense out of them]" (7). The semantic ambiguity of "vous me suivez?" indicates—like the English "you follow me?"—that two levels of meaning must be kept in mind here: the literal and the figural. It is by journeying with the narrator that we will also be able to grasp her meaning, to understand her attempt to give coherence to the story. Having enlisted the initial complicity of the reader, the narrator then guides the reading process and develops a perverse sort of intimacy, which is figured in the image of the young street urchin who is willing to accommodate any wishes a tourist might have, "une petite fille qui toisait du regard et du corps un touriste surpris, choqué [a little girl whose whole posture indicated that she was eyeing the surprised and shocked tourist from head to toe]" (5). Being thus placed in the position of a "tourist," the reader is challenged to go on the journey and to make efficient use of the *repères*, the allusions and clues, that will reveal both the inexorable logic of the narrative, its descent into an apocalyptic finale, and the narrator's dexterous ability to expose the operations that buttress this logic.

The pronoun *je*, however, and its direct address to a *vous* who is required to listen, to follow the story with an open mind, serves to reempower the postcolonial female subject, to allow her to slip out of a web of fatal circumstances, to expose "ces destinées maudites d'avance [these accursed and fateful lives]" (5), to testify if only long enough to express "cette hurlante envie de lancer ma voix, . . . de dire, de parler en un long flot sans reprendre haleine [this screaming need to shout out, . . . to tell, to talk breathlessly and without interruption]." In other words it is not so much the content of the testimony, its shape and its origin, its concrete details, that matter but its destination: "Que vous sachiez . . . [You should know . . .]." It is imperative that this *vous*, the reader, the other, the one who is put in the position of tourist, be able to recognize, acknowledge, and validate the voice itself: "Reconnaissez-moi, dans l'ombre fugitive que vous entrevoyez au coin de la rue [You must recognize me in the furtive shadow that appears on the street corner]." The impersonal nature of the shadow gives it greater symbolic and representative value as a figure for the oppressed female voice, for the way this voice has been silenced by representation and its protocols, by fictional discourse and its codes. To the extent that this process of novelization is shown to be a universal characteristic of literariness, it must thereby be unmasked through the use of an equally general and unspecific foil, the abstract and disembodied voice that alternately seduces the listener and keeps him at a distance, off balance, for fear that his scrutinizing gaze might paralyze the narrator, cut short her trajectory, and turn her to stone.

Since this voice chooses to braid its passive and active components—the codes that produce it and the means by which it deconstructs these codes—it also succeeds in creating an intersubjective space. Whereas traditional uses of urban characters as prostitutes may cast them as objects of a gaze, as stereotypical canvases to be filled, as plot lines to be fleshed out, as lacking therefore in subjective reality, the indeterminacy of the shadow on the street corner elicits a very definite and determinate engagement on the part of the interlocutor-reader: "Il y a partout et en tout d'étranges liens de continuité et de complicité, comme des fils entrelacés entre moi et moi, et vous et moi [Everywhere and in everything, there are strange links of continuity and complicity, like threads intertwining me and myself, and yourself and myself]" (7). To follow the narrator is to recognize her existence, to enter into a pact with her, and to occupy the same intermediate space that constitutes both the hearer and the listener as agents of knowledge engaged in a dialogue that reveals the transformational power of fictional discourse, its transgressive moves between the real and the imaginary, between male and female codes, between creative impulses and death wishes.

Rue La Poudrière thus forces us to acknowledge and recognize a subject that has heretofore been hidden under the blinding glare of romantic exoticism. The urban *devenir* of the narrator (34) is set in motion by the encounter between text and reader, and each new reading produces new levels of understanding, new spirals of meaning: "je me sens vieille, vieille, antique comme Port-Louis à la face de mendiante délurée et amène qui connaît trop de choses [I feel old, antique like Port-Louis, the city with the face of an alluring and pleasant beggar who knows too much]" (121). The unconventional knowledge that the city and the female subject both hold is the source of their powers of seduction and transformation. This in turn enables them to escape from the fixed subjectivities and confining categories of both tradition and modernization: "ma métamorphose s'accomplit tout doucement. . . . je déchire mes coutures, un autre moi s'élève comme un soleil noir" (34) [my metamorphosis is gently underway. . . . I tear at all my seams, another me is rising like a black sun]" (34).

This apparent metamorphosis serves to bring Paule in closer proximity to the obscure role her mother is assigned throughout the narrative. Described as powerful and malevolent, Marie—one of the few characters whose speech is realistically rendered in Creole—represents the "abject" in Julia Kristeva's sense of the word. The phenomenon of attraction/repulsion that is central to Paule's relationship to Marie is a classic case of the opposition between a *je* and an object that it perceives as internal to itself and thus threatening to its identity as subject. The abject is what contributes to the blurring of the boundary between inside and outside, same and other, life and death. It is what "disturbs identity, system, order. What does not respect borders, positions, rules. The in-between, the ambiguous, the composite."[21] The nondifferentiation that marks the relation of the narration to the real, the writer to the reader, Marie to Paule, Paule to the city, Paule to Edouard, is underscored in chapter 16, in which father, mother, and daughter seem to trade places in a silent parody of the concept of the Trinity.

Edouard, drunk, visits the bordello where Paule works. She is in her room, lost in her thoughts, and as she hears the footsteps of a customer coming closer to her door, she turns off the light and waits passively for the drunken assault to end. But as the man attempts to leave, father and daughter recognize each other, and Paule darts out the door, having become the abject object herself: "Il y avait une lèpre attachée à ma personne, une innommable contagion [There was leprosy stuck to my body, an unspeakable contamination]" (183). The boundaries of her universe once again collapse, and she searches for Marie, whose "magnétisme" is such that "elle était partout, en tout, uniforme et universelle [she was everywhere, in everything, uniform and universal]" (188).

As both mother and "mother-text," Marie represents the inescapable and universal forms of narrative within which this text—*Rue La Poudrière*—takes shape and from which it struggles to differentiate itself. Unable to escape the hold that this mother has on her, Paule can only disappear as the subject of her narrative, a story recounted in French but "contaminated" in parts by Creole, a language that seems destined to disappear in this world just as the arcane medical knowledge of Marie is bound to pass with her. It is as though the narrative traditions absorb all attempts to create an original *récit*. There is nothing "new" under the sun, only "self-consuming artifacts" that cross-contaminate each other.

Whereas Michelle Cliff's *Abeng* allows the narrator to retrieve the

---

[21]Julia Kristeva, *Pouvoirs de l'horreur: Essai sur l'abjection* (Paris: Seuil, 1980), 12; trans. Léon S. Roudiez as *Powers of Horror: An Essay on Abjection* (New York: Columbia University Press, 1982), 4.

collective dimensions of a repressed history, Devi's novel enacts the death of history, the murder of the city, and the poisoning of language in a universe where the subject's attempts to disentangle herself from the oppressive realms that determine her behavior lead to annihilation. In thus conflating the female's and the city's demise, Devi suggests that the postmodern nightmare of urban sprawl may in fact be the return of an old repressed: the postcolonial fin-de-siècle as a new age in which the female subject is at pains to re-present herself once again as an "idol of perversity" who nonetheless compels her readers to recognize their ambiguous relationship to the process of reading. Devi's novel powerfully enacts the vexed relationship between the postmodern and the postcolonial. The nihilistic final image of the book suggests that with global development come the ills of late capitalism and postmodernity. These now invade those postcolonial spaces where the female subject might have had a chance to invent herself anew had she not been tragically caught in a vise, as it were, between tradition (Marie) and corruption (Edouard) at the very moment when the boundaries between them were collapsing around her.

As subsequent chapters make clear, Maryse Condé and Leïla Sebbar show us the way out of such an impasse in their staging of postcolonial subjects whose nomadism allows them to elude the negativity of abjection and the stigmas that attach to boundary crossers. These subjects are the links that enable the articulation of a nontotalizing approach to a more inclusive form of humanism and agency.

3

Toward a New Antillean Humanism: Maryse Condé's *Traversée de la mangrove*

> Writing is the interminable, the incessant. The writer, it is said, gives up saying "I." . . . To write is to make oneself the echo of what cannot cease speaking. . . . The third person substituting for the "I": such is the solitude that comes to the writer on account of the work.
>
> —Maurice Blanchot, *The Space of Literature*

Since the publication of her first novel, *Heremakhonon*, in 1976, Maryse Condé has been a controversial figure, always retaining a very independent and skeptical intellectual attitude vis-à-vis the dominant ideological and aesthetic trends within the literature and culture of *la francophonie*. Her more recent novels *Traversée de la mangrove* (1989) and *Les Derniers Rois mages* (1992)—well conceived, well structured, and beautifully written—reveal the talent and control of a writer at the top of her form. These works provide an important bridge between the literary traditions of the United States and those of the Caribbean basin, and they contribute a unique perspective to our current understanding of the hybrid cultures of the New World.[1]

This chapter focuses on *Traversée de la mangrove*, a novel that illustrates the changing concerns of postcolonial thinkers, artists, and writers from Africa and the Caribbean who are not in quest of singularity, or of an absolute and irredeemable identity, but who would rather introduce aesthetic topologies and theoretical schemas that appeal to "an ethical universal."[2] This return to an ethical principle is mediated by an expanded notion of humanism, one that

---

[1]See Maryse Condé, *Heremakhonon*; *Traversée de la mangrove* (Paris: Mercure de France, 1989); and *Les Derniers Rois mages* (Paris: Mercure de France 1992). Page numbers for *Traversée* are given in the text.

[2]Kwame Anthony Appiah, "Is the Post- in Postmodernism the Post- in Postcolonial?" *Critical Inquiry* 17 (Winter 1991): 353.

is as opposed to the narrow nationalism of identity claims as it is to the colonizing and totalizing pseudo-universalism that allowed colonial empires to engage in the profound dehumanization of their subjects. Condé joins many intellectuals who are asking themselves what role literature now plays in contemporary Caribbean reality. The Haitian critics Yannick Lahens and Jacky Dahomay have posed the kinds of questions that are assuming broad dimensions in these intellectuals' reflections. Lahens asks: "Might our literature become the site in which individualism and humanism do not exclude one another? . . . What if we were to open up the territories of our *imaginaire* by first accepting exile, and thus the otherness within us?"[3] To accept this otherness often means taking up the problematics of the particular and the universal from a new angle, taking the long-standing cultural pluralism of the postcolonial world as a positive point of departure rather than as an aberrant form of cultural difference or homogeneized universality. Dahomay has also sought to show that "the ideology of difference and relativization" cannot satisfy the demands of liberty and "worlding" of the heterogeneous cultures of the Caribbean basin.[4] In *Traversée*, Condé offers a brilliant demonstration of her transposition into *narrative* practice of these theoretical questions, which she too has discussed in her critical essays.

Having left her native island in 1953 at the age of sixteen, Condé has always maintained an extremely ambivalent relationship to the Caribbean and to the nativist ideology that would restrict the writer to themes emphasizing only the cultural particularisms of her people. She did not return to live there until 1986, thirty-three years later. In the interim, she lived in France, Africa, and the United States. In a 1986 lecture given in Haiti, "Notes sur un retour au pays natal" (Notes on a return to the native land), Condé emphasized the feelings of boredom and oppression that had marked her adolescence in the "island-prison" of Guadeloupe; she maintained

[3] Yannick Lahens, "L'Exil: Entre écrire et habiter," *Chemins critiques* 1 (December 1989): 183.

[4] Jacky Dahomay, "Habiter la créolité ou le heurt de l'universel," *Chemins critiques* 1 (December 1989): 130, 109. Dahomay's phrase *devenir-monde* is rendered here as "worlding," in Martin Heidegger's sense (see "The Origin of the Work of Art," in *Poetry, Language, Thought*, trans. Albert Hofstadter [New York, 1977]), upon which Gayatri Spivak has elaborated in "Three Women's Texts and a Critique of Imperialism," *Critical Inquiry* 12 (Autumn 1985): 262.

that she had looked at the sea "only to have the desire to escape from the Caribbean," from a country that was nothing but a "vacuum" and a "nothingness" for her.[5] She echoed this sentiment in an interview published three years later: "It was so boring to be brought up in Guadeloupe during that era [that]...I wanted to break out; I was ripe for leaving, leaving the family, leaving the island."[6] An entire generation of intellectuals who likewise sought emigration at any cost has had to deal with the negative self-image of Antilleans, their difficult legacy of slavery and colonialism, and the assimilationist policies of France. Among those who preceded Condé, even Aimé Césaire cut a figure of intellectual alienation, a somewhat condescending one at that, without real ties to the culture of her island's people. For Césaire, as Condé points out, it is the writer who gives people "power, strength, unity, and faith." But this image of the writer-prophet who provides inspiration and guidance to "a vanquished people" never had any particular attraction for Condé.[7] This is why she concludes her "Notes sur un retour au pays natal" on a skeptical tone: "To be Antillean, in the end, I'm not always sure exactly what that means! Must a writer have a native land?...Could the writer not be a perpetual nomad, constantly wandering in search of other people?"[8]

Indeed, a form of wandering characterizes Condé's life and literary output in the 1970s and 1980s, from *Heremakhonon* to *Tree of Life*, from *Segu* to *I, Tituba, Black Witch of Salem*.[9] But in 1986, having acquired a degree of financial independence thanks to the success of *Segu*, she returned to live in her native land and to observe up close the changes that had taken place, from negritude to *antillanité*, from *antillanité* to *créolité*. Like the people of Guadeloupe, she now recognizes the value of the Creole language, of the indigenous dances and tales which, as she puts it, require acceptance "on their

---

[5]Maryse Condé, "Notes d'un retour au pays natal," *Conjonction: Revue franco-haïtienne* 176 (supp. 1987): 9–10.

[6]Vèvè Clark, " 'I Have Made Peace with My Island': An Interview with Maryse Condé," *Callaloo* 12 (1989): 94 (hereafter Condé, "Interview").

[7]Ibid., 111.

[8]Condé, "Notes," 23.

[9]Maryse Condé, *Segu*, trans. Barbara Bray (New York: Viking, 1987); *The Children of Segu*, trans. Linda Coverdale (New York: Viking, 1989); *Tree of Life*, trans. Victoria Reiter (New York: Ballantine Books, 1992); *I, Tituba, Black Witch of Salem*, trans. Richard Philcox (Charlottesville: University Press of Virginia, 1992).

own terms."[10] In an article published in 1989 she adopts a new point of view, asking what role a writer might play in Guadeloupean society, how a writer might derive sustenance from the sources of popular culture in order eventually to represent this milieu better and touch the readers who belong to it. Evidence of a new-found humility, this attitude also reflects Condé's desire to come to a better understanding of the lived experience of culture, to return to the oral traditions of a once disparaged—because poorly understood—popular tradition.[11] These questions seem to occupy the writer in a particularly pressing way:

> To live in this land is to learn to write all over again. To change almost entirely one's way of writing.
> To live in this land is also to learn a certain social fabric all over again.
> To live in this land is to solve an enigma, the enigma of the cultural particularisms which persist. . . .
> To live in this land is to speak of it in the present. It is to write of it in the present.
> And this leads me to reflect upon this question: what should we say in our books? . . .
> This is something very difficult: to find a way of speaking about this land as it is, to take account of its modernity and perhaps to integrate its modernity with its memories, the shreds of a past which is dear to us and which we would like to restore. A terribly difficult enterprise. To be at once present and depositor of a lost past without which the present would have no vitality, no flavor. . . . I think the writer must also supply dreams to those who approach him or her. . . . There is no reality without dreams, and the writer, in restoring life, also restores the dream. These are dimensions of literature which, for a certain period of time, we wanted to consider shameful. We privileged a certain type of writing. We neglected another type of literary work, and it seems to me that now we must acknowledge how absolutely inappropriate that was, because in the end the literary work must be as com-

---

[10]Condé, "Interview," 113.

[11]The sarcastic tone of *Heremakhonon* is particularly revealing on this point. See *AV*, chap. 5, "Happiness Deferred: Maryse Condé's *Hérémakhonon* and the Failure of Enunciation," and also Leah D. Hewitt, *Autobiographical Tightropes* (Lincoln: University of Nebraska Press, 1990), chap. 5, "Mediations of Identity through the Atlantic Triangle: Maryse Condé's *Hérémakhonon*."

plex as possible. It must integrate disparate aspects of reality, it must respond to all the exigencies of the human heart.

And so finally, to live in this land is to reflect a little on the literary work. It is to rethink the literary work. It is to rethink one's function as a writer.[12]

Glancing back over the path traveled by Condé, we can see the irony and cautious distance of the 1970s giving way to a "rootedness," to a focus on Antillean specificity. She distances herself from the kind of historical novel that fetishizes slavery, avoiding nostalgia in all its guises; she rejects aesthetic, exotic, or political prejudices that tend to fetishize the past and to idealize political activism, nature, or the people; and she denounces the *misérabiliste* ideology of her predecessors, which cast Guadeloupe as a marginal and oppressed land from which one could only be forced into exile. In *Traversée*, Guadeloupe has become a locus of *immigration* that attracts poorer Haitians and Dominicans who come looking for work, just as immigrants came from India in the nineteenth and early twentieth centuries. It is therefore an aspect of *post*colonial ideology that Condé deconstructs in this novel as she denounces the anti-Indian racism of Caribbean Creoles.[13] She undermines the familiar topoi of the literature of the 1960s and 1970s and represents the peasant culture, which seems to have best retained the traces of a unique cultural brew, the *créolité*, now being celebrated by many.[14]

Having settled in the countryside, in Montebello, where she spends part of the year (when she is not teaching in the United States), Condé has renewed contact with tropical nature, relearned the names of plants, and refamiliarized herself with rural culture. *Traversée* stages this rural world with considerable subtlety. Al-

[12]Maryse Condé, "Habiter ce pays, la Guadeloupe," *Chemins critiques* 1 (December 1989): 9, 11, 13.

[13]In the Caribbean, Indian immigrants are a cultural and ethnic minority. Condé cites a popular Creole song: "Kouli malaba / Isi dan / Pa peyiw" (Malabar coolie. This is not your country) which she "translates" for the French reader as: "Coolie malabar (injurieux). Ce pays n'est pas le vôtre" (19).

[14]I refer here to Jean Barnabé, Raphaël Confiant, and Patrick Chamoiseau, *Eloge de la créolité* (Paris: Gallimard, 1989); "In Praise of Creoleness," trans Mohamed B. Thaleb Khyar, *Callaloo* 13 (1990): 886–909. But see also the critique of her male colleagues' sententiousness in Maryse Condé, "Order, Disorder, Freedom, and the West Indian Writer," *Yale French Studies* 83 (1993): 121–35.

though published in Paris, like her previous books, *Traversée* is not written for a French public; for the first time, Condé seems to have a truly Caribbean audience in mind. Creole words and expressions are translated at the bottom of each page, but this was done after the fact, as a favor to the French reader and on the recommendation of Condé's editor. Aside from this linguistic *dépaysement*, the text offers no major cultural surprises: the cast of characters is a familiar one for a rural community, with its conflicts among families, its storytellers and teachers, its village idiot and its healer, its migrant workers and other outsiders who bear the brunt of xenophobic reactions on the part of long-time residents. These characters live, love, and die in Rivière au Sel as do humans everywhere. Because the village is isolated, it is possible to identify particularisms that have disappeared from more urban settings in other parts of the Caribbean—but by the same token, these rural characteristics are not unlike those that might be shared by a similarly isolated village in the heart of France's Berry region, for example.[15]

One might surmise, then, that an anthropologist looking for "culture" and difference in Rivière au Sel would initially be disappointed, as were Renato and Michelle Rosaldo when they did their fieldwork among Filipinos, who are generally viewed by anthropologists as "people without culture" because, having been "acculturated" by three and a half centuries of Spanish and then American colonial rule, they are not all that "different." They are "rational, not cultural," and "to the ethnographic gaze, these civilized people appear too transparent for study; they seem *just like us*: materialistic, greedy, and prejudiced." The point, of course, as Renato Rosaldo suggests, is that it is precisely those "zones of cul-

[15]The Berry is a mostly agricultural region of France, noted for its healers and storytellers. Marie-Blandine Ouedraogo makes a similar point about the shortcomings of ethnographic representations and the problems of the women's movement in Upper Volta: "Sometimes it seems that female ethnologists are not very interested in women's lives, . . . that they try, at all costs, to discover a system completely foreign to their own, that they insist on differentiating themselves from us. I think that if you were to compare an African woman with a European peasant woman, you would not see a whole lot of differences. Similarly, a white urban woman does not seem to me to be that different from an urban African woman. When the latter wants to communicate with a village woman, she encounters the same difficulties, the same level of suspicion as a European woman does" ("Paroles de Haute-Volta," interview conducted by Joële Meerstx in "L'Africaine: Sexes et signes," *Les Cahiers du Grif* 29 [Autumn 1984]: 33).

tural invisibility" that pose the most compelling questions for contemporary critics and theorists because that is where the transcultural process, through appropriation and contestation, manifests itself with clarity.[16] It is because "they" appear to be like "us" (Western readers), because "they" are involved in "universal" human problems, that the characters of *Traversée* are subversive: they undo that opposition between "us" and "them" which is indispensable to the representation of the exotic other in art, literature, or ethnography.[17] The villagers of *Traversée*, like Rosaldo's Filipinos, are human beings whose cultural production and consumption defy the West's attempt to exoticize them.

To refute the paradigms of exoticism and victimization, Condé skillfully depicts a self-sufficient community unburdened by crises of identity. She gives voice to each one of a series of characters with a unique perspective on the events that have caused them all to assemble at the wake for Francis Sancher, the stranger whose presence in Rivière au Sel caused some major changes in relations among the villagers. As a figure that allegorizes both the colonial process and the fate of nomadic intellectuals such as Maryse Condé herself, he is a cleverly drawn character who enters into a complicated relationship with the local *habitants*. He allows Condé to be self-reflexive about her writing, and about the role of writing in her own cultural context (203). Condé appropriates the technique of the novel within the novel to reflect upon the role of the writer as outsider, and of the outsider as catalyst or *pharmakon*, both poison and antidote, dangerous supplement, chronicler, and *aide-mémoire* of the community.[18]

This novel therefore represents for her an entirely new narrative

[16]See Renato Rosaldo "Ideology, Place, and People without Culture," *Cultural Anthropology* 3 (February 1988): 77–80 (my emphasis). The Rosaldos were studying the Ilongots, who "lacked the ethnographic staples of the day: lineages, villages, men's houses, elaborate rituals" (77–78).

[17]Hence, these characters are the counterpart of the *Man with a Bicycle* sculpture as described by Appiah (see Introduction, n. 20). On cultural and historical relativism, see Satya P. Mohanty, "Us and Them: On the Philosophical Bases of Political Criticism," *Yale Journal of Criticism* 2 (Spring 1989): 1–31.

[18]I use the term in the Greek sense made familiar by Jacques Derrida, "La Pharmacie de Platon," in *La Dissemination* (Paris: Seuil 1972), 126: "Le *pharmakon* est ce supplément dangereux qui entre par effraction dans cela même qui voudrait avoir pu s'en passer [The *pharmakon* is this dangerous supplement which enters forcibly where one would prefer to have been able to do without it]."

direction, the appropriation of a new locus of identity, the imple-
mentation of what might almost be called a new poetics, a "Guadeloupean aesthetic." To be a Guadeloupean writer is to attempt to
"write in the present," using the spoken idiom to emphasize local
particularisms but not becoming overburdened by the weight of a
certain *désiré historique*.[19] It also means to open oneself up to the
"exigencies of the human heart" and to exhibit the same flexibility
that characterizes the best of the great tradition of European realism
and humanism. But Condé's project also belongs in another, thor-
oughly Caribbean, tradition: that of nineteenth-century peasant literature, which easily became a political weapon in the hands of
Haitian writers such as Jacques Roumain and Jacques-Stephen
Alexis. Condé draws her reader into the daily life of a small village
that serves as a microcosm of Guadeloupean society. Here in Rivière au Sel, according to the author, culture "has never been so
alive"; it represents a sort of challenge; "because we are so small,
so insignificant, and yet despite all we remain absolutely different."[20] Instead of playing the role of wandering writer to which she
aspired twenty years earlier, Condé seems to have radically
switched courses, opting for a return to a tenacious difference and
to the oral traditions displaced by her education and her intellectual
nomadism, both more typical of a "global" citizen than of an is-
lander.[21]

Condé sets out to narrate this cultural specificity, this rediscovered difference, in order to highlight its originality but perhaps also
to suggest that it is only through the representation of local particularisms that the writer can capture a truly global dimension of
human experience. She reconstructs the Guadeloupean imaginary,
using a hybrid vocabulary—"francole" or "fréole"[22]—and a range

---

[19] The expression *désiré historique* is from Edouard Glissant, *Le Discours antillais*
(Paris: Seuil, 1984), 147. J. Michael Dash translates it as "longing for history" or
"longing for the ideal of history" (CD, 79). Condé ("Interview," 99) specifies that
"in order to avoid all demagoguery," she never "envisaged writing in Creole" but,
rather, wanted to introduce local inflections and metaphors into French.

[20] Condé, "Habiter," 11.

[21] Condé, "Au-delà des langues et des couleurs," *La Quinzaine Littéraire*, March
1985, 36.

[22] Antillean linguists have debated the merits of coining a new term combining
the words *français* and *créole* to identify a diglossic continuum. In a talk at the Conseil
International d'Etudes Francophones in Martinique, April 1990, Jean Bernabé dis-

of characters whose narrative voices singularize and concretize the real. She emphasizes the ways in which the experience of the inhabitants of this small locality can have a universal and timeless dimension, her principal themes being love, death, family strife, relations among neighbors, and the upset caused by the arrival of an outsider (who is not really a stranger but whose presence exposes the xenophobia and suspicions common to all rural communities). Condé's presentation tends to suggest that Guadeloupe, far from being a marginal land, is in fact a microcosm of the world; that the Guadeloupeans' practices of everyday life have value as examples; that their solutions to the problems of postcolonial life are sufficiently rich and nuanced to serve as a model for others. It seems to me that with *Traversée* Condé has indeed succeeded in staking out "the site in which individualism and humanism do not exclude one another," to use Yannick Lahens's formulation.

The language of the novel is permeated with sounds, images, and Creole turns of phrase that give the text a very special flavor. At the level of description, lexicon, and metaphor, *Traversée* is steeped in the Antillean environment:

Il y avait des hibiscus rose pâle dans le jardin et une tonnelle de maracuja. Je poussai la barrière et j'entrai . . . comme un cyclone qui a ramassé ses forces au-dessus de l'Atlantique et a enfin pris sa vitesse de pointe. (154).

Il n'avait jamais rencontré la mort elle-même. Lan-mo*. Il l'imaginait sous les traits d'une Négresse aux dents de perle, riant nacrées entre ses lèvre charnues, couleur d'aubergine black beauty et s'avançant avec un balancement mi taw, mi tan mwen** qui déchaînait le feu dans les entrailles.

* La mort
** Aguichant (166)

[There were pale pink hibiscus trees in the garden and a *maracuja* arbor. I pushed the gate and arrived like a cyclone that has gathered strength over the Atlantic and finally reached its cruising speed.

cussed this question of a hybrid language of indeterminate status, and the necessity felt by specialists to resemanticize the Antillean continuum within a new context.

He had never met death herself. *Lan-mo**. He imagined that she looked
like a black woman with pearl-white teeth shining between her thick
smily lips, dark like a black beauty eggplant and moving forward with
a swinging of the hips *mi taw, mi tan mwen*** that set his loins on fire.

* Death
** Seductive]

The words marked by asterisks are "translated" into French at
the bottom of the page, thereby supplying an *hors-texte* that suggests a certain linguistic opacity at the same moment that it is being
decoded for the non-Creolophone reader. A conception of the subject as multilingual and multicultural thus emerges from and per-
vades the realism of the description, preventing any simplistic
adherence to a static humanism, since the distance between the narrator and the reader is doubly articulated by this opacity and its
"translation." By making repeated use of the expression "There is
a time for everything . . . a time to live, and a time to die" (137), "a
time to love, a time to hate" (225), Condé apparently wants to portray a social environment where traditional values speak of patience and endurance, providing a source of stability. In the face of
changes brought on by modernity, the oral culture is not threatened
by dissolution, because it has this stable core. The choice of a rural
setting allows for the elimination of many superficial "metropolitan" influences that would be more visible in an urban milieu,
where assimilation and acculturation promote a greater dilution of
the local culture. What interests Condé in the rural setting, she
claims, is "the mechanism through which we integrate so many
things that appear so opposed to who we are, the mechanism
through which . . . we phagocytize them."[23]

This "mechanism," the cultural crossroads that fascinate Condé,
are the result of the phenomenon of appropriation and creolization
of outside cultures as they become grafted onto local practices.
Among the anthropologists and sociologists who have studied the
process of cultural adaptation and métissage, the sociologist Dominique Schnapper explains the phenomenon this way: "All culture,
. . . far from being a given, is the result of continual negotiation with

[23]Condé, "Habiter," 11.

the external world, negotiation through which, like a horizon, *an identity is affirmed which can only be defined as an ongoing creation.* Culture can only be conceived of as a condition and consequence of social action and interaction with the larger world society. Through these constant negotiations . . . culture forms a system (in the loose sense of the term); it constitutes a construction or dynamic which must be analyzed in terms of cultural reinterpretations."[24] Schnapper's reflections echo those of critics such as Edouard Glissant and James Clifford. For Glissant, the key concept is that of "identity-relation," which he opposes to "identity-root."[25] It is by means of his concept of "the Relation" that Glissant manages to think through the notion of cultural mixing without falling prey to the seductions of a "generalizing universal." Like Glissant, Clifford attempts to analyze the changes undergone by cultural systems over the course of colonization and decolonization and concludes that today all "identity is conjectural, not essential." What counts now, he adds, citing Edward Said, is that everyone be able to tell his or her story "in pieces, *as it is.*"[26]

In Condé's work, this fragmentation of identity is typically reflected in a narrative organization that does not necessarily create a postmodern dispersion or explosion of the subject. Fragmentation serves as a basis for the construction of cultural models appropriate to the contexts of postcolonial creolization, where exchanges and interferences produce a dynamic subject participating fully in the global process of métissage or transculturation, at the heart of which the Caribbean has been since the beginning of the colonial era.[27] Hence, to search for affiliation and origins (the traditional quest of classical heroes) would clearly result in an impasse for the Antillean subject, since her *imaginaire* can be successfully articulated only through nonlinear, egalitarian, and nonhierarchical cultural relations. This is not to say that dissymmetrical power relations do

[24]Dominique Schnapper, "Modernité et acculturations," *Communications* 43 (1986): 151 (my emphasis).

[25]Edouard Glissant, *Poétique de la relation* (Paris: Gallimard, 1990), 155; hereafter *PR*.

[26]James Clifford, *The Predicament of Culture: Twentieth Century Ethnography, Literature, and Art* (Cambridge: Harvard University Press, 1988), 11.

[27]See Nancy Morejón, *Nación y mestizaje en Nicolás Guillén* (Havana: Unión, 1982), chaps. 1–2; and *AV*, chap. 1.

not exist in this context. But the *imaginaire* of the writer seems to be able to invent a space in which new configurations can begin to be glimpsed.

This is why *Traversée de la mangrove* is a book whose story is told "in pieces," without intervention or mediation on the part of the author. The narrative aesthetic of the novel evokes a fragmented, dispersed consciousness, distributed among the different characters. Each character gives his or her own perspective on a diverse and ever changing reality. The sum of these perspectives does not present a totalizing vision of Guadeloupean reality; oñ the contrary, it brings to light the contradictions, discontinuities, and limits imposed on narrative when it attempts to deal with the everydayness of the real. Condé neither judges nor explains her characters; they are given to us as examples of the diversity found in concrete reality. The reality here stems from the events surrounding the life of Francis Sancher/Francisco Sanchez, the stranger who had arrived in the village several years earlier and whose death rends the social fabric of the small rural community. Like Lucien Evariste, who questions Francis—in vain—"in order to try, piece by piece, to put together the puzzle which constitutes his life" (236), readers are left unsatisfied: we cannot penetrate the irreducible, deliberate opacity of the character whose very life emphasized his singularity, his *strangeness*. The narrative harbors lacunae, and the death of Sancher underlines the fact that in reality as in fiction there are zones of nonknowledge and nonpower which the reader must learn to accept. The novel is not a completed whole but a rich open expanse of possibilities which assigns a multiplicity of meanings to the community. The latter, in the image of a literary text, can use the words of each of its members to construct a utopian universe in which differences are respected and do not lead to mutual negation.

Like the wake that assembles the characters, the narrative serves as a site of encounter and recognition, as a crucible in which the various cultures represented by the various characters sustain a mutual dialogue--among themselves and with the readers, who, if they are Creolophone, discover therein a reflection of their very own cultural history, as enigmatic and equivocal as the image of Francis/Francisco himself. As Patrick Chamoiseau remarked in his "Reflections," broadcast in Guadaloupe at the time of *Traversée*'s publication: "The character of Francisco Sanchez has an unclear genealogy; he isn't transparent, and we do not know where he comes from, where he was born, what he wants, what he fears. . . . But who among us can claim a distinct genealogy, with well defined, sketched, and recognized branches? Who among us can claim an unspoiled personal genesis without absences? What Creole person in the Caribbean today possesses a transparent past that would authorize certainty? An obscure character, whose obscure death is shrouded in enigmatic circumstances, Francisco Sanchez inscribes himself in the anthropological reality of our countries."[28]

Neither hero nor antihero, Sanchez is an "everyman": an archetypal inhabitant of the Caribbean archipelago, with his uncertain origins; his multiple geographic, emotional, and sexual attachments; his adventurous, rebellious nomadism; and the fragility that often characterizes a dissatisfied intellectual. The text of the novel thereby becomes the privileged site for this "continual creation" of a plural identity, as described by Schnapper. The encounter between the near and the far, the familiar and the other, the insular community and the outside world—shown from the point of view of each protagonist—reveals the ways in which the outside world in the person of Francis Sancher has exerted influence on, incorporated itself into, and left its mark upon local life.

With this novel, Condé gives herself access to a symbolic structure that constructs and deconstructs itself in the filigree of the characters' narrative. These "anecdotes without head or tail" (237) weave together the dynamic relations between the different narrators and social actors who represent various aspects of Guadeloupean culture: the Lameaulnes and Ramsaran families, one Creole, the other Indian; Man Sonson the healer; Moïse the pariah; Léocadie the schoolteacher; Cyrille the storyteller; Dodose and Sonny Pélagie; Lucien Evariste; Emile the historian; and Xantippe, a sort of community spirit who safeguards the memory of *tan lontan* (olden days). It is through their interactions that the narrative text encourages "the cultural reinterpretations" that influence in turn the network of representations and signification to which Antillean literature belongs: we are far removed from the monolithic heroes of

[28]Patrick Chamoiseau, "Reflections on Maryse Condé's *Traversée de la Mangrove*," *Callaloo* 14 (1991): 391–92.

Césaire, the tragic figure of Christophe, or the epic life of Delgrès. Here, the community is constructed in and through a shared space where ties among individuals are made and unmade, thereby working over and stretching the social fabric. Although this world is unique and has a very specific language, its human diversity evokes and suggests the universal characteristics that might allow for a successful communicative situation. In speaking to one another the characters never achieve "Cartesian" clarity, even if Lucien Evariste, for one, searches for it, submitting his interlocutors to an exhausting interrogation (239). Conversation is aimed not at some objective finality but at an understanding of the human dimensions of the "puzzle" that brings them all together for a wake that evening.

In sharing this meeting place, they neither lose their individuality nor resolve their differences, but their presence is an important concession. Because of the death of one whose life was a troubling enigma, they agree to recognize what they have in common, their shared humanity. It is interesting to note that what assembles them in this way is death. As Loulou Lameaulnes asks himself, "Why does death have this power? Why does it silence hatred, violence, rancor, and why does it force us down on both knees when it appears?" (130). Vilma Ramsaran echoes his sentiment: "Our ancestors used to say that death is nothing but a bridge thrown down between beings, a footbridge which brings them closer together, on which they meet halfway in order to whisper to one another all that they had not been able to share" (206). Since misfortune strikes blindly, the death of Francis Sancher serves as a catalyst for the rapprochement of the Lameaulnes and Ramsaran families, despite their racial differences. For Loulou, "misfortune has its own justice" (136), and "this justice descends from above, without needing to be sought out" (139), adds Sylvestre. Both Loulou's daughter Mira and Sylvestre's daughter Vilma had lived with Francis and found themselves pregnant by him; misfortune assigns the two families to the same rank, and their honor is saved by Francis's death. Mira, liberated in this way, does not hesitate to affirm: "My real life begins with his death" (245).

How then should we interpret the role of death in this novel? That we are all equal before death is in itself a trivial observation; as Robert Antelme says, if "we cannot detect any substantial differences in the face of nature and in the fact of death, we are obliged to say that there is but one human race."[29] But equality before fate is an almost revolutionary theme in Antillean literature, whose history abounds with portrayals of masters and servants. This theme imposes a reevaluation of the role of the community and the range of social ties available to its members. Sancher is not a messianic Césairean figure, and his death does not "save" this community, which was not even his own: "I don't belong to any camp" (134), he had said to Loulou. Nor do the inhabitants of Rivière au Sel harbor any illusions about the nature of their momentary *entente cordiale*. Loulou asks himself "what he [is] doing there, listening to these same stories for the hundredth time, these outrageous fibs, this hypocritical murmur of prayer" (130). The rapprochement does not eliminate their differences. It simply supplies the site in which a dialogue can be instigated.

For Condé, then, as for the philosopher Sarah Kofman, "affirming the unity of the species does not consist in eradicating differences, even opposition." Kofman sees the community "not founded on a specific difference or a shared essence, that is, reason, but on a shared power of choice, of incompatible, although correlated, choices, power to kill *and* power to respect, power to preserve the incommensurable distance, the relation without relationship [*le rapport sans rapport*]."[30]

What grounds the community of Rivière au Sel is the choice, freely accepted by all, to share life and death, both their own and Sancher's. The sharing is as precious as it is ineffable, ephemeral, and transitory; it lasts no longer than the wake, during which the presence of all gives legitimacy to the truths and secrets of the dead man. But death "hastens to transform people's minds" (130), and Loulou recognizes astutely that "soon, someone will begin to build a legend around Francis Sancher, and will make him into a misunderstood giant." The memory of the community feeds on myths and epics, and Antillean literature has a rich supply of works that build legends around events in the past. What is new in *Traversée* is Condé's deliberate effort to "write in the present," with the stated

---

[29]Robert Antelme, *L'Espèce humaine*, quoted in Sarah Kofman, *Paroles suffoquées* (Paris: Galilée, 1987), 76, in her fair and moving reflections on the world of the concentration camps.

[30]Kofman, *Paroles suffoquées*, 79.

goal of tracing out the always elusive possibility of creating "the relation without relationship." This is what Glissant calls "the lived of the Relation," because for him "it is the organizing principle of ethics" (PR, 207). The liberty of the community and the respect for difference is found in this consensual opacity. The text of *Traversée* is a site where these differences are not annulled through a transcendental rational synthesis but where humanism is conceived as a "punctual" response to a given crisis, the one the entire community is "traversing" at the moment. Condé has the rare virtue of being able to rethink humanism without romanticism or illusion, and so she opens up the literary field to currently unexplored thematic and stylistic possibilities.

Finally, one must note that the "creolized" language of the novel gives it a unique place in the Antillean literary corpus. If it is true that writers such as Jacques Roumain, Aimé Césaire, and Simone Schwarz-Bart were already innovating and changing the French language, it seems to me that Condé's originality lies in the fact that she goes beyond them in the creolization of French. Schwarz-Bart, for example, employed a syntactic "drift" that amounted to gallicization of Creole; as Jean Bernabé has argued convincingly in his study of French-Creole diglossia in Schwarz-Bart, she used Creole as a trace, inscribing Antillean proverbs into the French language of the novel, submitting "Creole to a variety of operations, thus filtering it, distilling it, erasing it." Certainly, the non-Creolophone reader has no need of a glossary in reading *Pluie et vent sur Télumée Miracle*.[31] The Creole perspective is translated into the French language, and French is changed with regard to its metaphoric structures. In effect, Schwarz-Bart brings about the phenomenon that Derrida, in a slightly different context, called "la dialectique dialectophage" of language.[32] Creole is written into the French text but in the process loses its specificity; it is "distilled," or even "erased." *Pluie et vent* offers us a reading of Guadeloupean

[31]Simone Schwarz-Bart, *Pluie et vent sur Télumée Miracle* (Paris: Gaillimard, 1972); *The Bridge of Beyond*, trans. Barbara Bray (London: Heinemann, 1982). Jean Bernabé, "Le Travail de l'écriture chez Simone Schwarz-Bart," *Présence Africaine* 121–22 (1982): 172.

[32]Jacques Derrida, *Glas I* (Paris: Denoël/Gonthier, 1981), 12; *Glas*, trans. John P. Leavey, Jr., and Richard Rand (Lincoln: University of Nebraska Press, 1986), 9: "The dialectic of language, of the tongue, is dialectophagy."

reality and lays the groundwork for the emergence of *créolité* and for the work of Patrick Chamoiseau, Raphaël Confiant, and Condé herself. There is continuity from *Pluie et vent* to *Traversée*. But whereas Schwarz-Bart places the Creole idiom "at the service of her literary strategy,"[33] which is to reconstruct a sort of epic or myth of origins, Condé is content to anchor the text in the "present" of the narrative enunciation and in the "space" of the wake. She thus brings all the characters together to supply a broad range of perspectives on Francis Sancher and daily life in the community of Rivière au Sel. Schwarz-Bart reconstructs a quasi-mythic history; Condé describes social reality in an extremely restrained manner in order to produce an anthropology of everyday life in Guadeloupe.

Condé's ethical and aesthetic concerns connect with those of many contemporary writers for whom literature is above all a way of understanding reality, of putting it into words in a way that opens up the possibility of self-reflexive awareness. In this way, a dialogue can be initiated between those who "live" the culture on a daily basis, on the one hand, and their often unconscious everyday practices—along with the imaginary structures that they implicitly reproduce—on the other hand. It is in this dialogue that the current dynamism of *créolité* presents itself in its most explosive form. Referring to a book by Georges Pérec, *La Vie, mode d'emploi*, Condé has declared: "Each of our novels replies to this question: life, how to? How to understand life, how to speak about life, how to, simply, live?"[34] *Traversée* seems to be Condé's reply to this question. But the ambivalence of her early novels has nevertheless not disappeared entirely: Francis Sancher also writes a book with the same title as Condé's, a title that astounds Vilma Ramsaran, who explains: "On ne traverse pas la mangrove. On s'empale sur les racines des palétuviers. On s'enterre et on étouffe dans la boue saumâtre [One does not cross the *mangrove*. One is impaled on the roots of the *palétuviers*. One is buried, suffocated in the briny mud]" (203).[35]

---

[33]Bernabé, "Travail," 175.

[34]Condé, "Habiter," 13.

[35]This passage presents special difficulties for the translator: the English word "mangrove," a tropical tree, is equivalent to the French *palétuvier*; the French word *mangrove* is an anglicism, referring to a very dense thicket of *palétuviers*.

Must one then see in this book a rethinking of "the Creole question" itself? Or is it a kind of self-criticism by an author who has not yet lost her prior skepticism? For the moment, it is clear that the character of Francis Sancher is an alter ego for the author, one who provides her access to "the otherness within," to cite Yannick Lahens's formulation once again. This character allows her to transcend the impasse of gender differences, as well as the dialectic of the particular and the universal, in order to suggest a new way of placing emphasis on that which can bring individuals and cultures closer together. The humanism she proclaims does not appeal to the forms of totalization and negation of otherness which underlie the hegemony of the Same in Western culture. On the contrary, this humanism throws "a bridge . . . a footbridge" over the abyss that separates individuals and cultures, thereby giving each one freedom of choice and the right to speak in a different voice within the dialogue that unites them.

4

Inscriptions of Exile: The Body's Knowledge and the Myth of Authenticity in Myriam Warner-Vieyra and Suzanne Dracius-Pinalie

To be a woman, and Antillean, is a destiny difficult to decipher.
> —Maryse Condé, "Interview"

I am a rudderless boat adrift in time and space.
> —Myriam Warner-Vieyra, *Juletane*

. . . embarking, as in this damned expedition, only on voyages of shame.
> —Suzanne Dracius-Pinalie, *L'Autre qui danse*

The death of a beautiful woman is, unquestionably, the most poetical topic in the world.
> —Edgar Allan Poe, *The Philosophy of Composition*

In her essay "Psychoanalysis and the Polis," Julia Kristeva has shown how and why the "abject can be understood in the sense of the horrible and fascinating abomination which is connoted in all cultures by the feminine." This happens, she explains, because the feminine represents a "partial object. . . . It becomes what culture, the *sacred*, must purge, separate and banish so that it may establish itself as such in the universal logic of catharsis."[1] The feminine body is paradoxically the text from which this logic is derived and upon which this catharsis is most glaringly written.[2] In postcolonial literature the gendered and racialized body of the female protagonist is consistently overdetermined; it is a partial object on which are written various cultural scripts and their death-dealing blows.

[1] Julia Kristeva, "Psychoanalysis and the Polis," in *The Kristeva Reader*, ed. Toril Moi (New York: Columbia University Press, 1986), 317.
[2] See John McCumber, "Aristotelian Catharsis and the Purgation of Woman," *Diacritics* 18 (Winter 1988): 53–67.

Burdened with religious and philosophical as well as psychoanalytic, sexual, and racial meanings, the body has long occupied a
prominent place in cultural discourses. In Greco-Roman antiquity,
when its beauty was emphasized by the sculptors, representations
of the healthy body were paramount. But in the Christian era the
symbolism underwent a profound transformation; now it is the
wounded and suffering body (emblematically presented in the form
of the crucified Christ) which inscribes itself in a new ideology, one
that emphasizes the notion of redemption through suffering and
death. The body thereby becomes a text on which pain can be read
as a necessary physical step on the road to a moral state, a destiny,
or a way of being. This in turn reveals a radical transformation
(generally considered positive) in the initial state of the individual
or her community.[3]

The motif of reformation and rebirth through suffering is, paradoxically, part of a philosophy of life which binds the mortification
of the flesh to a certain vital principle, a spiritual vigor through
which the individual may graduate to a higher plane of existence.
We know that slave societies in the New World exploited this
Christian ideology in order to keep at bay the specter of the sedition
and revolt they feared on the part of the oppressed. That is why
"Negro spirituals" often glorify death as a form of passage to the
hereafter, to the life of liberty and happiness denied the slaves on
earth. The internalization of a necrotic ideology is common in cases
of forced subjection and servitude. Women in particular, dominated
in every culture, are often victims of this syndrome. In literature,
it translates into passive and exploited female characters, often in-
capable of escaping unhealthy or degrading situations, or else messianic or maternal figures whose self-abnegation enables the
liberation of others.

Such is the case for the heroines of two novelists from the Caribbean diaspora, Myriam Warner-Vieyra and Suzanne Dracius-
Pinalie, whose work I examine in this chapter.[4] In the former's

---

[3] For an illuminating synthesis of many of these issues, see Leigh Gilmore, *Auto-
biographics: A Feminist Theory of Women's Self-Representation* (Ithaca: Cornell University Press, 1994), esp. chap. 4.

[4] Myriam Warner-Vieyra, *Le Quimboiseur l'avait dit . . .* (Paris: Présence Africaine,
1980), trans. Dorothy S. Blair as *As the Sorcerer Said . . .* (Essex: Longman, 1982), hereafter cited in the text as *Q/S*; *Juletane* (Paris: Présence Africaine, 1982), trans. Betty

Juletane and the latter's *L'Autre qui danse,* the tragic fate of the two principal characters, Juletane and Rehvana, underlines the social and sexual oppression they suffer, along with the continued political and economic exploitation of the French Antilles. But in counterpoint to these figures of victims, the characters of Hélène and Matildana are able to carry on productive, liberated, and satisfying lives. By opposing Juletane to Hélène and Rehvana to Matildana, the novelists outline narrative solutions to the problem of political domination: Juletane and Rehvana represent the search for the past, and with it a traditional form of life; Hélène and Matildana are sketches of a type of autonomous heroine who knows how to throw off the dead weight of archaic memory and thus refuses to internalize the sense of abjection and self-loathing that is repeatedly enacted by characters such as Juletane and Rehvana, in whom we find an echo of Ananda Devi's Paule.

In these novels the physical suffering of the main female characters functions as a code for denouncing an unsettling situation: the ambiguous status, legacy of a colonial past, of the French "Overseas departments" (Martinique, Guadeloupe, French Guiana, and Réunion). The suffering is the consequence of a spiritual quest that drives the heroines to exile in their search for lost origins. Juletane goes to Africa; Rehvana, whose family emigrated to Paris, tries to rediscover the Martinique of her childhood. But each becomes caught in a position of total dependence on a man, one whose initial seductive power came from a presumed ability to satisfy the woman's need for concrete ties to a long-lost African culture and identity. In Paris, Juletane marries Mamadou, a Muslim who takes her back to Africa, where her inability to bear children quickly pushes her to the margins of society. Rehvana, despite being pregnant by Jérémie, the bourgeois *négropolitain*[5] and business student at the Hautes Etudes Commerciales, follows Eric, the unfaithful and violent nomad, to the Caribbean, where she initiates herself into the local superstitions and customs, reimmerses herself in Creole, and lets herself be seduced by the dis-

---

Wilson as *Juletane* (London: Heinemann, 1987), cited as *J*; Suzanne Dracius-Pinalie, *L'Autre qui danse* (Paris: Seghers, 1989), cited as *L'A*. Published translations are modified in my text.

[5]*Négropolitain,* a negative slang term made up of the words *nègre* and *metropolitain,* refers to French blacks living in the *métropole*.

torting images of subjected femininity projected by the old legends. Self-castigated by her "de-culturation" and what she perceives to be a lack of "authenticity," each woman is in turn overwhelmed by a death wish.

These figures present a type of Caribbean woman who is both passive and masochistic, a *petite coque creuse* (empty little husk) drifting rudderless, having abandoned all rights and agency to the sovereign male (*L'A*, 81). Juletane and Rehvana both enter a self-imposed exile in the hope of finding an anchorage but lack the ability to integrate themselves into a genuine social milieu. If for them exile is an attempt to return to and renew old roots, their quest ends in nothing short of complete failure. For Juletane, arriving with her polygamous husband, "this homecoming to Africa, the land of [her] forefathers . . . become[s] a nightmare"(*J*, 15). For Rehvana, brought up in the suburbs of Paris, the "great return" is an attempt at rebirth which ends in disillusionment. The island of her birth, which appears initially as a promised land, quickly becomes a "calvaire pierreux d'ouvrages vains et d'élans infertiles [stony golgotha of wasted labour and barren effort]" (*L'A*, 190), where Eric's daily violence—subdued one day, explosive the next—leaves indelible marks on her now anorexic body.

When these themes of inertia and female dependence are combined with the search for origins and authenticity, rigidly defined and fixated on the past, we are in the presence of what Yannick Lahens has rightly called *l'esthétique de l'impuissance* (the aesthetics of impotence), to which (see Chapter 3) she wanted to oppose a new, more positive and creative opening to the future: "On the eve of the twenty-first century, it would appear possible, and even urgent, to rethink the question of identity, of nationality, and of origin, in such a way as to escape the inside/outside alternatives. How . . . can we continue to fetter creation by tying it to the question of territory, origin, or race? Have not the questions posed in these terms exhausted their aesthetic potential? . . . Will our writers know enough to weed out these referents in order to cultivate other aesthetic and political meanings? [Nos écrivains sauront-ils déporter ces référents pour qu'affleurent d'autres significances esthétiques et politiques?]"[6]

---

[6]Yannick Lahens, "L'Exil: Entre écrire et habiter," *Chemins critiques* 1 (December 1989): 183.

It is precisely these "other aesthetic and political meanings" that Warner-Vieyra and Dracius-Pinalie offer through their implicit critique of the passivity of their heroines. Their narrative strategies bring into play a double problematic—that of the origin and that of the future—and illustrate a new way of denouncing the illusion through which the return to the past and physical suffering can play a mediating role in the search for authenticity. For if there is a largely Western and Christian myth of suffering, it is particularly visible in the literary and musical traditions, either tragic or romantic, which idealize the suffering or dying female body (I am thinking here of opera heroines and of the poetic figure so dear to Edgar Allan Poe).[7] This romantic illusion, deeply rooted in Western literature, is simultaneously represented and deconstructed by Warner-Vieyra and Dracius-Pinalie. They highlight the more sordid dimension of an "aesthetic of impotence" founded on the idealization of suffering. It is this idealization that such a protagonist as Rehvana internalizes. In so doing, she lets herself be blinded by her desire to return to a destiny where fate rules and a woman must serve a man, her only link to the social world and public life.

The passivity exhibited by Juletane and Rehvana reflects the profound malaise that accompanies the ambiguous and uncertain status of the *domiens*.[8] In effect, while the rest of the world lives in what we now call the "postcolonial" era, it is far from evident that France's Overseas departments have truly emerged from their colonial status.[9] This is captured well in an exchange that takes place in Paris (in the 1960s) between two characters from Warner-Vieyra's *As the Sorcerer Said . . . .* The building caretaker opens the door for Rosemonde, who is returning from the Caribbean with her daughter Zétou, the narrator. This is her first encounter with the metropole:

[7]See Catherine Clément, *L'Opéra ou la défaite des femmes* (Paris: Grasset, 1979), trans. Betsy Wing as *Opera or the Undoing of Women* (Minneapolis: University of Minnesota Press, 1988); and the aphorism from Poe in the epigraph to this chapter.

[8]*Domien* is a neologism for an inhabitant of the Overseas departments, *départements d'Outre-mer* or D.O.M.

[9]One need only note the fatal turn of events in February–March 1991, in the Chaudron district of Saint-Denis, capital of Réunion, where Paris's banning of a pirate radio and television station provoked an outbreak of violence. The station often carried programming in Creole and catered to the most disadvantaged youth, among whom unemployment rates currently run between 30 and 35 percent. See Françoise Lionnet, "*Créolité* in the Indian Ocean: Two Models of Cultural Diversity," *Yale French Studies* 82 (1993): 101–12.

—Madame Rosemondé? Did you have a good trip?

—Yes, Madame Simone.

—How are things in the colonies?

Hm! I thought, "the colonies?" All these French people in France, don't they know we're a part of France, a French department . . . or at least an Overseas department? What's the difference between an Overseas department and a colony? Come now! . . . A colony means that you're colonised; that's the same as being dominated, controlled, domesticated. Brings to mind whips and kicks up the arse, forced labour, and that's only where the present times are concerned! If we talked about the past, it would take us too far back and we'd have to remember our ancestors, the period of slavery, and everything that that entails.

No, I prefer being "departmentalized," won over, it sounds nicer. It reminds me of Saint-Exupéry's *Little Prince*, with the fox who wanted to be tamed [apprivoisé]. (Q/S, 55/106)

It is interesting to note that dependence is presented here under the guise of taming: that is, as a relation of seduction, since being tamed amounts to being taken in, being lured in by one who holds a certain power but who strives to maintain the appearance of a democratic and egalitarian relationship. Such a situation inevitably provokes a sense of instability and unease, the discomfort at the heart of the search for identity which has characterized Caribbean literature from its beginnings in the eighteenth century.[10] This search was conducted less anxiously in the 1980s, which saw the introduction of a more serene, perhaps even triumphant, Creole identity. But the existential quest for selfhood, for an ego, and for a subject position marked both by colonization and by the difficulty in defining and delimiting one's own corporeality remains central among many writers of the Caribbean diaspora. Their search took a new direction with the publication of the works of such writers as Warner-Vieyra and Dracius-Pinalie.

For these women writers, the body serves to engage an ideological context within which they construct a narrative text that seeks to surpass or exceed this context. The body has therefore a double function: to represent the real, and to mediate the possible. This

[10]See Roger Toumson, *La Transgression des couleurs: Littérature et langage des Antilles, XVIIe, XIXe, XXe siècles* Vol. 1 and 2 (Paris: Caribéenne, 1989).

body, an emblematic space marked as much by the slave trade and métissage as by the constraints of its current social and sexual role, speaks and displays itself as the figure of the racial oppression of which it has been the victim throughout the course of colonial history. But the body's language is ambiguous and disturbing. The narrative emphasis on physical degeneration is in sharp contrast to the reductionist discourses of seductive and easy exoticism or to the tragic and romantic scenarios in which the death of the heroine serves as the main dramatic vehicle. As a canvas upon which historical problems of domination and physical or verbal violence, either latent or manifest, are sketched out, the body now reflects the strategic choices forced upon the alienated and colonized subject who wants to be "other" and who wanders in search of selfhood, looking toward other lands and other times.

In its relation to its other—European or African, real or possible, racial or sexual or cultural—this Caribbean body reveals its struggle for existence: the gestures and body language of the female characters are foregrounded in the narratives, and the bodily transformations they undergo are described in minute detail. These bodily descriptions are in stark contrast to the basically lifeless, distorted, or stereotypical representation of female protagonists created by male writers of the previous generation, such as Joseph Zobel or Edouard Glissant. As Ernest Pépin states:

> Women are accorded a large place in Caribbean literature, but this often takes account only of the social role of women. The Caribbean writer does not look at the Caribbean woman, he does not contemplate her, no doubt fearing a descent into exoticism. Women such as Fidéline (Zobel), Man Tine (Zobel), Mycéa (Glissant) do not really have bodies. They embody an abstract or disembodied type. There is still no sculptural representation of the Caribbean woman. It is as if the density of her reality engendered an absence of representation. [Il n'existe pas davantage une statuaire de la femme antillaise. Tout se passe comme si son trop plein d'existence engendrait un silence de la représentation.][11]

Absence perhaps, but only in the male texts. Warner-Vieyra and Dracius-Pinalie take up these questions by focusing both on lived

[11]Ernest Pépin, "La Femme antillaise et son corps," *Présence Africaine* 141 (1987): 193.

corporeality and on the symbolic images embedded in the cultural discourse. They give the female body a sensuousness and presence that are both striking and disturbing: victim of the entropy generating its slow disintegration, this body is a revealing text, one that draws attention to and denounces the necrotic ideology of Western culture.

The feminist critic Susan Gubar, investigating the question of female artistic creation, articulates clearly the perilous relation between the female author and her body, so often subjected to the gaze of numerous male artists who have reduced it to a mythic object. This is why a woman would seem to be obliged to perceive her body as both her own and as other. Furthermore, because this body is an intermediary between life and the domain of art, it seems that a woman is almost obliged to use her personal experiences to create, since her role models and artistic paradigms direct her back to her own corporeality. Gubar writes: "Like Kafka's victim in 'The Penal Colony,' women have had to experience cultural scripts in their lives by suffering them in their bodies. . . . For the artist, this sense that she is herself the text means that there is little distance between her life and her art."[12]

By using their personal experiences in their novels, Warner-Vieyra and Dracius-Pinalie bring into play very specific ties between the female body and cultural exile. For Warner-Vieyra, who has lived in Senegal for the last thirty years, the body is the privileged symbolic site serving to represent the conflicts that issue from the fatal clash of cultures: African and Caribbean, Islamic and Catholic. In *Juletane* the subject's distress translates into a steady diminution of her physical and mental capacities, a decline leading to a sort of "gentle death," since the character fades away into a tranquil forgetfulness.[13]

[12]Susan Gubar, " 'The Blank Page' and the Issues of Female Creativity," in *Writing and Sexual Difference*, ed. Elizabeth Abel (Chigago: University of Chicago Press, 1982), 81. My intent here is to suggest not that these novels are strictly autobiographical but rather that the personal experience of exile is translated by a representation of the female body which eliminates the distance between life and art, the lived and the imagined.

[13]It is worth noting that, by contrast, Sidonie (in Warner-Vieyra's *Femmes échouées* [Paris: Présence Africaine, 1987]), exiled to Paris, suffers a violent death following an act of vengeance against her husband, whom she castrates in a scene reminiscent

Juletane considers suicide because she cannot let herself be "tamed" either to the idea or the reality of the polygamous marriage that her husband, Mamadou, imposes upon her. She gives in to a self-destructive violence, which leads her to the brink of madness: "I began breaking everything in my room and banging my head against the walls" (*J*, 25) "I cut off all my hair, and put on mourning clothes" (*J*, 37). Looking at herself one day "in a broken bit of mirror," she gives a self-portrait that conveys her degenerate state: "There is a long diagonal scar across my forehead, a souvenir of my first depression. . . . My eyes, too shiny . . . my cheek-bones stand out above the hollows of my cheeks; my skin is without lustre. I look desperate, starved" (*J*, 66). She imposes upon herself a series of physical mortifications in a desperate and futile effort to master "a destiny over which [she] had no control" (*J*, 73).

Such an effort, according to the philosopher Susan Bordo, is an integral part of the psychology of women labeled "anorexic": that is, women who engage in self-destructive behavior in order to compensate for their lack of social power. Bordo, who draws inspiration from Michel Foucault's work on the discipline of the body and the history of cultural practices, argues that the anorexic is the victim of a philosophical dualism that we Westerners inherited from Plato, St. Augustine, and Descartes. This dualism places us in a radical dilemma, presenting us with the experience of our body both as the prison of the soul and as an object that constantly escapes the spirit's control and must therefore be mastered. If our self-image differs significantly from the one given to us by society, we will be tempted to exercise an even greater level of control over the rebellious body, to punish it through a variety of mortifications, including the various diets that so many women inflict upon themselves. Bordo is interested above all in the desire for perfection, the problem of a growing number of young women influenced by the power of advertising images that impose idealized physical norms.[14]

---

of Bessie Head's title short story in *The Collector of Treasures* (London: Heinemann, 1977); see Chapter 5.

[14]See Susan Bordo, "Anorexia Nervosa: Psychopathology as the Crystallization of Culture," in *Feminism and Foucault: Reflections on Resistance* (Boston: Northeastern University Press, 1988); 87–118.

Bordo's argument applies just as well in a mixed racial context, where ambiguity reigns and where the individual perceives herself (or is perceived by the society) as "not black enough," or "not exactly white." Juletane, for example, is called *toubabesse* (*J*, 42) by her co-wife Ndèye, who has nothing but disdain for this mixed-race woman from a culture more French than African: Ndèye even deprives her of "her identity as a black woman," Juletane says.[15] Rehvana, distressed that her hair is too straight (*L'A*, 25), compensates by exhibiting a "militant Caribbeanism [*antillanité militante*] . . . against anything which, in her eyes [does] not ̄ have the aura of incontestable authenticity" (*L'A*, 119). Her return to "nature" consists of archaism, violence, and the rejection of all technology, including electricity. She takes great pains to learn Creole cooking but eats nothing. She ruins her hands: "At the ends of her ragged fingernails, pared down by half, the flesh now forms cracked blisters"; her skin is "laced with bruises, legs and arms ulcerated with poorly healed sores" (*L'A*, 126). The search for redemptive spiritual authenticity translates into the gradual withering of the body, a symptom of her disturbing cultural realities. Here, violence is the work of men, but it is also a symptom of the lack of female solidarity: Rehvana and her daughter cannot be saved and quietly die of hunger in a housing project in the Paris suburbs, having voluntarily isolated themselves from one and all.

This discord between a particular idealized racial identity and the realities of the postcolonial world creates a rupture which encourages a deficit, a loss of being, a self-hatred comparable to that of the anorexic trapped in her fatal dualism, imposing impossibly high standards upon herself. For example, Rehvana belongs to a fanatic sect of young Parisian Caribbeans, *les Ebonis*, who demand fasting, flagellation, tattooing, and other bodily mutilation as means of purification and chastisement in order that they may feel closer to "mother Africa." Their regression to the stage of myth is accompanied by mockery from their brothers, the "pure-bred Africans," who "with sovereign disdain" are happy to ignore "these crazy *Ebonis*" (*L'A*, 57). Caught in an impasse, the *Ebonis* unknowingly

---

[15]*Toubabesse* is the feminine of *Toubab*, a term of Arabic origin used by native Africans to refer to white colonial administrators; in colloquial speech it simply means "white."

maintain the dualist illusion, thereby remaining trapped in the ideological system they had hoped to escape.

Warner-Vieyra and Dracius-Pinale's narratives thus enact both a real and a metaphoric exile, which culminates in the annihilation of the colonized subject. Younger sisters of Condé's heroine Véronica (in *Heremakhonon*), Juletane and Rehvana set out in search of a lost identity but never succeed in finding their proper place, the site of their mythic roots. Whereas Véronica has the composure, sarcasm, and intellectual means to live out her alienation and survive in her exile, Juletane and Rehvana fade away in solitude, victims of circumstances for which they themselves seem in part responsible. In my reading of these texts, the narrative strategies appear to highlight the considered passivity and impotence of the protagonists, who, feeling caught in an impasse, perhaps cannot imagine themselves other than as victims of the social order they reject.

This type of female character is common in the literature of the Caribbean basin.[16] At the center of the romantic aesthetic to which we are still heir, we find a heroine for whom seduction is synonymous with passivity, precariousness, or fragility. Vulnerable under the male gaze, which tries to "tame" the better to suffocate, the Caribbean heroine is often left without choice. Juletane feels obliged to remain in Africa, where she will eventually succumb to madness; and Rehvana is in a hopeless situation, her return ticket sold, her pride preventing her from asking her sister for help. The female subject, whose consciousness bears the double burden—material and ideological—of colonial and patriarchal society, has difficulty conceiving of herself as a subject who controls knowledge and, hence, as a subject endowed with either agency or power. The characters created by these novelists suffer the fate of victims because in that tradition there is not yet a literary model which allows the female subject genuinely to conceive of herself as both a speaking and an acting subject.

Nevertheless, two secondary characters suggest the possibility of

---

[16]The life of Rehvana, who follows Eric to Terres-Sainville in Martinique, evokes the atmosphere of Jean Rhys's book *Wide Sargasso Sea* (New York: Norton, 1982). The character of Man Cidalise, for example, echoes that of Christophine in the English novel; Rehvana evokes the sensuous yet dark and melancholy femininity of Antoinette Cosway.

an alternative scenario. *L'Autre qui danse* opposes Rehvana's misspent life to the well-regulated one of her sister Matildana: the younger sister is in search of an illusory identity, while "the gifted elder sister" is well anchored in reality. In *Juletane*, Hélène proves her independence, although it is to the detriment of the young African who seeks her hand. There does exist in both novels a feminine perspective that interprets reality for us, since Hélène is the reader of Juletane's diary, and Matildana's letters comment on the events in Rehvana's life. Their reactions serve as counterpoint to the narrativization of the degrading and abusive reality that makes up the daily life of the protagonists. Having learned to decode this reality, Hélène and Matildana can act in the capacity of *subjects* in the choices they make; they are not subservient to the social codes that Juletane and Rehvana have internalized. In the end, it is the death of the latter two that ransoms the liberty and independence of the former: a familiar theme of redemption written between the lines of both novels.

Thanks to feminist criticism and semiotic analysis, we have today acquired a more accurate understanding of the ambiguities that underpin the representation of the female body in all our cultural practices—textual or visual; in literature, advertising, cinema, or political discourse. In all these contexts the body remains a privileged code for a range of messages which, in the end, serve only to enslave this body to the ambiguous images that the cultural code carries, translates, or creates. As Ernest Pépin puts it:

The myth of a certain kind of passive femininity dies hard, and there are still many women who, seeking emancipation, find themselves trapped in a body which is both emblematic and dissimulative [*dissimulateur*]. After all, it is in and through her body that a woman arrives at self-consciousness; any inquiry which avoids this postulate is destined to wander about the twists and turns of futile debate. . . .

We cannot pass over the body, it is the inexorable of existence [*il est l'incontournable de l'être*]. . . . Inhibited bodies, alienated bodies, transcended bodies, no matter what the case, the image confronts the reality in a relentless one-on-one, in which psychological equilibrium is at stake [*un corps-à-corps sans merci dont l'enjeu est l'équilibre psycholo-*

gique]. In the end, the body, despite being the natural property of the subject, does not escape from society.[17]

If the subject's self-image is widely at variance with the social and cultural reality that surrounds her, if this reality is a mirror that casts back nothing but distorted reflections, the subject finds herself in a tragic impasse. It is this impasse that Warner-Vieyra and Dracius-Pinalie strive to describe. But they also make a point of showing the possibility of going beyond the mirror, of breaking the yoke of re-presentation and its mythic images. In contrasting the character of Rehvana to that of her more reasonable and well-adjusted sister, *L'Autre* sketches out a solution to the problems of identity. As a classics professor (like the author herself) and a linguist interested in Creole as much from a scientific as an affective perspective, Matildana represents the self-possessed Caribbean woman, comfortable with her body and able to negotiate the contradictions of her past and of her cultural and racial present. Clearly, this character is something of a self-portrait. But Dracius-Pinalie uses the famous phrase of Rimbaud, the nomad, as the book's epigraph: "Je est un autre" (I is an other), which echoes her chosen title. Perhaps this is an indication that Rehvana is the other, the "sister" whom the author carries within. This sister incorporates the temptation of a sometimes poorly repressed tradition and the lure of a passively lived femininity: these have not lost their resonance among contemporary Caribbean women.

As textual figures of the historical and identitary possibilities open to Caribbean women, Rehvana and Matildana are certainly two sides of the same character: the one who feels exiled and the one who feels anchored, the one who searches for origins and the one who comfortably assumes global citizenship. Similarly, Juletane and Hélène represent opposite ways of relating to men. These figures bring into play the familiar dialectic of departure and return, tradition and modernity, errancy and combat, dependency and autonomy. But they also redefine the traditional schema, displacing it onto a female subject whose identity was for too long dependent on distorted representations of the body that always limited her opportunities for emancipation. Like Condé, Warner-Vieyra and

[17]Pépin, "La femme antillaise," 181–82.

Dracius-Pinalie give their characters the possibility of discovering otherness within themselves. They thus invite us to reflect upon the different roads that have opened up for Caribbean women in the context of modernity and to share the aesthetic approach of many contemporary African and Caribbean artists, an aesthetic that corresponds to the *logiques métisses* of our postcolonial identities.[18]

[18]On this subject, see Jean Loup Amselle, *Logiques métisses: Anthropologie de l'identité en Afrique et ailleurs* (Paris: Payot, 1990); and this book's Introduction.

5

Geographies of Pain: Captive Bodies and Violent Acts in Myriam Warner-Vieyra, Gayl Jones, and Bessie Head

I am
the sun and the moon and forever hungry
the sharpened edge
where day and night shall meet
and not be
one.
>   —Audre Lorde, "From the House of Yemanjá"

Your hair fallen on your cheek, no longer in the semblance
>   of serpents,
Lifted in the gale; your mouth, that shrieked so, silent.
You, my scourge, my sister, lie asleep, like a child,
Who, after rage, for an hour quiet, sleeps out its tears.
>   —Louise Bogan, "The Sleeping Fury"

She did not know what essential parts of you stayed behind
no matter how violently you tried to dislodge them in order
to take them with you.
>   —Tsitsi Dangaremba, *Nervous Conditions*

Literature is a discursive practice that encodes and transmits as well as creates ideology. It is a mediating force in society, since narrative often structures our sense of the world, and stylistic conventions or plot resolutions serve either to sanction and perpetuate cultural myths or to create new mythologies that allow the writer and the reader to engage in a constructive rewriting of their social contexts. Women writers are often especially aware of their task as producers of images that both participate in the dominant representations of their culture and simultaneously undermine and subvert those images by offering a re-vision of familiar scripts. Thus, the nineteenth-century African American writer Harriet Jacobs uses the conventions of the seduction novel as well as the Victorian ideology of "true womanhood" in order to attract readership for her

Incidents in the Life of a Slave Girl. But she transforms those conventions by concluding her autobiographical tale with the statement "Reader, my story ends with freedom; not in the usual way, with marriage," thus placing a high value on a woman's need for independence and self-expression—a radical stance in 1861. Jacobs also stresses the right of her character, Linda Brent, to choose to act in a deliberately calculated way with a single purpose in mind—freedom—even if some of Linda's actions (such as sexual activity outside of marriage) are socially unacceptable and morally reprehensible to her readers. Here, for the female slave, the end clearly justifies the means, even if the means are morally suspect. As Jean Fagan Yellin points out in her preface to the book: "Instead of coupling unsanctioned female sexual activity with self-destruction and death, *Incidents* presents it as a mistaken tactic in the struggle for freedom. Jacob's narrator does not characterize herself conventionally as a passive female victim, but asserts that—even when young and a slave—she was an effective moral agent." Harriet Jacobs redefines morality by reframing the subject of woman's sexual oppression. She addresses the issue of feminine desire and sexual agency in a way that helps to demystify the ideology of feminine virtue as it was previously constructed in the mid-nineteenth century.[1]

As heirs to the tradition—exemplified by Jacobs—that recasts female subjectivity and agency by allowing women to name structures of oppression and to resist their debilitating effects, many twentieth-century black women writers in Africa and the diasporas have, since the 1970s, been equating marriage itself (or other forms of heterosexual alliance) with confinement and captivity, denouncing their culture's failure to offer models of sexual partnership that are not demeaning or degrading to women, *and* that allow for the mutual recognition of differences. These African and African American writers generally place the burden of responsibility for the insidious and gradual deterioration of gender relations on male characters whose indifference or aggression serve to perpetuate the structures of authority that contain, confine, and silence women within the domestic domain.[2] Though victimized by patriarchal so-

[1]Harriet Jacobs, *Incidents in the Life of a Slave Girl*, ed. Jean Fagan Yellin, (Cambridge: Harvard University Press, 1987), 201, xxx.

[2]I am foregrounding the gender issue and working under the well-understood

cial structures that perpetuate their invisibility and dehumanization, black female characters actively resist their objectification, to
the point of committing murder. This extreme step is often taken
after years of attempting to survive in an environment where they
are, at best, the victims of sheer neglect or, at worst, the objects of
violent abuse. Three contemporary writers, Gayl Jones, Bessie
Head, and Myriam Warner-Vieyra, use female murderers as protagonists, and the themes of disfiguration, castration, and imprisonment feature prominently in their texts. In this chapter, I attempt
to delineate the similarities among the fictions of these authors in
order to reach some theoretical conclusions about the symbolic
meaning of their choice of motifs and the cultural anxieties that
choice seems to reveal.[3]

For these writers too, the end justifies the means, when the end
is freedom from sexual oppression. Unlike Harriet Jacobs, however,
they have no illusions about the fate of women who take action to
save themselves: Jones's Eva and Head's Dikeledi are incarcerated;
Head's Life and Warner-Vieyra's Juletane and Sidonie die. But
whereas Jones and Head suggest that a certain utopian female community is to be found in the "other spaces," the heterotopias of
their protagonists' world (among other female inmates who are victims, like them, of criminal procedures that attribute guilt unjustly),
Warner-Vieyra's is a bleaker vision, anchored in the grim cultural
realities of a postcolonial world that links three different countries:
Guadeloupe, Senegal, and France. In the texts of Jones and Head,
revisions of the cultural script are mediated by a phantasmic resolution of differences, a retreat into the imaginary. For Warner-
Vieyra, however, madness and death seem to underscore the
triumphant reinscription of the symbolic order, since the heroine's
rebellion fails to dismantle or transpose the patriarchal narrative:
Juletane never actually loses the desire to please her husband Ma-

---

assumption that colonialism is the immediate historical context within which these
issues emerge. My purpose here, however, is to critique not colonialism but gender
dissymmetry. Colonialism has had its share of by now "canonical" critics, from
Nkrumah to Cabral, from C. L. R. James to Césaire and Fanon. My more specific
focus is the position taken by a few radical critics of black sexism.

[3]Gayl Jones, *Eva's Man* (Boston: Beacon Press, 1977), hereafter cited in the text as
EM; Bessie Head, *The Collector of Treasures* (London: Heinemann, 1977), cited as *CT*;
Myriam Warner-Vieyra, *Juletane*, and *Femmes échouées* (Paris: Présence Africaine,
1987), cited as *F*.

madou; and it is Sidonie's brother, Septime, who provides narrative closure after her death. Warner-Vieyra virtually reasserts and reinforces the traditional romantic ideology that revolves around the death of a heroine; by contrast, Jones and Head succeed in constructing an alternative space, a parallel world with utopian possibilities despite the restriction of movement that prison imposes.

Although the wide-ranging psychological and political problems resulting from colonialism or the slave trade are also invoked by these writers, the principal focus remains on sexual, familial, and domestic structures that uphold a particularly coercive order. As Bessie Head has pointed out: "Black women have a certain history of oppression within African culture . . . [where] women's problems are rooted in custom and tradition. What is certainly very dominant here is that the male had a superior position to the female . . . [and] the disregard of Garesego Mokopi [the husband in "The Collector of Treasures"] for his wife is based on the fact that he regards her as an inferior form of human life."[4] Bessie Head's stories—like those of her fellow Africans Buchi Emecheta, Ama Ata Aidoo, Mariama Bâ, Ken Bugul, and Assia Djebar, and, on this side of the Atlantic, those of Zora Neale Hurston, Gayl Jones, Maya Angelou, Alice Walker, Gloria Naylor, Toni Morrison, Audre Lorde, Paule Marshall, Simone Schwarz-Bart, and Maryse Condé—dramatize deep-seated cultural misogyny and the potentially fatal consequences of practices (such as de jure or de facto polygamy and quotidian forms of sexual slavery) which construct women as objects of exchange within the male economy. As Head likes to stress, the problem is not simply "political": that is, linked to the history of colonialism and to post-independence corruption, even though these aggravate economic conditions. Rather, she implies, the problem is rooted in ancient customs and traditions, for as Paul Thebolo in "The Collector of Treasures" is fond of saying, "The British only ruled us for eighty years" (CT, 96), and only a lucid and self-reflexive critique of tradition carried out from within the culture by those best acquainted with it will illuminate what Fatima Mernissi calls the "structural dissymmetry that runs all through and conditions the entire fabric of social and individual life."[5]

---

[4]Interview with Bessie Head in *Between the Lines*, ed. Craig Mackenzie and Cherry Clayton, (Grahamstown, South Africa: National English Literary Museum, 1989), 15.

[5]See Fatima Mernissi, *Beyond the Veil: Male-Female Dynamics in Modern Muslim Society* (Bloomington: Indiana University Press, 1987), ix. Head does not suggest (nor

The general human malaise stemming from dissymmetrical sexual arrangements has been superbly dissected and denounced by Paule Marshall.[6] Her book *Daughters* is her contribution to this rich tradition of feminist writing in Africa and the diaspora, and it continues to be extremely controversial because of its frank and, to some, biased depiction of gender conflicts.[7] Marshall's heroine, Ursa Mackenzie, is the textual daughter of Gayl Jones's Ursa and Eva, Bessie Head's Dikeledi, Mariama Bâ's Ramatoulaye, and Myriam Warner-Vieyra's Juletane and Sidonie, among others—all characters who struggle (often unsuccessfully) within the sexual and racial constraints of their post- or neocolonial societies to achieve a sense of dignity and freedom.

But it is important to stress that they are not meant to be in any way "representative" of a particular cross-section of "real" women. Rather, they are intended to function as *literary* figures (intertextually related to Jacob's Linda Brent or Zora Neale Hurston's Janie) whose extreme predicaments haunt the reader's imagination and help to crystallize awareness of gender oppression while problematizing these issues in reference to a specific cultural context. My purpose, then, is to focus on the *literarity* of a group of works whose thematic similarities are uncanny, although their narrative strategies differ considerably. What I am suggesting is that we should be wary of a too literal or sociological interpretation of these texts, which would lead us to infer from them a complete breakdown of communication between the sexes. Although the hearings preceding the confirmation of Clarence Thomas's appointment to the U.S. Supreme Court seemed to confirm the insights of women writers regarding the continued and outright dismissal of black women's

---

do I) that the impact of British colonialism on the fact of women's oppression is negligible. Rather, she stresses the larger historical and cultural picture, instead of simply opposing indigenous traditions to the colonizer's values.

[6]Paule Marshall, *Daughters* (New York: Atheneum, 1991), 407. Marshall suggests that Ursa's father, the powerful Primus Mackenzie, was born on the wrong side of the Atlantic: he has, in other words, retained the polygamous customs of his African ancestors.

[7]See Sven Birkerts's review, "The Black Woman's Burden," *Mirabella* (October 1991): "Marshall has written a powerful novel . . . [but] she has impaled the black man in the process" (76). He echoes other critics who believe, with him, that "black women writers appear to have declared open season on black men. In best-selling novels by Alice Walker, Toni Morrison, Gloria Naylor, and others, I hunt in vain to find males as strong, as honorable or as emotionally mature as their female counterparts" (78).

point of view in sexual matters, I tend to agree with Deborah Mc-
Dowell that "feminist critics run the risk of plunging their work
into cliché and triviality if they continue merely to focus on how
Black men treat Black women in literature."[8] Literary works, as the
Russian Formalists have shown, produce an effect of estrangement
and defamiliarization based on the application or subversion of
particular literary conventions and on the exaggeration of familiar
scenarios that can produce in readers the shock of recognition.
Knowledge of these conventions is central to the exchange of meaning between writers and readers, and by using formal methods of
comparative analysis we can perhaps elucidate certain crucial aspects of the cultural schema that subtends the works of these
women writers. As Mineke Schipper states: "In studying African
literature, one might certainly profit from the substantial progress
and the refinement of tools by literary theorists."[9] Rigorous textual
analysis can help us trace the somewhat puzzling, and disturbing,
commonalities among these writers, analyze the differences, and
outline the ways in which their narrative strategies deconstruct or
reinforce existing symbolic frameworks.

At the risk of collapsing together vastly different cultural arenas,
I am comparing a novel by an African American from Kentucky
(Jones), two short stories by a South African exiled to Botswana
(Head), and a novel and a short story by a Guadeloupean living in
Senegal (Warner-Vieyra). But I believe that the task of finding transatlantic connections is rendered all the more important by the fact
that these works evince a pattern of influence and cross-fertilization
in their use of themes and in their concern for the negative mythic
images of women (Medusa, Jezebel, Salome, the Furies, the Ama-
zon, the mad woman, the hysteric) which they exploit and translate
into powerfully subversive fictions. For whereas murder is generally considered to be a crime of the individual against society, in
these texts it is a symptom of society's crime against the female
individual. Struggle for the control of their own bodies determines
the ultimate act of resistance and survival performed by Eva, Jule-

---

[8]Deborah McDowell, "New Directions for Black Feminist Criticism," in *The New
Feminist Criticism: Essays on Women, Literature, and Theory,* ed. Elaine Showalter (New
York: Pantheon, 1985), 196.

[9]See Mineke Schipper, *Beyond the Boundaries: Text and Context in African Literature*
(Chicago: Ivan R. Dee, 1989), 7.

tane, Dikeledi, and Sidonie. The narratives thus construct each one as a heroine who takes justice into her own hands, revealing a profound conflict of values between the dominant culture and its "weaker" members. The women's subjection to forms of social control that further marginalizes them does not, however, succeed in annihilating their need for recognition and personal agency, even if this need manifests itself only in dramatically violent acts. The narrative representation of these acts provokes a reexamination of the doxa—the acceptable norms or moral codes—of their respective cultures, inviting the reader to rethink the role and the definition of "woman." The writers thus succeed in demystifying age-old traditions, providing a textual space where silence speaks and reveals a much more complex perspective on what constitutes criminality in both private and public domains. As Foucault has pointed out, "murder establishes the ambiguity of the lawful and the unlawful," and as a narrative catalyst it can serve to reorganize our cultural experiences and to blur cultural distinctions between arbitrary or relativistic norms of conduct and a truly ethical or universal moral code.[10]

Each text I examine refigures a cultural specificity (Kentucky, Botswana, Guadeloupe, Senegal), but taken together they create a series of what Pierre Nora has called *lieux de mémoire*, guiding the reader through some of the most sordid places in the labyrinth of colonial and postcolonial human sexual relationships. These sites record testimonies that memorialize the experiences of a gendered cultural "minority" and bring to representation the calculated— either subdued or explosive—violence that has been the mark of domestic life. Because they evoke the dystopian potential of oppressive and coercive gender arrangements, these sites also "anchor, condense, and express the exhausted capital of our collective memory," thus suggesting that on the global as well as the local level, some hypothesis about reciprocal meanings and dialogical encounters can be elaborated by comparing different cultural contexts. As Nora goes on to say, "contrary to historical objects, *lieux de mémoire* have no referent in reality; or, rather, they are their own

---

[10]Foucault is quoted and discussed in Joel Black, *The Aesthetics of Murder: A Study in Romantic Literature and Contemporary Culture* (Baltimore: Johns Hopkins University Press, 1991), 18.

referent: pure, exclusive, self-referential signs."[11] As such, then, narratives of murder by female characters open up a wide range of possible meanings: they are rhetorical resources, offering a "grammar of fictional situations" that can help us explore what Hortense Spillers has called "the politics of intimacy": that is, the myriad ways in which language and literature can "create an attitude of containment or liberation."[12]

It is important to deal with cross-cultural comparisons without falling into the trap either of essentialism or of false universalism. To state that comparisons are warranted on the theoretical basis of a certain understanding of *sites* of literarity and textuality is to bypass the culturalist/essentialist approach that naively tends to assume the existence of a common ground among these various fictions simply because their authors share some common "African" origin—which they all do, of course. But I want to stress that the similarities of theme in the works of Jones, Head, and Warner-Vieyra are the consequence not just of their shared "Africanness" but of a performative intertextuality that is a function of the ideological and cultural matrix that generates the works.[13] The dialectic of the particular and the universal which exists within the interpretive space of textuality has been understood as the foundation of literariness in the Western context. Now that the definition of literature is finally expanding to include the contributions of women and colonized peoples, it is becoming increasingly clear that this inclusion will inflect the accepted meaning of universality: since literature and literary criticism give us "a clue to the text of our own experience," as Spillers says, it also broadens this expe-

---

[11]Pierre Nora, "Between Memory and History: *Les Lieux de Mémoire*," *Representations* 26 (Spring 1989): 24, 23. The "minority" to which I refer is not numerical but cultural: that is, one whose point of view is not part of the "majority" culture.

[12]See Hortense Spillers, "The Politics of Intimacy: A Discussion," in *Sturdy Black Bridges: Visions of Black Women in Literature*, ed. Roseann P. Bell, Bettye J. Parker, and Beverly Guy-Sheftall (Garden City, N.Y.: Anchor Books, 1979), 89.

[13]See Jean Bessière, *Dire le littéraire: Points de vue théoriques* (Liège: Pierre Mardaga, 1990), 310–11: 'The perfect validity of discourse would seem to reside in the fact that it is a *singular universal....* The validity of the literary stems from a series of sentences that are specific universes, and as many marks of idiomatic difference.... Literary discourse ... does not clarify, but it maps out the places of speech. It is necessarily fictive because it is this interpretive repetition that prefigures, by means of textuality and in a variable way, the witnesses, the moments, the spaces of speech. The literary matters here because it presupposes a *common understanding.*'

rience in light of the alternative models and strategies proposed by heretofore muted groups.[14] By focusing on such an extreme issue as murder, Jones, Head, and Warner-Vieyra refuse to be relegated to a relativistic theory of literature and culture; they demand to be taken seriously on the grounds that their concerns are universal ones, that the issues raised by their fictions are the same as those that have compelled the human imagination since Sophocles and Euripides entertained fellow Athenians with tragic tales of murder and suicide.

But these writers do make it obvious that Africans and African Americans have their own particular perspective to add to the concert of voices that have dealt with such issues. As the Africanist critic Bernard Mouralis has stated, "As soon as the peoples of Africa and the Diaspora started to engage in literary creation, and to use literature as a means of revelation and demystification, the west found itself confronted with these unexpected texts written, furthermore, in its own languages. Westerners simultaneously discovered that it would no longer be possible to continue speaking for those who had produced such texts." Indeed, to read these narratives is to be provided with the woman's own perspective on gender dissymmetry within African and diasporic contexts. Furthermore, it is the intertextual references among the texts that underscore their status as literature. As Mouralis adds: "Literature is both a social object—with a specific institutional configuration—and another (or an other) object which can be reduced neither to a reflection of reality nor to the discourses on reality that ideology constructs]."[15]

A commonality of theme—what I call a geography of pain—and the production of a specifically female literary vision unite the works of Jones, Head, and Warner-Vieyra. All three write with meticulous attention to realistic detail and the paradoxical desire to communicate in the most honest way possible the radically subjective, and thus generally uncommunicable, experience of pain. Elaine Scarry has studied the "language-destroying" attribute of physical pain and torture and its political consequences: namely,

---

[14]Spillers, "The Politics of Intimacy," 88.
[15]Bernard Mouralis, "Réflexions sur l'enseignement des littératures africaines," *Nouvelles du Sud* (1985): 10, 12.

that pain makes "overt precisely what is at stake in 'inexpressibility' " and thus "begin[s] to expose by inversion the essential character of 'expressibility,' whether verbal or material." Scarry's project, which intersects with that of the women writers under study here, is a phenomenology of pain; it is "about the way other persons become visible to us, or to cease to be visible to us. It is about the way we make ourselves (and the originally interior facts of sentience) available to one another through verbal and material artifacts."[16] Eva, Dikeledi, Juletane, and Sidonie (much like Firdaus in Nawal El Saadawi's *Woman at Point Zero;* see Chapter 6) are characters who come to feel that they are being denied the most elementary form of recognition and visibility; they are thus driven to murder as a result of the "inexpressibility" and cultural invisibility of their pain and dehumanization.

Jones, Head, and Warner-Vieyra are adept at representing the containment and imprisonment of their female characters within a social and textual space that stifles and silences them. Restricted movement and confined locales are the principal topoi of these narratives: the hotel room where Davis keeps Eva; the village compound that circumscribes Dikeledi's life; the bedroom and then the hospital room where Juletane's madness develops; the small Paris apartment where Sidonie, the invalid, witnesses her husband's infidelities. In this carceral world the women's thought processes as well as their activities are controlled and policed by structures of domination that involve complex networks of power vested primarily in the male characters, but at times reinforced by other female characters, such as Juletane's co-wife Ndèye.

Disfiguration and Castration: Juletane and Sidonie

Published in 1982 and 1988 respectively, *Juletane* and *Femmes échouées* (which includes the story "Sidonie") are the most recent of these stories of murder. It is not clear whether Myriam Warner-Vieyra had read Gayl Jones's *Eva's Man* or Bessie Head's *The Collector of Treasures* before or while she was writing her own.

[16]Elaine Scarry, *The Body in Pain: The Making and Unmaking of the World* (New York: Oxford University Press, 1985), 19, 22.

Warner-Vieyra does not seem to know English; her only interviews do not refer to any specific literary influences on her creative choices.[17] Although Bessie Head's stories have not been translated into French, a translation of Jones's *Eva* was published under the title *Meurtrière* by the Editions des femmes in Paris in 1977. Whether Warner-Vieyra was influenced by Jones and Head is impossible to determine at this point, but these works all belong to a period marked by intense feminist questionings around the world and culminating in the United Nations Decade for Women Conference in Nairobi in 1985. By translating these international concerns into very private and personal narratives that reflect her own experience as a displaced Guadeloupean woman, Warner-Vieyra looks at culture from a dual perspective: that of the Western educated woman (she has lived and worked as a hospital librarian in Senegal for more than thirty years, after studying in Paris for a brief period), who then marries an African intellectual (filmmaker Paulin Vieyra) and follows him "home." She is thus acutely aware of the difficulties faced by Antillean women who, like Juletane, experience culture shock in an African milieu that is overwhelmingly Muslim.

Juletane relies heavily on the principle of doubling, in both theme and structure. The text constructs a dialogue between Juletane's diary and Helene's reading; it is thanks to the personal narrative of a fellow Guadeloupean that Hélène recognizes her own "face" and her own predicament in the mirror of the story.[18] Doubling also occurs among the three co-wives, Juletane, Ndèye, and Awa, in a way that suggests the echoing patterns of disfiguration, death, and castration which are at the center of Warner-Vieyra's works.

Feeling exiled in an inhospitable land, Juletane progressively loses her ability to function in the family compound that she shares with Awa and Ndèye. She literally shuts herself off from the community, depriving herself of food and gradually sinking into mental illness: "I remained locked in our room without eating or drinking" (*J*, 24). After a nervous breakdown and a violent outburst

---

[17]I thank Anne Adams for sending me a taped conversation in French that she had with Warner-Vieyra in 1988. See also Mildred Mortimer, "An Interview with Myriam Warner-Vieyra," *Callaloo* 16 (1993): 108–15.

[18]See Jonathan Ngaté, "Reading Warner-Vieyra's *Juletane*," *Callaloo* 9 (1986): 553–63. Ngaté's careful study of the *mise en abyme* of the effect of reading has stressed this dialogical encounter.

caused by her inability to adapt to her husband's polygamous culture, she spends time in a mental hospital, then has a miscarriage
as a consequence of an accident, becomes sterile, and thus is alienated completely from the household: "I have buried once and for
all everything that goes on outside this house. My life unfolds in a
room five paces by four and under the mango tree in the yard
where I eat my meals" (J, 26–27). This *manguier stérile* [barren tree]
(J, 134/74) is significant: it does not bear any fruit, and planted in
the middle of the courtyard it is a nagging reminder of Juletane's
own "shortcomings" as a sterile wife. She denies her own physical
needs, begins to think of suicide, goes for days without food, shaves
her head, begins to see Mamadou as a monster, and displaces her
fears onto every other human face she sees: "I looked at the people
who surrounded me; they were frightful giants, with monstrous
faces" (J, 36–39). She even harbors thoughts of killing Mamadou:
"Pour me venger, je l'imaginais mort, une belle dépouille de cra-
pule puante sur laquelle je crachais [To get revenge, I imagined
him dead, nothing but a fine stinking corpse, on which I spat]" (J,
75/39).

Her conflicts with Ndèye escalate to the point where the latter,
calling her a *toubabesse*, denies her the very identity she had come
to Africa to claim: that of a black woman (J, 79/42). When Ndèye
destroys Juletane's recording of Beethoven's Ninth Symphony and
violently slaps her face, she propels Juletane on a violent course
of her own: "That slap in the face was the last drop that made my
cup of passivity overflow and transformed my patience into a rag-
ing torrent" (J, 50). Awa's children are found dead the following
morning, and a week later Juletane literally disfigures Ndèye by
pouring hot oil on her face (J, 73), an incident that occurs after she
had spent some time imagining herself sharpening the long kitchen
knife, stabbing Ndèye to death, and watching her face become "un
masque hideux aux yeux vitreux [a hideous death mask, her eyes
... glassy]" (J, 124/69). After being confined to a mental hospital,
she dreams of visiting a cemetery with her father and seeing her
own gravestone, with no name on it. Feeling ever more like a
"zombi" (J, 39) from the Caribbean, she has the impression "d'être
à la fois au-dessus et en dessous [of being inside and outside the
grave]" (J, 139/77), of being a traveler between the worlds of the
living and the dead. Narrative closure is finally provided by her

actual death three months later in the hospital, a death that appears to redeem Hélène, the reader in the text, from her own coldness and unfeeling existence as a displaced Guadeloupean.

If, as Paul de Man has written, "the autobiographical moment happens as an alignment between the two subjects involved in the process of reading in which they determine each other by mutual reflexive substitution," then the death of the displaced postcolonial female subject is emblematic here of a much broader cultural phenomenon. Juletane's loss of identity and effective disfiguration and unnaming are a function of her own liminal positionality as both active and passive agent in the text. Clearly, there is a certain "mutual reflexive substitution" between Hélène and Juletane, since reading Juletane's diary transforms Hélène's life. More important, though, it is among the three co-wives that textual specularity is established in a nonbinary fashion: if Ndèye and Awa are each other's opposites—the modern, superficially educated, vulgar, spendthrift, urbanized wife and the illiterate but refined traditional African rural wife—they are also two figures whose fates incorporate elements of Juletane's own predicament. Awa commits suicide by jumping into a well, while Juletane feels trapped in a well of loneliness and despair, "ce puits de misère, où git mon corps depuis quelques années [this well of misery, where my body has been lying for years]" (J, 18/5). And Juletane appears to enact her own anxieties about her loss of self by disfiguring Ndèye. Juletane's diary thus constructs each of her co-wives, in de Man's terms, as a "substitutive exchange that constitutes [her as] subject," since the specular structure of their relationships points to Juletane's implicit recognition of their shared predicament as faceless and nameless women occupying the position "wife," and hence easily substitutable or permutable within the familiar economy. Self-writing or autobiography for Juletane thus serves to reinforce her sense of defacement and confirms de Man's view that "death is a displaced name for a linguistic predicament, and the restoration of mortality by autobiography . . . deprives and disfigures to the precise extent that it restores. Autobiography veils a defacement of the mind of which it is itself the cause."[19] Indeed, the loss of self experienced

[19]Paul de Man, "Autobiography as De-Facement," *Modern Language Notes* 94 (1979): 921, 930.

by Juletane is reinforced by the writing of the diary. Although writing does allow her to take stock of her situation—"writing does me good"; "perhaps it is good therapy for my anxieties" (J, 46, 51)—it also participates in the process of unnaming: the attribution of "monstrosity" slides from Mamadou to Juletane herself as the narrative progresses—"Etais-je ce monstre de douleur? [Was I this monster of pain?]" (J, 135/75)—just as the death of Awa and the disfiguration of Ndèye prefigure Juletane's own predicament in the end.

Furthermore, Juletane's madness, her feminine disorder, the fact that she ostensibly goes crazy and "loses her head," could be seen as a form of effective decapitation brought about by the patriarchal system which she finds herself up against but which her transgressive behavior threatens. Her resounding, hysterical laughter, Hélène Cixous's "laugh of the Medusa," marks two crucial moments in the story.[20] The first occurs when she imagines Mamadou dead: "Cette vision me fit éclater de rire, un rire absurde et démentiel, jusqu'à perdre le souffle [This image made me burst out laughing, a ridiculous, demented laugh that left me breathless]" (J, 75/39); the second, when she fantasizes killing Ndèye: "J'éclate de rire en pensant à tout ce beau sang rouge qui s'échappe de la poitrine de Ndèye. . . . Quelle belle farce, la préférée de Mamadou hors du circuit! [I burst out laughing at the thought of all that beautiful red blood flowing from Ndeye's side. . . . What a lovely joke, Mamadou's favourite out of the running!]" (J, 125/69). Her laughter momentarily liberates her from Mamadou's hold. As Hélène Cixous knows so well, it is *laughter* that allows women to function outside the male economy, and that is why it needs to be contained. In her essay "Castration or Decapitation," Cixous relates a story about unruly Chinese women who literally have to choose between being beheaded and keeping absolutely quiet: "It's a question of submitting feminine disorder, its laughter . . . to the threat of decapitation. If man operates under the threat of castration, if masculinity is culturally ordered by the castration complex, it might be said that the backlash, the return, on women of this castration anxiety is its dis-

[20]Hélène Cixous, "The Laugh of the Medusa," in *New French Feminisms: An Anthology*, ed. Elaine Marks and Isabelle de Courtivron (Amherst: University of Massachusetts Press, 1980), 245–64.

placement as decapitation, execution, of woman, as loss of her head." Driven to madness by the circumstances surrounding her induction into the economy of polygamy, Juletane, like the women in Cixous's story, does not actually lose her head by the sword; the women only keep their heads "*on condition that they lose them . . .* to complete silence."[21] Thus, having "lost her head" to what is labeled "madness," Juletane is committed to the psychiatric hospital, but there she refuses to say anything to the doctor who questions her (J, 76). Silence is her retreat, her escape, as it is for Gayl Jones's Eva. Although imposed upon them, silence becomes, for these protagonists, their "loophole of retreat," as Linda Brent said of her life in the garret.[22]

If, as Cixous argues, the disfiguration and decapitation to which patriarchy subjects women is a displacement of male castration anxiety, then Myriam Warner-Vieyra's writings constitute an interesting attempt to work out this problematic in structural as well as thematic terms. In her short story "Sidonie," a double crime links castration and disfiguration. The castrated husband musters enough strength to strangle his invalid wife, who is confined to a wheelchair. Here, although Warner-Vieyra uses free indirect discourse to enter into the minds of several characters, it is Sidonie's brother Septime whose perspective dominates the third-person narrative, his interior monologue that frames the beginning and the end of the tale. Septime's self-centered concern for his personal loss at the death of his sister reveals a damning shallowness and callousness. There is an unequal and dissymmetrical presentation of perspectives which mirrors the relative power of the characters. Each one's interior monologue allows the reader some insight into Sidonie's life and feelings—her reasons for writing, her jealous nature, her relationship with Bernard, the car accident that paralyzed her, and her feelings toward the young woman her husband has made pregnant—but we are never allowed into her own consciousness, and it is truly her silence that is resounding here. No one really knows her. She writes, but the reader does not have access

[21] Hélène Cixous, "Castration or Decapitation," in *Out There: Marginalization and Contemporary Cultures*, ed. Russell Ferguson, Martha Gever, Trinh T. Minh-ha, and Cornel West (New York and Cambridge: New Museum of Contemporary Art and MIT Press, 1990), 346.

[22] Jacobs, *Incidents*, 114.

to her notebooks. Yolène "thought she knew Sidonie well, and would never have believed her capable of so much determination and barbaric violence" (*F*, 144). Bernard sees "son visage luisant de sueur, déformé par un rictus démentiel [her sweat-covered face, deformed by a mad grin]" and hears her "fou rire hystérique [hysterical laughter]" just before he strangles her. His hands around her neck below the mad, deformed face suggest a beheading, actually confirming Cixous's suspicion about decapitation: the text clearly uses it as a form of punishment or retaliation for Bernard's castration.

Furthermore, there is no interpretation of Bernard's own actions and reactions; only Sidonie's unruly behavior gets the benefit of the other characters' speculations and judgment. If the surface coherence of the texts strongly implies that Sidonie has gone mad, an equally powerful countercoherence emerges from the radical and disruptive force of the uninterpreted events of the story; it is up to the reader to examine these structural dissymmetries and to understand the unstated social inequalities in the vision of each character. Sidonie is perhaps a "victim" gone mad, but just as Juletane's delusions make it hard to determine what degree of agency she is capable of, here it becomes clear that the very notion of agency needs to be redefined to accommodate those situations where extreme pain is *the* condition of subjectivity, of a "radical subjectivity" that imprisons humans in an utterly incommunicable experience.[23] Juletane and Sidonie are locked in a private and painful world that remains largely inarticulate, and eruptions of violence are their only means of acting out their pain.

Thematically and textually, narrative closure is reached in death: the death of the title character. This is a very traditional way to provide closure and to restore order to the community. One might argue, then, that Warner-Vieyra's texts equivocate: that is, they disown on a constructional level what they embrace on an ideological one.[24] Since Juletane regrets that Mamadou has died before being able to read her journal, she appears to have reached a state of "rationality" and accommodation that would allow her final re-

[23]Scarry, *The Body in Pain*, 50.

[24]D. A. Miller, *Narrative and Its Discontents: Problems of Closure in the Traditional Novel* (Princeton: University Press, 1981), 48, discusses this phenomenon in the works of Jane Austen.

entry into the symbolic realm of patriarchal culture; she no longer wants to live: *"Hélène had subsequently learned that since her husband's death, Juletane had ceased to react"* (*J*, 78–79). And it is suggested that Hélène becomes a more gentle, tender, accommodating, and "feminine" woman after reading the diary. In effect, then, the structure of the work reinforces traditional notions of femininity in the end, despite the strong ideological critique of female alienation that it contains. Warner-Vieyra seems to want to do an about-face that will not antagonize traditional readers who constitute the majority of literate Africans capable of reading her works. This, of course, has been a familiar tactic since Harriet Jacob's *Incidents*. It is even clearer in "Sidonie," where Septime's point of view is more sympathetic to Bernard's awful "mutilation" (*F*, 146) than to his sister's crippled body and death. Male solidarity triumphs over female hysteria, and the social order remains intact.

Medusa's Silence: Eva

Castration and hysteria are central to the narrative of *Eva's Man*. Unlike those of the two previous texts, Gayl Jones's title seems to focus on the man in/of the story. It is after all Davis's death that the story attempts to explain without, however, requiring that the murderess have a believable rational motive. Eva's subjectivity is filled with the voices of others; it is a kind of echo chamber in which her self-representations are always mediated by the words and actions of others,[25] by the cultural discourses that attribute certain nominative properties to women.[26] Although *Eva's Man* is a first-person narrative, it does not present a coherent perspective. Much like Condé's *Véronica*, who embraces the epithet "Marilisse" despite its negative connotations,[27] Eva interrogates the terms of address that construct women as "Eve," "Medusa," "Salome," or

[25]Cf. Maryse Condé's handling of Véronica, the protagonist in *Heremakhonon*; see also *AV*, chap. 5.

[26]See Hortense Spillers's discussion of what she calls "overdetermined nominative properties" in "Mama's Baby, Papa's Maybe: An American Grammar Book," *Diacritics* 17 (Spring 1987): 65–81.

[27]*H*, 42, 130/20, 71. The term refers to a black woman who "sells out" by associating with white men.

"Queen Bee" by pushing these representations to their logical extreme.

Her story begins at the end: "The police came and found arsenic in the glass" (*EM*, 3). A crime has been committed, but the arsenic does not yet explain why "a lot of people like to go . . . and see where the crime happened." The reader's first impression of Eva is mediated by her cellmate Elvira's reported speech: "Elvira said they had my picture [in the paper] and my hair was all uncombed and they had me looking like a wild woman." The figure of Medusa looms behind our initial encounter with Eva, and the impression is confirmed as the story progresses: her lover, Davis "wouldn't let [her] comb [her] hair" (*EM*, 10), and he is explicit about her appearance: "You look like a lion, all that hair . . . a male lion . . . Eva Medusa's a lion" (*EM*, 16). To which Eva replies that her name is Eva Medina. Later on, he calls her "Eve," and again she angrily corrects him, but he continues to associate her with women who are fatal to men, women whose gaze is a lethal lure: "There was something in your eyes"; "Don't look at me that way" (*EM*, 44, 46, 47). Elvira, on the other hand, sarcastically brings up the image of Salomé: "Just like in that Bible story, ain't it? Except got his *dick* on a platter" (*EM*, 47). And finally, Eva herself brings the point home when she says to the prison psychiatrist who questions her about her motives for killing Davis and her reasons for castrating him after his death: "My hair looks like snakes, doesn't it?" (*EM*, 77). This echoes Elvira's initial question, "Do you kill every man you go with?" (*EM*, 17), which overdetermines the reader's understanding of Eva from the beginning. When Eva bites off Davis's penis after having poisoned him, she explicitly relates the event to Eve's biting into the apple of knowledge: "I got back on the bed and squeezed his dick hard in my teeth. I bit down hard. My teeth in an apple" (*EM*, 128). All the cultural symbols that construct woman as a dangerous temptress, a bewitching snare, are brought together at the scene of Davis's castration.

Thus, Eva's self-representation, as well as the way she feels about herself and her actions, cannot be separated from the cultural images of women which are common currency around her. Consequently, when the psychiatrist who tries to "help" her asks her how she feels, she can only recall other instances of people asking her and other women how "it feels" (*EM*, 77), for how is a woman

supposed to feel about her own sexuality when its value is repeatedly denied, when she knows nothing about her own desires, and
when male sexuality expresses itself in the form of sexual harass-
ment? The doctor is an obvious composite of the male protagonists
who have used her in the past: his name is David Smoot, recalling
young Freddy Smoot as well as Davis Carter himself. In fact, just
as Eva is made to represent a certain stereotype of fatal woman, all
the men eventually merge into one single paradigm of male dom-
inance, the voice of "all them Dr. Frauds" (*EM*, 148) which, since
Freud, keeps on interrogating femininity: "Why won't you talk
about yourself?" "Why did you kill him?" "What did he do?"
"What happened?" "Did you want to do anything you did?" (*EM*,
67, 167, 169, 170, 173). This is the same voice that has always puz-
zled over "what a woman wants." Like Juletane or Saadawi's Firdaus, Eva refuses to explain herself: "I don't like to talk about
myself" (*EM*, 73), and this is the only way she has of resisting the
dominant discourses that imprison her inside certain labels: "Her
silences are . . . ways of maintaining . . . autonomy," Gayl Jones has
said.[28] Her seemingly passive compliance is a way of resisting the
double bind, what Cixous has called the "phallocentric represen-
tationalism" that distorts and objectifies.[29] "You keep all your secrets, don't you?" (*EM*, 101), Davis says, when there are in fact no
"secrets" to keep, only the impossibility for the woman to accede
to the symbolic realm of language without simultaneously putting
herself under erasure, risking misunderstanding, or confirming the
patriarchal representations that preexist her speech: "A motive was
never given. She never said anything. She just took the sentence"
(*EM*, 153). It is this apparent "serenity" that leads to the insanity
plea: "When a woman done something like you done and serene
like that, no wonder they think you crazy" (*EM*, 155), Elvira explains. Eva instinctively knows that what a black woman might feel
and what she might want are so inconceivable to the imagination
of a partriarchal nation, so threatening, that she must be neutralized
by stereotypical accusations of feminine instability and unreli-
ability.

---

[28]See Gayl Jones, interview with Claudia Tate, in *Black Women Writers at Work*
(New York: Continuum, 1983), 97.
  [29]Cixous, "Laugh," 254.

If Eva conforms to the damaging stereotypes and plays the part with a vengeance, it is in large measure her way of escaping behind the negative images, of protecting her own autonomy, as Jones suggests, of accepting the defacement of those names in order to better subvert the system. She does not attempt to rename or refigure herself; she remains silent and refuses the psychiatrist's representations: "Don't you explain me" (*EM*, 173, 174). Unlike Eva, however, Elvira has the "madness" of feminine excess: her "problem" is "hysteria" (*EM*, 45); she is defined by her laughter (*EM*, 10, 16, 45) and by the fact that she is allowed to travel between the inside (jail) and the outside (society), returning with stories of what is being said in the papers about Eva (*EM*, 3). Elvira stands outside the symbolic framework, can retreat into the imaginary by letting her body talk, and can relate to Eva on the intersubjective level that remakes them both into a new image of femininity, one no longer implicated into the morbid erotic economy of masculine desire triggered by fear. Previously silenced by the (male) other's presence— "I wanted to tell him how I was feeling. But I never would tell him" (*EM*, 158)—Eva is now able to recognize her own desire, to "speak her pleasure" (in Cixous's terms), and to accept Elvira's offer of lesbian sexuality (*EM*, 177). Her sexual desire is no longer desire-for-the-other; rather, it is desire-in-itself and does not need to be verbalized, since it is in stillness and secrecy that it can manifest itself without being recuperated by patriarchy. As Cixous explains, "Silence is the mark of hysteria. The great hysterics have lost speech, they are aphonic, and at times have lost more than speech: they are pushed to the point of choking, nothing gets through. They are decapitated, their tongues are cut off and what talks isn't heard because it is the body that talks, and the man doesn't hear the body. In the end, the woman pushed to hysteria is the woman who disturbs and is nothing but disturbance."[30] Eva's disturbance, like Juletane's, is her way of eluding power by means of violent acts that inscribe female agency on the interpretive text of patriarchy, resisting her construction as a "zombi," as one of the "demon women" whose trancelike passivity belies a deep determination to escape from the stereotype (*EM*, 148).

On a structural level, Jones makes no attempt to placate her read-

[30]Cixous, "Castration," 353, 352.

ers: *Eva's Man* is a difficult book, a tale of great intensity that resists closure. As I suggested above, it is a story about men, about their obsessive sexuality and exploitative relationships. Eva's own personal story is not really told, since most of what we know of her is what the men in her life (Freddy, Mr. Logan, John Canada, Tyrone, Davis, Alfonso, Moses Tripp, James Hunn, and finally David Smoot) have done to the women she knows. The narrative shows how they have made Eva herself into a "little evil devil bitch," a "sweet [castrating] bitch" (*EM*, 35, 64, 127, 138, 139, 173). The narrative fragments do not add up to a coherent picture of the past, and the novel thematizes its structural discontinuities by stressing the gaps and the fissures in Eva's memory, suggesting that it is thanks to those gaps that she can manage to slip out of the symbolic domain and disrupt the culture's master narrative.

It is interesting to note that the name Eva is contained within the name *ElVirA*, seeming to suggest that Eva is meant to be reincorporated into the different economy—that of a woman-identified sexuality—into which Elvira will finally initiate her. If Elvira can absorb and contain Eva, this icon of all the negative representations of women, then perhaps she can also reengender her as a new female subject. Eva finds in her imprisonment the key to her liberation, since it allows her to discover a female community in the transitional space of the psychiatric ward, in the "in-between" where, "according to Cixous, different subjects knowing one another and beginning one another anew only form the living boundaries of the other"; it is in this process of exchange that, the "newly born woman" can begin to reject the demeaning cultural values she has internalized.[31] In that space she can envisage a world where a "lesbian continuum," as defined by Adrienne Rich, can replace the violence of compulsory heterosexuality and female sexual slavery.[32] In the end, Eva realizes that what she wants is "nothing [he] can give" (*EM*, 176). She displaces her focus to a space outside the politics of (male) aggression and power, offering passive resistance to the cultural scenarios that frame her as a *femme fatale*. Thus, the "Now" she utters as she surrenders to Elvira (*EM*, 177) brings her

---

[31]Cixous, "Laugh," 254.

[32]Adrienne Rich, "Compulsory Heterosexuality and Lesbian Existence," in *Blood, Bread, and Poetry: Selected Prose, 1979–1985* (New York: Norton, 1986), 51, 43.

into a present that suggests an alternative to her passive submission to and acceptance of the other's will to pleasure.

Finding "Gold Amidst the Ash": Life and Dikeledi

Like Warner-Vieyra, Bessie Head was an exile who willingly talked about her personal experiences and how they affected her creative choices—unlike Jones, who prefers to retain a degree of anonymity and distance from her reading public. Head's works explore the question of marginality from the perspective of a stateless person. Born in an asylum and forced to live as a stateless exiled person in Botswana for many years, Head, who died in 1986, was the mixed-race daughter of a wealthy South African woman of Scottish descent and a black stable boy. Her mother had been committed to the asylum because of the interracial love affair, and at her death she left money to be used for Bessie's education. First cared for by a foster family who soon rejected her, Bessie ended up in a mission school, where she became very close to one of her teachers.

This aspect of her personal life formed the basis of her novel *Maru*, as well as *A Question of Power*, another autobiographical novel which was written during a period of great stress and depression in the late 1960s, after an unhappy marriage and divorce. But in the short stories that make up *The Collector of Treasures*, published after the novels, she writes about village life in Botswana in a clear prose that is rich in evocative and realistic details and full of humor and tenderness. It is with those tales that Bessie Head truly acquired the "cool stance" and "detachment" that she considered her goals as a writer. Her tragic tales of domestic horror focus attention on the mental and physical plight of women who find themselves trapped in the very institution that is supposed to protect and nurture them and their children. She leads us, says Mieke Bal, "to realize how deeply violence is anchored in the domestic domain."[33] But her characters, male and female, are depicted with a great deal of affection and concern. She avoids any simplistic

---

[33]Mieke Bal, *Death and Dissymmetry: The Politics of Coherence in the Book of Judges* (Chicago: University of Chicago Press, 1988), 231.

polarization of the issues: for her it is not just the advent of modernity or the aftermath of colonialism that causes the breakdown of the family but deep and specific cultural realities that must be correctly "read," interpreted, and understood before one can propose to act on them.

Indeed, though Head is clearly sympathetic to her women protagonists, one cannot say that she offers a one-sided view of the social picture: her male characters are not uniformly evil—far from it. "As a storyteller [you can] shape the future," she has said, and asserts that although she borrows her "basic plot" from life, she likes to add positive male figures that she hopes can serve as role models for other young men. Paul Thebolo in "The Collector of Treasures" is such a man, this *"huge* majestic man [who] moves into the story [and is] going to solve all the problems of family life." As Head insists, "there's a kind of coolness and detachment in my work . . . The cool stance means: you are up on a horizon, you have the biggest view possible. The storyteller has to have that. It's not so much a question of being black as of having got control of life's learning. . . . I shape the future with this cool stance, the view that's above everything."[34] Her strong belief in the performative powers of narrative places her among those African writers for whom writing is "an essential gesture" that helps to break the long-standing silence of, and about, women and to expose oppressive cultural taboos and archaic customs.[35]

Beyond the simple suggestion that murder is an inevitable act of resistance for the female protagonist who has reached the end of her rope and can no longer endure her condition of overt or subtle oppression, Head also raises the issue of agency: she is well aware of the all too easy copout of representing the third world woman as the monolithic "victim" of both *universal* patriarchy and *specific* black male exploitation. She prefers, instead, to give us some insights into the social configurations of power that drive women to make desperate decisions when they are trapped in dead-end situations. As an outsider to the culture of Botswana, she had the kind of freedom from her immediate environment that allowed her to

---

[34]Head interview in Mackenzie and Clayton, *Between the Lines*, 14, 12–13.

[35]Nadine Gordimer, *The Essential Gesture: Writing, Politics, and Places*, ed. Stephen Clingman (New York: Knopf, 1988).

apprehend individual pain and suffering without feeling hemmed in by customs and traditions that might be used to justify or defend the status quo. This allowed her to play the role of social satirist, to write stories that place her within the European narrative tradition of a seventeenth century "moralist."

Two of the stories, "Life" and "The Collector of Treasures," offer interesting contrasts, although they both deal with the changing village economy and with domestic conflicts that are resolved violently. The weapon is a kitchen knife, used in one case by Lesego to stab his wife, Life, and in the other by Dikeledi to castrate her husband. The events that lead to Dikeledi's calmly premeditated act suggest that the supportive community women build around themselves gives them the courage to oppose the male social order and to jeopardize their own lives and freedom. These communities function on a principle of exchange and barter which gives the women an independence that is gradually undermined by the advent of capitalism.

In "Life," the "beer-brewing women were a gay and lovable crowd who had emancipated themselves some time ago" (CT, 39). Much like Cixous's transgressive figures, they "talked and laughed loudly and slapped each other on the back and *had developed a language all their own*" (my emphasis). Men, in this context, are parasites who "[hang] around, [live] on the resources of the women." It is they who become objects of exchange, shared by the women: "Many men passed through their lives." Life introduces prostitution in the village, bringing a more mercenary approach to a system that had functioned on the principle of the friendly trade of goods and services. This causes her eventual downfall, as she is too "bold," too "free," and too indifferent to rural "social taboos" to put up with a traditional married life in which "she found no one with whom she could communicate what had become an actual physical pain" (CT, 40, 44). Her fun-loving urban ways introduce dissymmetry in her relationships with the people of the village. As the omniscient narrator suggests: "Village people reacted in their own way; what they liked, and what was beneficial to them, they absorbed. . . . what was harmful to them, they rejected. The murder of Life had this complicated undertone of rejection" (CT, 37). When she comes back to the village after ten years in the city and marries a "dull" shepherd, Life puts herself in a situation of acquiring ostensibly unacceptable power because of her ability to make money by using her body. Money becomes the sign of a disturbing independence for the villagers; it is a destabilizing force that undermines the order of things, and she has to be neutralized. Like the money she makes, she becomes a sign that severely disrupts both the gender economy and the system of barter particular to that village.

Enter the justice system and the courts: after Life's death Lesego, who is apparently a "straightforward, uncomplicated" man, proves to be a master of signs as well: "The judge who was a white man, and therefore not involved in Tswana customs and its debates, was as much impressed by Lesego's manner as all the village men had been"; he gives Lesego a much reduced sentence (five years) because "this is a crime of passion" (*CT*, 46). Lesego's authoritative "manner," his ability to pass judgment and to interpret reality, has the desired effect on the white judge. Here, it seems to me, Head underscores universal male solidarity against irrational female behavior; indeed, the text's suggestion that *"wild anger* was driving [Life] to break out of a way of life that was like death to her" (*CT*, 44) contrasts sharply with Lesego's "logical" and "rational" explanation of his own behavior, an explanation that convinces all the men present. This is "the fundamental struggle to enforce and strengthen dissymmetrical (unequal) power relations" that Mieke Bal has analyzed in another context: Lesego knows how to use language as an instrument of power, how to put the judge on his side. He "interprets" Life's lived reality the better to reduce her to silence.[36]

By contrast, in "The Collector of Treasures," Dikeledi gets a life sentence. No one argues in her favor for a reduced sentence based on self-defense or a "crime of passion." In fact, the workings of the court are not even made visible in this story; it is as though the female defendant is completely invisible to the justice system. The narrative begins with the image of the "crumpled" heap, "oblivious to everything but her pain" during the long journey in the police truck to "the long-term central state prison in the south" (*CT*, 87). If the text later makes clear that Dikeledi is a brave and innocent woman, a patient and methodical worker who accomplishes her

[36]See Bal, *Death and Dissymmetry,* 18.

crime in her own conscientious way ("With the precision and skill of her hard-working hands, she grasped hold of his genitals and cut them off with one stroke" [*CT*, 103]), thus putting the reader's sympathies on her side, it also suggests that she has no means of access to the interpretive system that grants power to those who can manipulate it. She is a socially silenced subject whose ability to act as an effective moral agent to protect herself and her children recalls Linda Brent's familiar predicament in the American slave-owning South.

Dikeledi is one of a community of supportive women friends who exchange goods and services. Kenalepe, with whom she has "one of those deep, affectionate, sharing-everything kind of friendships that only women know how to have," even offers her husband when Dikeledi's husband has left her: "I can loan Paul to you if you like" (*CT*, 94, 96). The text suggests that this generous and sharing attitude contrasts with that of the misguided women who, allowing themselves to be divided by the men who use them, chase their unfaithful husbands "from one hut to another [in order to] beat up the girlfriends" (*CT*, 95). "We must help each other" (*CT*, 91) is the message Bessie Head's women give to other women, and Dikeledi can count on Paul Thebolo and Kenalepe to take care of her children after she is sent to jail. As in "Life," it is interesting to note that money is the primary cause of social disturbance: it is because Dikeledi is "short on R20.00 to cover the fees" (*CT*, 99) for her son's school that she appeals to Garesego for help; it is because he expects her to be sexually available to him if he is going to help financially that she finally rebels against "defilement by an evil man" (*CT*, 101) and castrates him.

What is most significant about these female characters is the degree of independence and agency that they succeed in maintaining throughout the narratives. Unlike Warner-Vieyra and Jones, Head shows a certain indomitable optimism. To be sure, Life dies and Dikeledi is serving a life sentence, but Head trusts her reader to share her views about the fundamental inequities that she dramatizes in those stories. She believes, like Dikeledi, that our task as human beings is to attempt to find "gold amidst the ash," to rise above the arbitrary moral codes of a given culture, and to exonerate the victims for whom the end must justify the means. She appeals to a form of classical humanism based on moral standards that transcend cultural epiphenomena. Dikeledi finds a community in jail; she puts her numerous skills to good use, building friendships behind bars as she had in the village, believing in female solidarity, and finding "deep loves that had joined her heart to the heart of others" (CT, 91).

If this is an idealized picture of prison life, it nonetheless suggests the possibility that the role of literature is to reinforce the belief in the "universal" qualities of creativity and generosity that Dikeledi demonstrates. It is thus fair to say that Head would probably subscribe to a recent statement made by the critic Guy Ossito Midiohouan about African literature: "As the expression of a creativity that ceaselessly strives to reinvent society, culture and history in an impulse that renders us more conscious of ourselves and of the world around us, . . . modern African literature collectively profiles our identity and helps make us into peoples who, while being carried along by the currents of history and attending to the life of the world, are not assimilated into an impoverishing, planet-wide uniformity but, on the contrary, contribute to the Universal, which can only be rich by virtue of the variety that different peoples bring to it."[37] However encouraging such a view may be, a question remains: what degree of specificity can be translated into a universal language when the specificity in question is that of the grave physical and emotional pain which generally—"planet-wide"—remains invisible because its victims are only women?

As a privileged symbolic space, the "body in pain" translates cultural conflicts into a visible representational frame: the words that describe Dikeledi as she is carried away to the state prison underscore the extent to which she has been dehumanized: "crawl-[ing] painfully forward in silence," "more like a skeleton than a human being" (CT, 88, 89). But if women's pain and suffering remain marginal in most cultures, then Dikeledi—like Life, Juletane, and Eva—is locked into a form of subjectivity that annuls our interpretive possibilities. If women's pain cannot be articulated, verbalized, interpreted, and communicated in a language that makes it visible to "universal" patriarchy, then the women protagonists of these stories are in a position of radical dissymmetry with respect

---

[37]See Guy Ossito Midiohouan, "Modern Literature and the Flourishing of Culture in Black Africa, "*Research in African Literatures* 22 (Spring 1991): 96.

to the rest of us, writers and critics, who are in command of the interpretive means that can give larger significance to their lives. This is the contradiction inherent in the relationship between textuality and reality: it emphasizes that the problematics of universalism in the context of women's literatures remains a dead letter so long as women's silences and body languages continue to be ignored or recuperated by the symbolic order, thus becoming the "black holes" (so to speak) within and against which all interpretive discourses can only come to a halting stop.

6

Dissymmetry Embodied:
Nawal El Saadawi's
Woman at Point Zero
and the Practice of Excision

> What is most needed is some kind of special illumination of
> the structural dissymmetry that runs all through and condi-
> tions the entire fabric of social and individual life.
> —Fatima Mernissi, *Beyond the Veil: Male-Female
> Dynamics in Modern Muslim Society*

In this chapter I examine the discursive contexts of a specific
ritual practice in order to test the ideology of cultural relativism.
The phenomena of female excision and infibulation that are performed in parts of Africa and the Middle East constitutes important
aspects of the gendered cultural identity of some Islamic women.[1]
These ritual practices, often defined as various forms of sexual mutilation, have since colonial times been denounced by missionaries,
colonial administrators, Western media, feminist critics, and health
service professionals. They have decried such "ethnic" customs as
"barbaric" or "anachronistic," using terms that often smack of racist, anti-Islamic rhetoric. In the 1970s—especially after 1976, which
was declared International Women's Year by the United Nations—
the issue suddenly mobilized European and American feminists; as
Renée Saurel claimed in 1979, those practices "have caused much
blood to be shed for thousands of years, and much ink for the past
two."[2]

[1]There are three main types of female circumcision. *Sunna* (Arabic: "tradition")
circumcision, considered the equivalent of male circumcision, consists in the removal
of the prepuce of the clitoris. Excision is the removal of the prepuce, the clitoris
itself, and the labia minora. Infibulation consists in the removal of the clitoris, "the
whole of labiae minora and majora, and the stitching together (suturing) of the two
sides of the vulva leaving a very small orifice to permit the flow of urine and men-
strual discharge" (Olayinka Koso-Thomas, *The Circumcision of Women: A Strategy for
Eradication* [London: Zed Books, 1987], 16–17).
[2]Renée Saurel, *L'Enterrée vive* (Geneva: Slatkine, 1981), 20. Discussion of these

In contemporary Western medical and anthropological literature, and in journalistic reports, the subject of excision is often treated peremptorily, in an impassioned, reductionist, or ethnocentric mode that represents the peoples who practice it as backward, misogynistic, and generally lacking in humane and compassionate inclinations. In other words, as has always been the case with respect to Africa and Africans, the dominant rhetoric emphasizes lack, absence, failure, inhumanity, and greed.[3] Unfortunately, counterarguments also tend to use inflammatory language. In an interview Mamadou Kante links the interest of Europeans in the sexual lives of African women to a desire to control the African birth rate: "Everyone knows that if they [the Western powers] succeed in controlling women under one pretext or another, then the birth-rate in Africa will be under control. Under the misleading pretext of excision, that is the hidden agenda. That is the realm of occult political forces."[4]

Kante may well be justified in questioning the motives behind the campaign for birth control; the concern about "galloping demography" in nonwhite countries is indeed laced with racist fears and instincts for self-preservation stemming from the fact that whites are a global minority, and a wealthy one, intent on curbing growth among those generally poorer than they are. But is it really fair to link the fight against excision to the racist wish to control nonwhite women's reproductive capabilities? Or does this accusation simply blur the real issue, marginalizing the female victims while the two opposing sides trade abuse and insults? Statistics do show that excision and infibulation can have lethal side effects that contribute to increased mortality rates for mothers and infants at the moment of delivery.[5] But to conflate Western fears about higher birth rates in the "third world" with the human rights issue of

issues culminated at the 1985 Nairobi conference marking the last year of the UN Decade for Women.

[3] See Anne de Villeneuve, "Etude sur une coutume somali: Les Femmes cousues," *Journal de la Société des Africanistes* 7, no. 1 (1937): 15–32; Fran Hosken, *The Hosken Report: Genital and Sexual Mutilation of Females* (Lexington, Mass.: Women's International Network News, 1982), 201; and Françoise Lionnet, "Identity, Sexuality, Criminality: 'Universal Rights' and the Debate around the Practice of Female Excision in France," *Contemporary French Civilization* 16 (Summer 1992): 294–307.

[4] Mamadou Kante, "L'Excision," *Présence Africaine* 142 (1987): 180.

[5] See Michel Erlich, *La Femme blessée: Essai sur les mutilations sexuelles féminines* (Paris: L'Harmattan, 1986), 132–33; and Koso-Thomas *Circumcision of Women*, 27.

maternal and infant health seems to be a downright contradiction. Of course, birth control information did make its entrance into Africa with the same health care professionals who have denounced genital mutilations in moralizing terms. The attitude of suspicion exemplified by Kante is easy to understand, even if one cannot agree with it.

Unfortunately, the generally offensive rhetoric leaves little room for the careful examination of two competing claims: on the one hand, the campaign for the abolition of all such ritual practices on the basis of a universal ethical imperative against the physical torture and psychological impairment of millions of women;[6] on the other hand, the advocacy of respect for the cultural autonomy of African societies that denounce any feminist intervention as "acculturation" to Western standards.

African women themselves have, in no uncertain terms, proclaimed that the issue is theirs to debate and discuss. Of several recent texts by African women who examine the problem with great care, three are particularly noteworthy: *The Circumcision of Women: A Strategy for Eradication*, by Olayinka Koso-Thomas, is a well-researched document, focused on Sierra Leone, which outlines a twenty-year plan for eliminating the practice; *La Parole aux négresses*, by Awa Thiam, is a compilation of interviews with women from Francophone and Anglophone West African states (Ivory Coast, Guinea, Mali, Senegal, Ghana, and Nigeria); and *The Hidden Face of Eve*, by Nawal El Saadawi, raises the issue as it relates to North Africa and the Middle East. Saadawi's novel *Woman at Point Zero* is, with Evelyne Accad's *L'Excisée*, among the few fictional accounts written with moving sincerity and autobiographical details. It is a more effective and convincing denunciation than many pragmatic or political treatises because it allows the reader to enter into the subjective processes of the individual, to adopt her stance.[7]

These writers are all Western-trained feminist intellectuals or sci-

---

[6]There are approximately 80,000,000 to 100,000,000 excised women in the world today, of whom about 5,000,000 have also undergone infibulation. See Erlich, *Femme blessée*, 277; and Alice Walker, *Possessing the Secret of Joy* (New York: Harcourt Brace Jovanovich, 1992), 281.

[7]Koso-Thomas, *The Circumcision of Women*; Awa Thiam, *La Parole aux négresses* (Paris: Denoël/Gonthier, 1978); Nawal El Saadawi, *The Hidden Face of Eve: Women in the Arab World*, trans. Sherif Hetata (London: Zed, 1980), and *Woman at Point Zero* (1975), trans. Sherif Hetata (London: Zed, 1983); Evelyne Accad, *L'Excisée* (Paris: L'Harmattan, 1982). Page numbers for *Woman at Point Zero* appear in the text.

entists (Koso-Thomas and Saadawi are physicians) who denounce the practice from the vantage point of the educated elite—hence, some have argued, from a perspective more "Western" than "African" and thus alienated from the common people who would neither read them nor sympathize with their views. There is, in other words, a dissymmetry of class and ideology between them and the uneducated masses, an inevitable dissymmetry, since literacy and education remain, to a large extent, steps that favor Westernization. But there are important indications that "progress" is being made. Arguments in favor of a form of cultural relativism that would excuse excision on strictly cultural grounds do not have as much currency as some vocal critics of interventionism might lead us to believe.

Indeed, a close examination of some defenses of excision reveals inconsistencies. For example, although Joséphine Guidy Wandja argues in favor of the specificity of African sexuality and stresses the deep meaning (*signification profonde*) of traditional African rituals, declaring that "the African model of sexuality cannot be . . . the same as the European model," she nonetheless must conclude her essay in defense of particularism with a "universally" valid statement that grounds sexuality in the materiality of the body. She does so despite her earlier emphasis on the *optique spiritualiste* of secular African traditions, which she had contrasted to the mechanistic and materialist approach of the Americans William Masters and Virginia Johnson. She asks: "Indeed, how is it possible to explain the age-old customs of a people on the basis of very recent discoveries (20th century)? One can read, for example, that *excision suppresses women's right to experience pleasure*, but in their research, *specialists* would have to give a unanimous definition of *pleasure*."[8]

If the issue is one of defining what constitutes "pleasure," then it seems acceptable to relativize the definition according to sociocultural context or sexual preference. But Wandja never questions *le droit au plaisir*, the right of women to be sensually and sexually fulfilled. As a matter of fact, in grounding the ethical problem in the physicality of the body, she universalizes the well-being (if not the full integrity) of the body. Hence, one might argue, her position does not invalidate the search for an ethical imperative. Moreover,

---

[8]Joséphine Guidy Wandja, "Excision? mutilation sexuelle? mythe ou réalité?" *Présence Africaine* 142 (1987): 58, 56.

Wandja falls into what is perilously close to contradiction, for the other side of the coin remains the question of pain: how is it possible to reconcile the fundamental human right to pleasure with the willful infliction of pain on the body of the female child?[9] Her particularist approach fails to justify relativism.

There are practices in all cultures, however, that aim at regulating, transforming, and "improving" the body. I would be falling into the ethnocentric trap if I did not point out that in the West the pursuit of an elusive ideal of femininity has also been mediated by *pain* (inflicted by the corset, for example). French-speaking female children grow up hearing that "il faut souffrir pour être belle [you must suffer to be beautiful]," and the pain of childbirth has generally been considered the "normal" fulfillment of a woman's destiny—a rite of passage, a difficult but necessary ritual. Similarly, excision and circumcision are considered rites of passage, initiatory practices one purpose of which is precisely to test the mettle of the individual, her endurance of pain, her ability to remain impassive and stoic in the face of severe discomfort. It is a "character-building" experience. It creates solidarity, closeness, and sisterhood among the initiates. Thus, as Wandja puts it, a successful initiation confers respect and dignity on the child now become woman. As an initiatory practice, excision serves the same purpose as other forms of ritualized violence in many different cultures (fraternity hazing, for example, and its occasionally fatal consequences). Furthermore, excision is an operation that has an aesthetic function—on a par with plastic surgery and other (Western) forms of self-denial: what Susan Bordo has called the "normalizing disciplines of diet, make-up, and dress ... [through which] we are rendered more ... focused on self-modification.... [These] practices of femininity may lead us to utter demoralization, debilitation, and death."[10]

---

[9]Need I say that all published oral testimonies of educated *and* illiterate women dwell on the painful aspect of the procedure and its sequels, even if some interviewees maintain that their ability to experience orgasm is not affected? Chantal Patterson, "Les Mutilations sexuelles féminines: L'Excision en question," *Présence Africaine* 142 (1987): 165, stresses two points: "(1) Different civilizations live, practice, and conceptualize eroticism and sensuality differently. (2) If there is any mutilation, a system of compensation must be set in motion by the body, this extraordinary machine."

[10]Wandja, "Excision?" 57. Susan R. Bordo, "The Body and The Reproduction of Femininity: A Feminist Appropriation of Foucault," in *Gender/Body/Knowledge: Fem-*

That is why, I would argue, it is quite possible to link excision to the general cultural paradigm of the reproduction of femininity and its concomitant depersonalizing effects. Marie Bonaparte, who had the opportunity to examine many excised women in Egypt in the 1930s, speculated, with Freud, that the practice stemmed from a wish to maximally "feminize the female" by removing the clitoris—"this cardinal vestige of her masculinity"—and to intimidate and suppress the child's sexuality. But she also noted that "the physical intimidation of the girl's sexuality by this cruel excision would not achieve the aim of feminizing, vaginalizing her, any better than the psychical intimidation of the clitoridal masturbation of European little girls."[11] Since the operation suppresses genital structures that are "phallic," the ethnopsychiatrist Michel Erlich adds, the psychological dimension of these operations is "inscribed as the specific manifestation of masculine castration anxiety in front of the 'castrated' female sexual organ." In this reading of the practice, male fears of women's sexuality would be the unconscious motivation for exaggerating, and thus controlling, femininity. But infibulation, paradoxically, which might first appear to be a "hyperfeminization" of the genitalia, can also on the contrary be interpreted as a *phallisation* of the vulva, which has been rendered smooth and convex, thus evoking "a phantasmatic phallus." These conflicting yet complementary interpretations underscore the arbitrariness with which a visually based and apparently "objective" interpretive grid can be used. The ambiguities and indeterminacies stressed by Erlich point toward the "thickness" or polyvalent nature of all symbolic systems, as Clifford Geertz has shown.[12] It is clear that there are embedded incoherences in the signifying text of culture; there can be no simple cause of and therefore no simple "solution" to the complex cultural phenomena of genital mutilation. As Tobe Levin declares, "Western activists must learn to enter the value system

---

inist *Reconstructions of Being and Knowing*, ed. Alison M. Jaggar and Susan R. Bordo (New Brunswick, N.J.: Rutgers University Press, 1989), 14. See Erlich, *Femme blessée*, 183, for a comprehensive survey of the "aesthetic" argument.

[11]Marie Bonaparte, *Female Sexuality*, trans. John Rodker (New York: International Universities Press, 1953), 207.

[12]Erlich, *Femme blessée*, 14; Clifford Geertz, *The Interpretation of Cultures* (New York: Basic Books, 1973).

of the 'circumcised' to avoid the counter-productive approach based on ignorance and indignation alone."[13]

It is by pointing out some of the incoherences in cultural practices that we can begin to make sense of them. Indeed, the "official" discourse—on both sides of the ideological fence separating abolitionists from traditionalists—tends to overemphasize coherence: in the one case by appealing to abstract humanitarian notions, in the other by claiming the importance of cultural autonomy and specificity. In 1985 the president of Senegal, Abdou Diouf, stated the position of his government:

> Female mutilation is a subject that is taboo. . . . But let us not rush into the error of condemning [genital mutilations] as uncivilized and sanguinary practices. One must beware of describing what is merely an aspect of difference in culture as barbarous. In traditional Africa, sexual mutilations evolved out of *a coherent system*, with its own values, beliefs, cultural and ritual conduct. They were a necessary ordeal in life because they completed the process incorporating the child in society. These practices, however, raise a problem today because our societies are in a process of major transformation and are coming up against *new socio-cultural dynamic forces in which such practices have no place* or appear to be relics of the past. What is therefore needed are measures to quicken their demise. The main part of this struggle will be waged by education rather than by anathema and from the inside rather than from the outside. I hope that this struggle will make women free and "disalienated," personifying respect for the eminent dignity of life.[14]

President Diouf invokes a "coherent system" of traditions to which he opposes the "new socio-cultural dynamic forces in which [the old practices] have no place." In other words, two symmetrical and coherent systems seem to be opposed, the new displacing the old, the need to disalienate women taking precedence over the physical ordeal of excision. But one might contend that the so-called coherent systems are in fact already undermined by what Mieke Bal has

---

[13]Tobe Levin, "Women as Scapegoat of Culture and Cult: An Activist's View of Female Circumcision in Ngugi's *The River Between,*" in *Ngambika: Studies of Woman in African Literature,* ed. Carole Boyce Davies and Anne Adams Graves (Trenton, N.J.: Africa World Press, 1986), 208.

[14]Quoted in Koso-Thomas, *Circumcision of Women,* app. 5, 106 (my emphasis).

called a *countercoherence*, the coherence of dissymmetry, of unequal power relations based on and reinforced by the use of language as an instrument of control, as a weapon capable of ensuring power-lessness in the victims.[15]

Consider, for example, that in many parts of Islamic Africa, no-tably the Sudan and Somalia, the worst form of insult is to call someone "a gaping vulva." There, speech acts perform tradition, reinforcing the doxa, the meaning of age-old practices. Words, laden with ideology, contribute to ensuring powerlessness before the social system so that women may take their rightful place as subjected objects of desire. Women are named and defined by men who thus shape their self-understanding. Female self-knowledge is mediated by social perceptions conditioned by patriarchal culture.

Saadawi gives us an intimate and shocking look at this predica-ment in *Woman at Point Zero*. The protagonist, Firdaus, whose name means "paradise" in Arabic, is taught the alphabet by her sexually abusive uncle (15). Later on, when she is living the life of a pros-titute, the men to whom she submits also name and define her. They call her "slut," "bitch," "street walker," "prostitute," "not respectable" (50, 49, 62, 70), and she begins to use those words herself (50), having internalized the vision conveyed by the speech acts that help perpetuate the status quo. For Saadawi, the construc-tion of female subjectivity is clearly a process of gradual internali-zation of social knowledge—an internalization that engenders a split, a *Spaltung*, such as the one identified by psychoanalytic critics. For Saadawi too, the female subject is a site of conflict between an imposed social identity and a shared feminine identification, me-diated by the intimate experience of physical and verbal abuse, ex-cision, and insult.

If, as Elizabeth Abel has argued, "it is too early for feminism to foreclose on psychoanalysis," then Saadawi provides us with a powerful example of the uses to which psychoanalysis can be put when we are attempting to understand, interpret, and resist certain debilitating cultural practices. As Abel puts it, "The urgency of the-orizing subjectivity within a range of social contexts has made it less productive to reiterate old oppositions within psychoanalytic

---

[15]Mieke Bal, *Death and Dissymmetry: The Politics of Coherence in the Book of Judges* (Chicago: University of Chicago Press, 1988), 18, 23, 138.

feminism, or between psychoanalysis and contemporary feminism, than to imagine more fluid intersections."[16] Indeed, Saadawi's work as a psychiatrist and a novelist highlights the productive ways in which psychoanalysis, when it is not insulated from social and discursive practices, can help us make sense of, and indeed resist, those discourses that perpetuate women's oppression.

Firdaus realizes that words have a substance that is "palpable," "tangible," a materiality and a weight as real as that of the bodies that arouse and abuse her. As her powerful anger makes clear, words can be means of control, abuse, and torture: "The words continued to echo in my ears . . . buried themselves in my head like some *palpable* material object, like *a body as sharp as the edge of a knife which had cut its way through my ears, and the bones of my head to the brain inside*. . . . I could almost see them as they traversed the space separating his lips from my ears, like *tangible* things with a well-defined surface, exactly like *blobs of spit*, as though he had aimed them at me from between his lips" (70–71; my emphasis). These words are sharp and cutting, instruments of contempt and disdain, ejaculations ("blobs of spit") that defile and contaminate the hearer, as in an act of rape. Words maintain the dissymmetry of power between the sexes by entering the woman's consciousness, serving as scalpel in a metaphoric lobotomy that mirrors the genital excision: "the knife . . . had cut its way through my ears . . . to the brain inside." The soft tissue of the ear with its orifice that leads to the brain has an unmistakable sexual connotation. Words rape as surely as the penis, or the knife that the groom must use on his wedding night to open his bride's vulva and consummate the marriage. Saadawi thus conflates the act of speech and the act of sex in a way that clarifies and buttresses Bal's claims about dissymmetry.

Furthermore, words—uttered or written—have the same power as money: they are akin to paper money ("a mere piece of paper" [66], "the whole ten pound note" [65]), contact with which produces in Firdaus a physical sensation as violent and as sudden as the unexpected orgasms provoked by her abusive uncle and clients.

---

[16]Elizabeth Abel, "Race, Class, Psychoanalysis? Opening Questions," in *Conflicts in Feminism*, ed. Marianne Hirsch and Evelyn Fox Keller (New York: Routledge, Chapman & Hall, 1990), 199.

The symbolic value of words and money is thus conflated in a way that underscores their respective worth as currency, as means of exchange within a system that attributes to women a similar exchange value, depending on their physical conformity to patriarchal standards of sexual beauty and purity. These standards are themselves based on a distortion of the idea of the cultural *symmetry* that is presumed to exist between male and female processes of acculturation of the body.

Indeed, the question of symmetry is so often raised by traditionalists (Wandja, for example) who want to emphasize either the equivalence between circumcision and excision or the need to leave cultural interpretations of Africa to Africans (or both) that we must examine its tenets. I have already mentioned that the dissymmetry "educated" versus "illiterate" is evoked whenever feminist points of view are brought into focus, especially because feminism is considered to be a foreign—that is, Western—import.[17] The fact is that there is an obvious analogy between circumcision and excision: they both consist in the ablation of a part of the body for the ostensible purposes of hygiene and sexual attractiveness, and as a means of correcting the primal androgyny, or original bisexuality, of each being, a belief held by some Nilotic peoples and by the Mande and Kwa of western Africa.[18] Hence, for both sexes the operation is meant to *inscribe* a particular sexual identity on the body, to mark it as cultural, to give it symbolic meaning—that is, to *differentiate* it. In Foucault's terminology, excision is part of a network of practices that "discipline" the body, functioning as means of social control and reproducing unequal relations of power along with gender identity. Mary Douglas has shown that there are symbolic relationships between the human body and the social body, that rituals can be interpreted in terms that link purity with order, impurity with disorder, the latter being a sign of danger and power.[19] Excision, like circumcision, thus "purifies" the body, renders it fit to belong to its assigned place within the social order, which it no longer threatens by its impure, abject nature—that is,

---

[17]See the critique of Thiam in Patterson, "Les Mutilations sexuelles," 165.

[18]Erlich, *Femme blessée*, 210–18.

[19]Michel Foucault, *Discipline and Punish: The Birth of the Prison*, trans. Alan Sheridan (New York: Vintage Books, 1979); Mary Douglas, *Natural Symbols* (New York: Pantheon, 1982), and *Purity and Danger* (London: Routledge & Kegan Paul, 1966).

its undifferentiated, dangerous sexuality. The painful ordeal to which the individual is subjected becomes a sign that the body can transcend pain, can endure. It is proof that the flesh is under the control of the spirit, that the embodied self can become sufficiently detached from its physical sensations to attain the state of "pure" and heroic subjectivity.

But there ends the expected symmetry. It becomes a *dis*symmetry when the focus is once again placed on the body. From a strictly anatomical perspective, only a piece of flesh is removed from the male member, whereas in the case of the female, a sexual organ is cut off. By all accounts, the infliction of pain through circumcision cannot even begin to compare with that of excision and infibulation. In *The Hidden Face of Eve*, making a confession that can be juxtaposed to the silent testimonial of Firdaus in *Woman at Point Zero*, Saadawi graphically describes her own experience of the knife:

I was six years old that night when I lay in my bed, warm and peaceful in that pleasurable state which lies half way between wakefulness and sleep, with the rosy dreams of childhood flitting by, like gentle fairies in quick succession. I felt something move under the blankets, something like *a huge hand, cold and rough*, fumbling over my body, as though looking for something. Almost simultaneously another hand, as cold and as rough and as big as the first one, was clapped over my mouth, to prevent me from screaming.

They carried me to the bathroom. *I do not know how many of them there were*, nor do I remember their faces, or whether they were men or women. *The world to me seemed enveloped in a dark fog which prevented me from seeing....* All I remember is that I was frightened and that *there were many of them*, and that something like an *iron grasp* caught hold of my hand and my arms and my thighs, so that I became unable to resist or even to move. I also remember the icy touch of the bathroom tiles under my naked body, and *unknown voices and humming sounds interrupted now and again by a rasping metallic sound* which reminded me of the butcher when he used to sharpen his knife before slaughtering a sheep for the *Eid*.

My blood was frozen in my veins....

I imagined the thing that was making the rasping sound coming closer and closer to me. Somehow it was not approaching my neck as I had expected but another part of my body. Somewhere below my belly, as though seeking something buried between my thighs. At that very moment I realized that my thighs had been pulled wide apart, and that each of my lower limbs was being held as far away from the other as possible, gripped by *steel fingers* that never relinquished their pressure. . . . Then suddenly *the sharp metallic edge* seemed to drop between my thighs and there cut off a piece of flesh from my body.

I screamed with pain despite the tight hand held over my mouth, for the pain was not just a pain, it was like a searing flame that went through my whole body. After a few moments, I saw a red pool of blood around my hips. . . .

I did not know what they had cut off from my body. . . . *I just wept, and called out to my mother for help. But the worst shock of all was when I looked around and found her standing by my side. Yes it was her, I could not be mistaken, in flesh and blood, right in the midst of these strangers, talking to them and smiling at them,* as though they had not participated in slaughtering her daughter just a few moments ago.[20]

If we follow Elaine Scarry in her argument that the pain of torture is a process that "unmakes" the world and the self, dissolving the boundary between inside and outside, conflating in an almost obscene way private and public, then the experience described by Saadawi underscores the "unmaking" of the child's environment.[21] Visual and auditory perceptions become blurred; trust is forever destroyed as the mother's smiling face denies the reality of the shock and the pain. The strangers are described as body parts: a huge hand, cold and rough, an iron grasp, unknown voices, steel fingers. The child's own body reacts to the cold bathroom floor, to the rasping sound of metal being sharpened, to the metallic edge of the knife, and to the searing flame of pain that envelops her.

But the disjunction and depersonalization caused by the pain is replaced by a strong sense of urgency and agency when she sees her sister being carried away to the same fate. A mirroring effect comes into play when sisters' eyes meet, and they are united by the memory of a past and future pain: "They carried me to my bed. I saw them catch hold of my sister, who was two years younger, in exactly the same way they had caught hold of me a few minutes earlier. I cried out with all my might. No! No! I could see my sister's face held between the big rough hands. It had a deathly pallor and

[20]Saadawi, *Eve*, 7–8 (my emphasis).
[21]Elaine Scarry, *The Body in Pain: The Making and Unmaking of the World* (New York: Oxford University Press, 1985), 53.

her wide black eyes met mine for a split second, a glance of dark terror which I can never forget.''[22] The remarkable anger voiced by the six-year-old child who protests on behalf of her younger sister is an almost mythical example of the agency and autonomy manifested by the body despite its disintegrative suffering. Here symmetry exists powerfully: the excised child sees herself in her sister and *feels with* the sister. The empathy is complete and total. And in *Woman at Point Zero* it is precisely this question of empathy that will haunt the adult narrator as she first resists identification with Firdaus, struggling to understand her position vis-à-vis this "other" whose lower-class status and identity as a murderer, the narrator initially feels, invalidates any comparison between them as symmetrical female subjects.

Woman at Point Zero is a lyrical testimonial that exemplifies the countercoherence of dissymmetry, the possibility of resistance to hegemonic pressures and to the cultural master narrative. Here, the countercoherence of "the body in pain" manifests itself in a feeling of irretrievable loss that opposes sensations to language and ideology, subjective structures to cultural doxa. It is emblematic of issues raised by the work of Gayatri C. Spivak: the name of "the other woman," and the relationship between autobiography and "truth." In an interview with Sneja Gunew, Spivak has pointed out that "if one looks at the history of post-Enlightenment theory, the major problem has been the problem of autobiography: how subjective structures can, in fact, give objective truth."[23]

These issues continue to be widely debated in feminist theory. Saadawi's work is an excellent example of the self-reflexive questioning that can make feminist criticism sensitive to the way scholarly discourse names "the other woman" and appropriates her voice, for *Woman at Point Zero* is itself the appropriation of another woman's story by a scholar whose research on female offenders brings her into close contact with the painful experiences of an extraordinary woman. This association between the educated researcher and the "(un)common criminal" changes the terms of the equation between "self" and "other" or "subjective" and "objec-

---

[22]Saadawi, *Eve*, 8 (my emphasis).
[23]Gayatri C. Spirak, interview with Sneja Gunew, in *Women's Writing in Exile*, ed. Mary Lynn Broe and Angela Ingram (Chapel Hill: University of North Carolina Press, 1989), 420.

tive," enacting a transfer of values and feelings, locating the practice of writing at the intersection of multiple forms of knowledge.

Now my own purpose here is also to make a scholarly appropriation: to scrutinize Saadawi's text, to examine the way it contrasts and collapses the language of patriarchy and the language of the body, to bring into focus those aspects of the narrative that might allow for its redefinition as self-portrait. By appropriating Firdaus's voice yet allowing intersubjective communication to occur, Saadawi raises the hope that it is in fact possible to come to an acceptable compromise regarding interpretation and the role of "intervention" in the local practices of certain African societies. If autobiography is the means by which women represent themselves, then to understand their subjective experience of excision and its affective and cultural ramifications, we need to look for traces of these preoccupations in their texts and to listen to their silences.

Saadawi's work often has a hypnotic, incantatory quality that draws the reader into its world. If, as Spivak puts it, "subjective structures can, in fact, give objective truth," then Saadawi's struggle in *Woman at Point Zero* to come to terms with Firdaus, "the real woman" (1) whose story she tells, testifies to her efforts to elevate this case study to the status of an exemplary narrative of female oppression and emancipation—in other words, to give universal appeal to the story of this Cairo prostitute who is awaiting execution in Qanatir Prison for the murder of her pimp.

In the author's preface, Saadawi states: "Firdaus is the story of a woman driven by despair to the darkest of ends. This woman, despite her misery and despair, evoked in all those who, like me, witnessed the final moments of [her] life, a need to challenge and to overcome those forces that deprive human beings of their right to live, to love and to real freedom" (iv). The author is emphasizing generally unproblematic values here, but these values could hardly be taken for granted in Anwar Sadat's Egypt. What makes her story compelling, then, is the highly personal tone, the erosion of distance between the authorial self and the narrating "I" of Firdaus. Indeed, if Saadawi is first drawn to Firdaus because of her exceptional nature, the focus soon shifts to their shared experience of oppression as women in a patriarchal culture. What the text puts in motion is a strategy of displacement and identification between two women who are "objectively" very different in their respective social class, education, and profession, but whose intimate experiences as women are uncannily similar. The narrative suggests that the universal can be known only through the particular or the personal: it is the concrete subjective experience of this "other woman" that allows the scholar to relate to her as woman and sister, and to bring her back to life through her writing.

There is, finally, an ironic parallel. Six years after the publication of her book, on September 5, 1981, Saadawi herself became a political prisoner, along with a thousand other people who were alleged to have committed crimes against the state and whom President Sadat considered threats to the stability of his regime. The telling of Firdaus's story thus becomes a rehearsal for Saadawi's own descent into the hell of an Egyptian prison. Saadawi is, and will become, Firdaus, the double that compels her. To tell Firdaus's story is to give voice to the "other" that haunts her, to see her own face in the contours of the prostitute's narrative, and to be provided with a moving link to her own experiences as an excised woman.

Trained as a research scientist, Saadawi initially distances herself from Firdaus, struggling to remain faithful to the (male) scholarly principles of "objectivity" which she has learned to value in her profession. She tries to maintain her calm, her detachment as a scientist, while stressing the disturbing and depersonalizing impact of emotion: "Subjective feelings such as those that had taken hold of me were not worthy of a researcher in science. I almost smiled at myself as I opened the door of my car. The touch of its surface helped *to restore my identity, my self-esteem as a doctor*" (5; my emphasis). The researcher in her exhibits a Western and male belief in the importance of autonomy and rationality. As Jessica Benjamin has argued: "Both in theory and practice [Western] culture knows only one form of individuality: the male stance of overdifferentiation, of splitting off and denying the tendencies toward sameness, merging, and reciprocal responsiveness"[24] That is why Saadawi tries to negate the value of sensory perceptions in the acquisition of knowledge: when the prison warder tells her that she "senses"

---

[24]Jessica Benjamin, "The Bonds of Love: Rational Violence and Erotic Domination," in *The Future of Difference*, ed. Esther Eisenstein and Alice Jardine (New Brunswick, N.J.: Rutgers University Press, 1985), 46.

that Firdaus "knows" Saadawi, the author ponders, "Why should that indicate that Firdaus really knew me?" (5). Because Saadawi is powerfully attracted to Firdaus, she fears for her own autonomy and objectivity. But her discovery of the "sameness" of their experiences militates against her continued adherence to male standards of rationality. Her self-doubts signal a move toward *indifferentiation*: Firdaus becomes a figure for the sister whose eyes succeeded in bringing Saadawi's disintegrative self/world back to a coherent point where agency—in the form of resistance to excision, as well as in the act of storytelling—became possible again because she identified and merged with the feelings of her sister.

Firdaus first refuses to see Saadawi, and this rejection threatens to undermine the doctor's self-confidence, her faith in her work: "Compared to her, I was nothing but a small insect crawling upon the land amidst millions of other insects" (3). Yet however much she may try to distance herself, Saadawi cannot escape the gradual but ineluctable fusion with her case study. The narrative sets this course in motion from the very beginning: both women experience feelings of self-doubt for which they compensate by expressing a need to "feel superior to everyone else" (11). Although Saadawi understands that Firdaus's refusals are directed not at her personally "but against the world and everybody in it" (5), she feels threatened by the other woman's strength. When Firdaus finally agrees to talk, and the physician is called back, Saadawi lyrically describes her feelings of jubilation: "I walked with a rapid, effortless pace, as though my legs were no longer carrying my body. I was full of a wonderful feeling, proud, elated, happy. The sky was blue with a blueness I could capture in my eyes. I held the whole world in my hands; it was mine. It was a feeling I had known only once before, many years ago. I was on my way to meet the first man I loved" (6).

Saadawi's dependence on Firdaus's acceptance of her erodes all her attempts to keep her distance. A doubling occurs and functions as a metonymic displacement between author and narrator, whose voices so echo each other that it is hard for the reader to know who speaks. Saadawi's journey takes her into Firdaus's world, under Firdaus's control: when she enters the cell to talk, it is Firdaus who orders her to "sit down on the ground"(7) and who demands, "Let me speak. Do not interrupt me" (11). Saadawi loses her sense of reality, does not feel the cold and bare ground under her; she becomes completely absorbed in "the voice of Firdaus," as if entering a dream or a trance like state of complete self-dissociation. The first and the last parts of the book, framing Firdaus's actual autobiographical tale, respectively end and begin with the same passage describing the author's entry into an oceanic state: "It was the cold of the sea in a dream. I swam through its waters. I was naked and knew not how to swim. But I neither felt its cold nor drowned in its waters" (7, 107).

The novel thus begins and ends by blurring the distinctions between "subject" and "object," psychiatrist and case study, author and prisoner, biography and autobiography, fiction and documentary. The narrative seems to enact a pattern which, according to Rita Felski, is common to the genre of the feminine confession and to its authors: namely, "their overwhelming yearning for intimacy." Felski asks: "What . . . are the reasons for this blurring of the distinction between autobiography and fiction in feminist literature? Feminist confession exemplifies the intersection between the autobiographical imperative to communicate the truth of unique individuality, and the feminist concern with the representative and intersubjective elements of women's experience . . . Feminist confession often reveals particularly clearly the contradictions between the desire for total intimacy and union, which seeks to erase all boundaries between desire and its object, and the act of writing as a continuing deferral of any such identity."[25] In *Woman at Point Zero* the desire for intimacy is first of all the author's. Saadawi develops a strong need to be close to Firdaus, to understand her and be accepted by her. The decision to write a novel is an attempt to deal with the interest and fascination that had developed during the interviews Saadawi carried out in the prison cell: "[Firdaus] vibrated within me, or sometimes lay quiet, until the day when I put her down in ink on paper, and gave her life after she had died." (iii).

"Until I put her down on paper": by writing down and giving back the other woman's life, Saadawi assumes control over the obsession that had consumed her. But Firdaus too yearns for intimacy.

---

[25]Rita Felski, *Beyond Feminist Aesthetics: Feminist Literature and Social Change* (Cambridge: Harvard University Press, 1989), 109, 93, 108.

When she meets Sharifa Salah el Dine, the madam who becomes her mentor, or when she talks of her love for Ibrahim, a co-worker, it is in terms similar to those used by Saadawi: "The sky over our heads was as blue as the bluest sky" (51); "It was as though I held the whole world captive in my hands. It seemed to grow bigger, to expand, and the sun shone brighter than ever before. Everything around me floated in a radiant light" (82). The repetitions form a leitmotif that interweaves Saadawi's subjectivity with Firdaus's. Both voices merge into one; both bodies experience the same feelings of loss and detachment from surrounding reality with occasional and fleeting experiences of fulfillment. Past and present, self and other mirror each other, and the narrative accentuates the interchangeability of speaker and listener as intimate and private experiences point to a common sense of loss and betrayal deeply rooted in their memories.

The preface and the first and last parts of the narrative relate the author's personal reactions to Firdaus and situate the middle part as a first-person retelling of Firdaus's oral confession; thus, to read the novel is to be twice removed from the original story, which is, however, retold in a way that preserves the flavor of the oral exchange. The almost obsessive use of repetition as a narrative device allows the reader to enter into the consciousness of both subjects, to take part in an organic process of storytelling in which it becomes impossible to separate the teller from the tale.[26] Saadawi/ Firdaus tells a story that unmasks an ancient truth about patriarchy: namely, that women need not fear what enslaves them, that freedom and "reciprocal responsiveness" are possible. Even if the outcome is death, the story is a posthumous lesson in courage—a lesson that Saadawi also gives us as an activist and a writer of "resistance literature" whose books are banned in her own country.[27]

[26]As Trinh T. Minh-ha has observed: "In this chain and continuum, I am but one link. The story is me, neither me, nor mine. . . . My story, no doubt, is me, but it is also, no doubt, older than me" (Woman, Native, Other: Writing, Postcoloniality, and Feminism [Bloomington: Indiana University Press, 1989], 122–23).

[27]See Barbara Harlow, Resistance Literature (New York: Methuen, 1987), 137–40. See also "Living the Struggle: Nawal el Saadawi Talks about Writing and Resistance with Sherif Hetata and Peter Hitchcock," Transition 61 (1994): 170–79. Saadawi discusses her role in forming the Arab Women's Solidarity Association (AWSA) and the continued censorship in Egypt of some of her works.

As she explains in her introduction to the *The Hidden Face of Eve*, Saadawi sees her writing as having a social function that is bound to disturb and unsettle those in power: "It was also natural that a small minority express their fear, or even panic, at words written by *a pen sharp as a scalpel that cuts through tissue to expose the throbbing nerves* and arteries embedded deep in a body. ... My pen will continue to lay bare the facts, clarify the issues, and identify what I believe is the truth."[28] Using her pen as a scalpel, Saadawi turns back on society the instrument of torture that is used on her. Like her, Firdaus was marked at a very young age by the mutilation of excision, by the intervention of the mother and her accomplice, the woman who carries "a small knife or maybe a razor blade" (13). Firdaus mentions this initial trauma without any commentary. It is a brief parenthesis, a secret no sooner shared than buried in the enveloping silence of the text; the act is never again mentioned. But what returns is the insistent questioning of the body, of its sensations of pleasure and pain, "a pleasure [she] ... had lived in another life ... or in another body that was not [her] body" (48). Identical terms appear seven times in the narrative (14, 22, 26, 33, 48, 56, 78) to describe these sensuous physical impressions. Firdaus's confession uses this refrain to underline the link between her unfulfilled desire for intimacy and the erotic awakenings that set her body adrift toward innumerable male bodies, toward prostitution—accepted passively at first, then freely chosen because "as a prostitute [she] had been looked upon with more respect" (75) than when she was a "respectable" (70) employee.

Firdaus's silence is in sharp contrast to Saadawi's graphic confession (cited earlier), which fills in the blanks of the novel. In both cases, the mother is cast as an instrument of the patriarchy, as the means by which "femininity" is initially reproduced, thus allowing the system to perpetuate its hold on each generation of girls. For Firdaus, the betrayal of the mother and the loss of intimacy are metaphorized throughout in the use of a recurring trope: it is the image of two eyes, "two rings of intense white around two circles of intense black" in which each color grows more intense, more engulfing. Firdaus is overcome by the gaze,

---

[28]Saadawi, *Eve*, 3 (my emphasis).

which is linked at first to her mother's enveloping, supportive presence: "Two eyes to which I clung with all my might. Two eyes that alone seemed to hold me up" (17). Later, these eyes are evoked when she meets Iqbal, a schoolteacher, and the feeling is one of intense, nameless pleasure: "I held her eyes in mine, took her hand in mine. The feeling of our hands touching was strange, sudden. It was a feeling that made my body tremble with a deep distant pleasure, more distant than the age of my remembered life, deeper than the consciousness I had carried with me throughout" (29–30). This "deep distant pleasure" is articulated as a "memory," as the trace within the body of "something no sooner remembered than forgotten" (33), intangible yet real, a loss of physical being which motivates and subtends her later denunciations of the familial, social, and political structures that maintain sexual oppression.

It is particularly interesting that the pervasive and undefined sense of loss communicated by Firdaus should correspond so precisely to what object relation theorists have articulated as an archaic yearning for the mother's body, for the plenitude of indifferentiation. In her discussion of mother-infant relationships, for example, Nancy Chodorow has argued that this early relationship, with its issues of "primary intimacy and merging," is crucial in establishing the foundation for future adult relationships.[29] Adults all have some aspect of self that wants to recreate the experience of primary love, the feeling of comfort and satisfaction derived from the sense of identification with another. As Michael Balint has suggested, "This primary tendency . . . is the final aim of all erotic striving."[30] In Saadawi's narrative, the mother-daughter relationship is based on a fundamental lack, the lack of trust, the lack of physical continuity between the two, which contrasts sharply with the lateral, sisterly identification described at the scene of excision in *The Hidden Face of Eve*. This lack engenders a desire for nurturance which is trans-

[29]Nancy Chodorow, *The Reproduction of Mothering: Psychoanalysis and the Sociology of Gender* (Berkeley: University of California Press, 1978), 79.

[30]Quoted in ibid. As Abel has noted, "Feminist object relations theory . . . explicitly locates the production of gendered subjectivity in historically specific and socially variable caretaking arrangements" ("Race, Class, Psychoanalysis?" 185). It thus seems highly appropriate to use Chodorow to interpret Saadawi's novel.

lated into an erotic longing for intimacy with Iqbal, Sharifa, or Ibrahim.

It must be noted that the death of Firdaus's mother is immediately followed by a move from the familial home and the native village to the city and the uncle's apartment, where she has her first glimpse of herself in a mirror: the scene is one of misrecognition which fills her "with a deep hatred for the mirror" (21) and for the features of her face that remind her of either her father ("the big ugly rounded nose") or her mother ("this thin-lipped mouth" [20]). Fragmented by disconnections, her image of herself points to the inaugurating experience of the self-portraitist as described by Michel Beaujour: "emptiness and absence."[31] Separation from her rural home breeds self-hatred and propels Firdaus on a search for other experiences of love and closeness which will reproduce the primary intimacy of early childhood, the experience of what Chodorow calls "boundary confusion or equation of self and other."[32]

Also worth noting is Saadawi's first encounter with Firdaus, which actually places Firdaus in an ambiguous position in relation to gender, suggesting that her sexual identity is androgynous and therefore disruptive and disturbing to the social order. Thus, when the prison doctor first describes her to the author-narrator, Saadawi reports his words in indirect speech: "[He] told me that this woman had been sentenced to death for killing a man. Yet she was not like the other *female* murderers held in prison" (1; my emphasis). It is through his words that the reader and the narrator first encounter Firdaus. He inscribes her as a feminine presence/absence, an enigmatic and silent figure ("She . . . won't speak to anyone. . . . She asked for pen and paper. . . . Perhaps she was not writing anything at all"), sensual and duplicitous ("If you look into her face, her eyes, you will never believe that so gentle a woman can commit murder" [1]). But, by contrast, what the narrator *hears* is a strong, highly masculine voice: "The voice was hers, steady, cutting deep down inside, cold as a knife. Not the slightest wavering in its tone"

[31]Michael Beaujour, *Miroirs d'encre* (Paris: Seuil, 1980), 9.

[32]Nancy Chodorow, "Family Structure and Feminine Personality," in *Woman, Culture and Society*, ed. Michelle Z. Rosaldo and Louise Lamphere (Palo Alto, Calif.: Stanford University Press, 1974), 57–58.

(6). This voice connotes an instrument: the knife that foreshadows the murder of the pimp. The cold-blooded murder is the ultimate act of resistance and liberation on the part of Firdaus, an act comparable in fact to the act of writing for Saadawi, since writing produces similar consequences—imprisonment, solitary confinement—and since Firdaus's description of the murder echoes Saadawi's metaphors for writing: "I raised the knife and buried it deep in his neck. . . . I stuck the knife into almost every part of his body. I was astonished to find how easily my hand moved as I thrust the knife into his flesh, and pulled it out almost without effort. . . . I realized that I had been afraid, and that the fear had been within me all the time, until the fleeting moment when I read fear in his eyes" (95).

To infer a parallel between the act of writing and the act of murder allows us to further the comparison and identification between Saadawi and Firdaus. There is dissymmetry between the act of writing, which is an act of creation, and the act of murder, which is a form of suppression; but there is also symmetry in the movements of the hand that guides the pen on the paper or the knife into the flesh. To write (for a woman) and to kill are both forms of social transgression that lead to jail. The pen that inscribes words on the page and the knife that indelibly marks the body are means of control, tools whereby power can be appropriated. Since the foundational sign of appropriation and power is, of course, the masculine gesture of sexual possession, in which the penis can be used as a weapon (as in an act of rape), it becomes clear why Firdaus is such a subversive figure. Her fundamental transgression is that she reverses the traditional social roles on a symbolic as well as a real level: she trespasses on male sexual territory by using the knife as a means of penetration. Similarly, Saadawi's inscription of a woman's text on the masculine fabric of Egyptian culture is a form of trespass that deserves punishment because it interferes with the culturally acceptable codes of femininity.

What motivates Saadawi's writing is her hope for the future, her desire to "lay bare the facts." Similarly, when Firdaus talks about exchanging secrets and sharing stories with her school friend Wafeya, she does so in order to paint a picture of the future which can give them both hope and courage: "If I had something to say, therefore, it could only concern the future. For the future was still mine to paint in the colours I desired. Still mine to decide about freely, and change as I saw fit. . . . Sometimes I imagined that I would become a doctor, or an engineer. . . . I kept imagining myself as a great leader or head of state" (25). To appropriate the knife or pen is to appropriate the future, to dream of its possible configurations beyond the limitations of gender and class and, most of all, beyond the limitations of mutilation. Saadawi's desire for an "objective" stance parallels Firdaus's wish for a "masculine" role. But each woman needs an interlocutor to legitimate her quest, to provide reciprocity and intersubjective exchange. This reveals each woman's preoccupation with issues central to the relational nature of female subjectivity, to what Chodorow calls "the lost feeling of oneness."[33] Firdaus moves through the text with a physical yearning for the "paradise" of childhood, which is associated here with a time "before"—that is, before the betrayal by the mother and the torture of excision.

In contrast to her feelings of having a body that she does not experience as her own, her description of male bodies gives them a materiality and a specificity that borders on caricature. There is the ostentatious piety of the village fathers as they come out of the mosque every Friday, "nodding their heads, or rubbing their hands one against the other, or coughing, or clearing their throats with a rasping noise, or constantly scratching under the armpits and between the thighs" (13). Her image of the father who eats alone in front of his starving children has echoes of Ousmane Sembene's depiction of the polygamous husband in his movie *Mandabi*: "His mouth was like that of a camel, with a big opening and wide jaws. . . . His tongue kept rolling round and round in his mouth as though it also was chewing, darting out every now and then to lick off some particle of food that had stuck to his lips, or dropped on his chin" (19). Her old husband has a disgusting face with an open and smelly sore; her clients, whether clean or dirty, rich or poor, are nothing but heavy bodies under which she closes her eyes and waits.

Physically and verbally battered, Firdaus feels a rage that culminates in the scene of the murder. This cathartic moment helps her realize that anger sets her free to *reappropriate* language, to face

---

[33]Chodorow, *Reproduction of Mothering*, 79.

"the savage, primitive truths" (102), and to be beyond fear and death. Firdaus finally names herself: refusing to be a victim, she is willing to be a criminal because she prefers, as she puts it, "to die for a crime I have committed rather than to die for one of the crimes *you* have committed" (101). This *you* names the ultimate *other*, the one who creates *my* hell.[34]

To Spivak's question "How am I naming [the other woman]? How does she name me?" Saadawi might answer in the words of Roland Barthes and Nadine Gordimer: that a "writer's enterprise— his [sic] work—is his [sic] essential gesture as a social being" and that writers "take risks they themselves do not know if they would."[35] When Saadawi braids her identity with that of Firdaus because of their shared experience of pain and betrayal, she gives us a powerful example of feminine textuality as what I call *métissage*, as dialogical hybrid that fuses heterogeneous elements.[36] Because Saadawi's use of the pen lands her in jail just as surely as does Firdaus's use of her knife, we are in the presence of a mutual and reciprocal "naming" that effaces differences in order to point to an *essential* truth: beyond their social differences the two women share a nominal essence *qua* excised women.[37] Since this sexual mutilation is the most important cultural signifier of femininity, "biological" femininity becomes a culturally determined fact, linked to specific local practices. When Saadawi denounces those practices, she puts herself in jeopardy. By appealing to universal human rights, she attempts to build bridges across cultures, showing the validity of a "Western" mode of analysis (psychoanalytic object relation theory) which allows her to name her subjective experience of pain and to situate it within an *inter*subjective context. As a critic who does not belong to the Islamic Egyptian culture, I am nonetheless interpellated by this dimension of the narrative, and I must respond to it in a way that "universalizes" the integrity of the body.

---

[34]I allude here to Jean-Paul Sartre's famous statement "L'enfer, c'est les autres [Hell is—other people]," from his play *Huis clos* (*No Exit*).

[35]Nadine Gordimer, *The Essential Gesture: Writing, Politics, and Places* (New York: Knopf, 1988), 286–87, using Roland Barthes's formulation in *Writing Degree Zero*, in *Barthes: Selected Writings*, ed. Susan Sontag (London: Fontana, 1983), 31.

[36]See *AV*, chap 1.

[37]See Diana Fuss, "Reading Like a Feminist," *differences* 1 (Summer 1989): 78, and *Essentially Speaking: Feminism, Nature, and Difference* (New York: Routledge, Chapman & Hall, 1989).

But, I would argue, this form of universalism does not objectify the other and subsume her into my world view; what it does is create a relational space where intersubjectivity and reciprocity become possible.

7
The Limits of Universalism:
Identity, Sexuality, and Criminality

Believe that even in my deliberateness I was not deliberate.
—Gwendolyn Brooks, "the mother"

I am trying to create a genre of legal writing to fill the gaps
of traditional legal scholarship, . . . to write in a way that reveals the intersubjectivity of legal constructions. . . . One of
the most important results of reconceptualizing from "objective truth" to rhetorical event will be a more nuanced sense
of legal and social responsibility.
—Patricia J. Williams, *The Alchemy of Race and Rights*

Further discussion of the issue of female genital excision, which
exemplifies the clash of cultures resulting from the postcolonial migrations of the late twentieth century, may help to "illuminate" the
social contexts within which the "structural dissymmetry" of gender is embedded.[1] This chapter examines the issue in the context of
the culture of immigrants from Mali who now live in France.

Excision has come to the attention of public opinion in France,
and other western European countries, because immigrants are
having it performed on their daughters. Medical and school professionals, social workers and lawyers, anthropologists and psy-
chiatrists have been called upon to attest to the existence of the
practice, to interpret its meaning, to testify to its effects on the physical and mental health of children, and to speculate about the merits
of criminalizing it through the courts. Viewed as intolerable by
Western critics since early colonial times, excision can be fatal and
is increasingly considered—in the West—a violation of basic human rights.[2]

The fact that the practice exists in Europe began to surface at a

---

[1] Fatima Mernissi, *Beyond the Veil: Male-Female Dynamics in Modern Muslim Society*
(Bloomington: Indiana University Press, 1987), ix.

[2] See esp. Allison T. Slack, "Female Circumcision: A Critical Appraisal, "*Human
Rights Quarterly* 10 (1988): 437–86.

time when the rights of all children were being widely debated and legislation enacted to protect them from various forms of physical and sexual abuse. On 2 February 1981 a new law was introduced into the French penal code with the express purpose of repressing violence against minors. Article 312-3 of the code specifies the various legal sanctions that can be used to punish those found guilty of assault and battery on minors, or "coups et blessures volontaires à enfants de moins de 15 ans." In 1993, Article 229-10 was added to the new penal code, stating that those who inflict "bodily mutilation" on a child under the age of fifteen can be sentenced to a fifteen-year prison term for a criminal offense. Since then, judicial cases tried on the basis of this law have raised complex cultural questions. They have all involved African families whose daughters had been subjected to excision.

This rite of passage is meant to mark entrance into adulthood and is normally accompanied by extensive psychological preparation in the form of religious teachings and ritualized observances. When transferred by immigrants from their own countries to their new homeland in France, however, much of the ritual apparatus is absent, and the operation is sometimes performed at an extremely young age, which may result in death. Mantessa Baradji, a five-week-old baby girl, died of a slow hemorrhage on 3 April 1983, the day after she had been excised. This case, as well as two nonfatal ones—involving Batou Doukara and Assa Traore, excised respectively at the ages of three months in 1980 and one week in 1984—were tried in criminal court, and suspended jail terms of one to three years were given to the parents. The justice system is becoming ever more severe in its attempt to suppress the practice.[3] But at the same time, a serious legal controversy has emerged around these decisions.

The debate opposes two apparently conflicting versions of human rights, one based on the Enlightenment notion of the sovereign individual subject, and the other on a notion of collective identity grounded in cultural solidarity. Critics of the Enlightenment ver-

[3]See "Les Mutilations sexuelles: L'Excision," *Droit et Cultures* 25 (1993): 135. On 10 January 1993 the *New York Times* reported that under this article a Gambian woman, Mrs. Teneng Jahate, had been sentenced to five years' imprisonment, four of them suspended, on charges of causing the wounding and mutilation of her two baby daughters, aged one and two years.

sion of human rights have opposed to it more culturally specific concepts of human dignity. These can vary, as Rhonda Howard points out: "They are embedded in cultural views of the nature of human beings, which in turn reflect the social organizations of particular societies;" she adds that "in Africa, idealized versions of human dignity reflect idealized interpretations of pre-colonial structure."[4] When emphasis is on the group, protection of the individual *qua* sovereign individual subject can be at odds with her development as a fully functioning member of her own society. By criminalizing the practice of excision and sending the parents to jail, the French courts have judged individuals guilty of an act of violence, when in fact they had no intention of committing violence; their behavior was in accord with deeply held sociocultural and religious beliefs about the nature of femininity and the function of sexuality in their respective collectivities. Anthropologists and social critics have argued that legal sanctions will have little if any positive impact, since families may continue to have excisions performed either clandestinely in France (and with greater risk to the girls' life and health) or back in Africa during school vacations.

Geneviève Giudicelli-Delage has pointed out that France is the only European country that actually prosecutes "les auteurs et complices d'excision [those who operate or aid and abet in the operation of excision]." This, she says, may involve the judicial system in serious blunders, because "le prétoire pénal est le lieu où l'on juge exclusivement des comportements individuels et non un lieu où l'on débat de pratiques collectives [the criminal court is the place where individual behavior only is to be judged, it is not an arena for debate about collective practices]."[5] Nevertheless, a jury trial in Paris in March 1991 concluded with a harsher punishment than any previously imposed: a five-year jail term for Aramata Keita, a resident of France and a member of the caste of women ironworkers who traditionally perform excision in Mali; and five years' suspended sentence with two years' probation for the parents, Sory and Sémité Coulibaly, who had had their six daughters excised by Keita in 1982 and 1983.

[4]Rhonda E. Howard, *Human Rights in Commonwealth Africa* (Lanham, Md.: Rowman & Littlefield, 1986), 17.
[5]Geneviève Giudicelli-Delage, "Excision et droit pénal," *Droit et Cultures* 20 (1990): 207, 208.

As *Le Monde* reported in its coverage of the trial, the presence of the three accused in the dock would have seemed but "a pretext, were it not for the fact that they were risking imprisonment," for the courts seemed to be trying the practice rather than the persons involved: "The three accused listened to proceedings without understanding them. Their two interpreters did not translate the debate being conducted in court—which occasionally took on the air of a symposium." The woman public prosecutor dismissed experts' arguments regarding the pressures of ethnic customs and the ways in which such a practice forms part of a whole social system. Stressing the fact that Keita had received a financial reward for her services (ostensibly the symbolic and documented offering of a *pagne* [cloth] and some soap, but presumably unacknowledged monies as well, totaling approximately one hundred francs), the prosecutor demanded—and got—an exemplary decision from the jury: "From today on, it must be made quite clear to every African family that excision has become a money making activity which risks incurring a very heavy sentence."[6] Under the guise of protecting young girls from a "barbaric mutilation," the French legal system thus victimized three individuals who were not themselves treated as persons in their own right during the trial, since it was clear that their intentions, motivations, and responsibility—which are the foundations of individual guilt before the law—could not be interpreted as criminal.[7] As the respected ethnopsychiatrist Michel Erlich has explained, the reasons for the continued performance of this practice are compelling psychosexual ones for those involved, since it is embedded in a cultural context that encodes it as a beautifying and enriching phenomenon without which girls do not become women and will therefore never be able to marry, have some degree of economic security, and lead "full" female lives.[8]

Many women and men in Africa and the Middle East have denounced excision, (see Chapter 6), putting in place complex "strat-

[6]See the articles by Maurice Peyrot, "L'Excision, crime coutumier," *Le Monde*, 8 March 1991; "Ethnologie comparée à la cour d'assises," *Le Monde*, 9 March 1991; and "Une Condamnation pour l'exemple," *Le Monde*, 10–11 March 1991, trans. as "Tribal Practices Pose Dilemma for Western Society," *Guardian Weekly*, 24 March 1991.

[7]See Giudicelli-Delage, "Excision," 205.

[8]Michel Erlich, *La Femme blessée: Essai sur les mutilations sexuelles féminines* (Paris: L'Harmattan, 1986).

egies for eradication," in Olayinka Koso-Thomas's words, in such countries as Senegal, Sierra Leone, and Egypt.[9] But those who object to the practice agree that education remains the essential tool. Legal action cannot be justified, because no law in France specifically forbids excision; the penal code must be *interpreted* as relevant to these particular cases. The social, economic, and psychological consequences of jail for the families of the condemned parties are ignored by the courts, which thus manifest a blatant disregard for collective, familial, and community values and, under the pretext of protecting the abstract rights of an individual child, penalize the child by arbitrarily sentencing her parents for the purpose of making an example of them.

To reflect upon the contradictions and difficulties arising from these complex human rights issues, a working group called Atelier Droits des Peuples et Droits de l'Homme was organized at the Centre Droit et Cultures of the University of Paris, Nanterre. The preliminary results of this workshop published as a series of essays in the journal of the center, *Droit et Cultures*, are important because they help to define the discourse about identity and sexuality within immigrant communities in France, and because they reopen the question of universal rights in an unprecedented way.

The increasing diversity and plurality of French society have given rise to cultural conflicts that continue to erupt around such topics as citizenship, habitation, schooling, dress, and the rhetoric of difference and equality, or integration and xenophobia, that characterized political discourse in the 1980s. These conflicts are forcing a reexamination of the principles of universal democracy and natural rights that had theoretically been taken for granted since the French Revolution of 1789. As Raymond Verdier explains, it has become necessary to rethink the familiar Western dialectic based on the oppositional paradigm of the individual versus society, and to conceptualize in its place "des droits dits de la solidarité [rights based in the concept of solidarity]":

The approach we propose would not take the individual subject as its point of departure, but would look at the human being as a member

---

[9]See Olayinka Koso-Thomas, *The Circumcision of Women: A Strategy for Eradication.* (London: Zed Books, 1987).

of a diversified community. This would avoid the recourse to either the pure cultural relativism that undermines the unity of the human race or the totalitarian pseudo-universalism that would refuse the right to difference and lead to the negation of all cultural and religious identity, in keeping with "the modern individualist configuration of values."

This is a difficult conciliation, and it requires a deep understanding of cultural traditions, of their evolution and transformation, on the one hand, and, on the other, a critical look at the notion of identity so as to avoid falling into the traps of ethnocentrism.[10]

The practice of female excision is a kind of ideal test case, since it apparently illustrates absolute and total cultural conflict between the rights of the individual to bodily integrity and the individual's need to be satisfactorily integrated into a community. As Michel Erlich reminds us, the right to bodily integrity is by no means an absolute value even in Western society, since male circumcision, tonsilectomy, and appendectomy--which can be viewed as ritual forms of surgery comparable to ethnic "mutilations," and which have been the object of controversy among medical professionals— *are* culturally acceptable and thus do not fall under the structures of the French penal code.[11] Furthermore, under what Erlich calls a form of *misogynie médicalisée* (medicalized mysogyny), excision was frequently performed (as were ovariectomy and hysterectomy) from the seventeenth to the early twentieth century to treat nymphomania, hypertrophy of the female genitalia, masturbation, and lesbianism. A famous seventeenth-century French surgeon named Dionis is credited with being the first to recommend excision "as a remedy against female lasciviousness."[12] To defend excision on

[10]Raymond Verdier, "Chercher remède à l'excision: Une Nécessaire concertation," *Droit et Cultures* 20 (1990): 149.

[11]Michel Erlich, "Notions de mutilation et criminalisation de l'excision en France," *Droit et Cultures* 20 (1990): 151–62.

[12]Erlich adds: "Adopted by Levret, this radical medical solution inaugurates a strategy of repression of female sexuality the sadism of which will be on the increase during all of the nineteenth century. Clitoridectomy was first used in 1822 by Graefe to treat 'masturbatory madness,' and forty years later, it was chosen as a panacea by Barker-Brown, the famed British surgeon who will be remembered by posterity as the champion of 'therapeutic' excision. At about the same time, Battey, an American, and another great mutilator, proposes ovariectomy, that is female castration, which he defines as 'normal,' as a means of treatment for a number of nervous ailments. This medicalized form of misogyny culminates in England during the Vic-

strictly cultural relativist grounds is thus as misguided as to condemn it on universalist and humanitarian ones, since complex psychosocial phenomena both in Europe and elsewhere have motivated its existence, and only education and information combined with an open and tolerant approach to different definitions of identity and sexuality may eventually succeed in eradicating it.

Can one oppose the practice on a feminist epistemological ground? Can one argue that in all the foregoing cases the common denominator was conscious or unconscious, individual or collective misogyny aimed at curbing all manifestations of female sexuality and thus representing a universal fear and hatred of women, which must be countered by the appeal to a universal approach to human rights, the only means of protection for female children in misogynist cultures? Ideally, perhaps one can. But to condemn excision as a violation of human rights is to presume that such a practice is the only culturally sanctioned form of violence that deserves to be denounced, whereas we know that many other forms of violence are not repressed by law in the Western context, and that some of our own practices are objectionable and shocking to Africans.

Erlich, expressing doubts about some radical Western feminist arguments, states that it is "un étrange paradoxe" that women's right to pleasure and to the integrity of their bodies "is linked to a legislation that legitimates abortion, a major mutilation the legalization of which did indeed contribute to female liberation in our society, but which is still considered a crime by many and judged as such in those cultures that practice mutilations, which our humanitarian activism has decided to treat with mutilating means."[13] To accept the legality of abortion but criminally repress the performance of excision is one of those paradoxes of contemporary legal practice that seem arbitrarily to condemn "exotic" or "foreign" barbaric practices, regardless of predecents in our own culture that are legal and acceptable to a majority because they are situated within a particular framework of rights and gender that no longer shock our sense of fairness or interfere with our freedom

torian era, but in the United States, it will continue to be performed during the twentieth century, and some doctors will still be prescribing it into the 1950s. This is how the medical uses of sexual mutilation evolve from the domain of physical pathology to that of psychological pathology" (ibid., 156).

    [13]Ibid., 161.

to live according to our own values. Although Erlich does not elaborate on the parallel he draws with abortion, the suggestion is provocative and compelling because it sets the abortion issue within a context of reproductive rights that forces a reexamination of both feminist individualism and modern notions of freedom of choice.

Given the social stigma that still attaches to unwed motherhood among the middle classes, and the financial and emotional difficulties in which a single parent will continue to be involved so long as the responsibility for raising a child is primarily the mother's, one might argue that there is no real "freedom of choice" for many women who decide to have an abortion. Indeed, don't some of them—like the African women influenced by their communities' views on excision—decide to have an abortion because it is either the only possible solution in an economic and cultural context that may force them to choose between earning a living and motherhood, or the only way to gain acceptance within their own social or professional communities as women who are truly in charge of their own lives and reproductive capacities? The rhetoric in favor of abortion has stressed the rights of women to choose, and that is why the law should protect that right and sustain the legality of the procedure. Note also that the parallel Erlich draws between abortion and excision is based *not* on a religious view of the fetus as a "person" whose rights are in conflict with those of the mother (as the fundamentalist Christian right would have it) but on a view of pregnancy as a "natural" consequence of female sexuality, just as we might see the clitoris as a "natural" part of the female body. In this view, abortion, like excision, simply imposes cultural constraints on physical reality, and both procedures can arguably be defended by their proponents as cultural steps taken to avoid biological determinism.

The question of choice thus remains problematic when one focuses not just on individual rights but on the way such rights may conflict with the broader social, religious, or communitarian values to which an individual woman must subscribe if she is to remain a respected member of her community, as opposed to being a "free" agent in our increasingly atomized capitalist culture. Here again, the modern individualist view of freedom leaves much to be desired, since identity remains closely linked to particularist views of reproductive rights and sexual choices and, in the case of women choosing motherhood, to their (by no means universal) right to health care, day care, and social programs that will help in the task of raising children.

What all this suggests is that radical individualism is an empty word for women, whether they live in "traditional" societies whose practices are shocking to citizens of modern states that theoretically protect human rights, or *are* such citizens living under a comforting illusion of choice that does not sustain critical scrutiny if we examine the supposedly "voluntary" acts involving sexuality and reproduction. Similarly, ritual practices are not adhered to "voluntarily": the mother who, like Sémité Coulibaly, solicits the services of a woman to excise her daughters believes that she is conforming to the traditions of her community and that failing to do so would jeopardize her daughters' chances of being accepted by their community of origin. Furthermore, refusal to allow excision of the daughter could endanger the mother's opportunity to engage in the slow process of liberation that now allows African women living in France to oppose polygamy, to work, and to enroll in literacy programs *so long as* they are not perceived by the immigrant community to be imposing these "new" values on their own daughters: "If on top of all this we seem to be appropriating the girls, we'll be rejected by everyone, sent back to the village," one woman exclaimed. Her fear is echoed by most of the Soninké of Mali who participated in a study conducted in Paris by Catherine Quiminal.[14]

At stake is the definition of tradition itself, the way it forms part of a network of power within which notions of freedom, community, and authority conflict. As Quiminal points out: "Like all traditions, the sexual mutilation of women is a 'tradition' only to the extent that the women concerned have no choice but to submit to it or else be excluded from their community. As soon as they are contested, traditions are revealed to be but the expression of power relations, arguments of authority."[15] Excision makes clear how power relations are inscribed on the female body by virtue of its subjection to particular sexual traditions. As noted above, the

---

[14]Catherine Quiminal, "Les Soninké en France et au Mali: Le Débat sur les mutilations sexuelles," *Droit et Cultures* 20 (1990): 190.
[15]Ibid., 183.

reasons for this practice have to do with complex definitions of masculinity and femininity that construct the clitoris and the male prepuce as vestiges of the opposite sex which must be eliminated for a "proper" sexual identity to exist. Thus, the female body is considered "too masculine" and socially unacceptable when not marked by excision. Malian women are culturally dependent on this view of sexuality; it forms the basis of their feminine identity. This situation illustrates Michel Foucault's insight that "the political technology of the body" amounts to a "system of subjection" of individual persons within a specific cultural code.[16]

It is interesting to note that in the African context the discourse on female sexuality defines femininity in terms of binary *cultural* inscriptions (male circumcision/female excision) rather than purely biological categories of male/female. One is not simply born "a woman"; one becomes a female person after having submitted to a cultural process. Similarly, a "person" is not a person until he or she has been marked by society in a way that confers dignity and social status within a specific ethnic group. Isaac Nguema has stressed that throughout "traditional" Africa "la personne humaine n'a de valeur qu'à l'intérieur de son groupe ethnique. . . . la personalité juridique . . . s'acquiert au fur et à mesure que la personne franchit les étapes de la vie: à l'occasion de la circoncision, . . . du mariage, . . . de la naissance des enfants [the person has value only as a member of her own ethnic group. . . . the legal personality . . . develops as one goes through different stages of life: on the occasion of circumcision, . . . marriage, . . . and the birth of children]."[17] Thus, he argues, the African notion of "person" is more interactive and dynamic than the Western one, which he sees as "abstract, mechanistic, static, materialistic," and intolerant of genuine solidarity, since an absolute view of individual rights necessarily conflicts with a genuine form of familial or cultural solidarity.

Problems then arise because the power of Malian culture to invest meaning in the individual body is at odds with the power of the French state to construct that body's biological integrity according to modern notions of individual rights. When Malians fall un-

[16]Michel Foucault, *Discipline and Punish: The Birth of the Prison*, trans. Alan Sheridan (New York: Vintage Books, 1979), 26.

[17]Isaac Nguema, "Universalité et spécificité des droits de l'homme en Afrique: La Conception traditionnelle de la personne humaine," *Droit et Cultures* 19 (1990): 215.

der the authority of the French courts on French territory, their bodies are invested with full responsibility for their actions and intentions, and they become liable to imprisonment not so much because performing or abetting the performance of excision is a violation of the rights of children (as the application of Article 312-3 would suggest) but because the state locates meaning and identity in the individual, autonomous body of its *citizens*. Because the Coulibalys reside in France, it is the authority and sovereignty of the French courts that are exercised; the Coulibaly's identity as immigrants supersedes their "Africanness." Sylvie Fainzang is well aware of the specifically legal aspect of a dilemma increasingly familiar in a pluralistic society, one that faces all those who live in two cultures with a foot in each world: "Excision is thus performed in order to obey a law; it results from the need to conform to a collective practice, and from the fact of being subjected to a social constraint. Individuals are thus caught as in a vise between two opposing laws: to obey the one ipso facto leads to breaking the other."[18] The two laws represent two systems of power which hold sway over individual responsibility, undermining the very possibility of assigning individual blame. These cases demystify the fiction of the sovereign subject, since the subjectivity of the defendants can easily be shown to be the site of conflicting and contradictory constraints. In Foucault's terms, the "power-knowledge relations" created by the courts' intransigence is a reflection of the absolute noncommensurability of the two cultural systems that interface in these cases.

Indeed, since excision can very well be defined as a "custom" in the technical sense allowed by French law (according to Article 327 of the penal code), it should be exempt from criminalization, just as corporal punishment of children is exempt because it is considered an acceptable form of parental behavior sanctioned by "custom" as understood by this law.[19] The crux of the matter is clearly a question of which juridiction has authority over the persons accused, and what constitutes "custom" or tradition or precedent under that jurisdiction.

Giudicelli-Delage puts it clearly: "Just as our public order/sys-

---

[18]Sylvie Fainzang, "Excision et ordre social," *Droit et Cultures* 20 (1990): 180.
[19]See Philippe Merle and André Vitu, *Traité de droit criminel* (Paris: Cujas, 1984).

tem of law and order could not accommodate an opposing order based on a foreign system of laws, it cannot tolerate a foreign and opposed practice/custom. Within the conflict of cultures that excision foregrounds, any position that might suggest a tolerant attitude toward this practice on French territory is condemned in the name of our own internal public order, and of fundamental human principles. Our culture can only proclaim its vigorous opposition to excision. But by which means can it do so? The judicial way, as is currently done, the legislative way, or yet a 'third way'?" For Giudicelli-Delage, there is no doubt that the only worthwhile and effective approach is the "third" one: that is, cooperation with those African countries that are slowly struggling to put new cultural forms in place by educational, not repressive, means: "Il faut pour chasser une ancienne coutume qu'une nouvelle prenne sa place, qu'une nouvelle culture se forge at non se voit imposer [The way to phase out an ancient custom is to allow a new one to replace it, to let a new culture forge itself, not to impose one from above]."[20] To apply abstract Enlightenment values in a rigidly intolerant legal way is to undermine the system's own claim to universality, since it thereby condemns practices that form part of a network of social values upon which rests the global equilibrium of a *different* culture. These practices are not just irrational and aberrant abuses, as many uninformed Western critics would like to believe. It is in fact possible to see them as part of a coherent, rational, and workable system—albeit one as flawed and unfair to women as our own can be.

The 8 March 1991 ruling marks the Coulibalys as subjected inhabitants of the French state. Their identity is thus reconstructed by the same set of legal rules that will apply when the decision is made to grant them citizenship in accordance with the rights of immigrants. In fact, because the right of immigrant families to citizenship is not clear, immigrants acquire different "national" identities (and the customs that go with them) as a result of the same kinds of power relations that arbitrate either in the case of rulings penalizing excision or when the need to impose a certain construction of sexual identity supports the practice of excision. As Sylvie Fainzang explains, "The analysis of discourses relating to this practice reveals that sexual mutilations are a means of disciplining in-

---

[20]Giudicelli-Delage, "Excision," 203, 206–7, 210.

dividuals, of rendering them fit for the social role which is reserved for them because of their gender. This sexual differentiation is motivated by the will to distinguish among different statuses. . . . The sexual marking provided by excision is the necessary condition of access to a specific social status, that of *woman subjected to the authority of man*. The practice of excision thus depends on the will to create the (physical) conditions of the (social) domination of woman by man."[21] On the one hand we have immigrants who are subordinated to French law; on the other, females brought under the authority of males. In either case, it would seem that we are very far indeed from any individualist conception of rights. It is a conception of identity as subordinate to either the state (France) or the ruling patriarchy (in Mali) that governs the legitimacy of parental behavior. It is therefore pointless to claim that the issue opposes communitarian values to universal ones; the actual conflict hinges on the opposing claims of two different communities, one of which would like to believe that its culture is a "universal" one.

What does appear to be "universal" when we carefully examine the whole cultural contexts within which the debate is situated is the way in which *different* cultures, for better or for worse, impose *similar* constraints on the bodies of their members, especially when those bodies are already marked by the sign of the feminine. Both cultures—-the French and the African—have ways of disciplining and socializing the body that denote highly complex sociocultural organizations, and the work done by the Centre Droit et Cultures attests to the long-term educational process that still needs to take place in order for African immigrants to liberate themselves from age-old customs *and* for the French legal system to accommodate the increasing diversity that is now French society. This diversity has the incontestable merit of underscoring the injustices and inequities of our own culture and of reminding us that "'le barbare, c'est d'abord l'homme qui croit à la barbarie [the barbarian is first and foremost the one who believes in barbarism]," as Claude Lévi-Strauss once put it.[22]

[21]Fainzang, "Excision," 177–78.
[22]Claude Lévi-Strauss, *Race et histoire* (Paris: Gonthier, 1961), 22.

8

Narrative Journeys: The Reconstruction of Histories in Leïla Sebbar's *Les Carnets de Shérazade*

Exoticism . . . shows well its fundamental justification, which is to deny any identification by History.
—Roland Barthes, *Mythologies*

Our history (or more precisely our histories) is shipwrecked in colonial history.
—Jean Bernabé, Raphaël Confiant, and Patrick Chamoiseau, "In Praise of Creoleness"

In all her novels, Leïla Sebbar successfully stages the contemporary diversity of French society and the survival strategies deployed by immigrants in their attempts to stake out a cultural terrain. In her *Shérazade* trilogy she explores the fascination that exoticism and Orientalism exert upon the imagination of her heroine, a young *beure* (an Arab born in France of immigrant parents) who works her way across France and through its museums, discovering there for the first time a representation of her own cultural heritage. This journey is a cultural itinerary that succeeds in establishing a set of seductive relations between a mythic France and an equally mythic Orient, at the crossroads of which Shérazade engages in self-discovery through self-displacement.[1]

Shérazade, who insists on this nontraditional spelling of her name, is a paradigmatically postcolonial subject who constructs her *monde diffracté mais recomposé* (diffracted, but recomposed world), and her identity, through her own work of oral storytelling.[2] The

[1]Leïla Sebbar, *Shérazade* (Paris: Stock, 1982); *Shérazade*, trans. Dorothy Blair (London: Quartet Books, 1991); both cited as *Sh*; *Les Carnets de Shérazade* (Paris: Stock, 1985), cited as *CS*; and *Le Fou de Shérazade* (Paris Stock, 1991).

[2]See Jean Bernabé, Raphaël Confiant, and Patrick Chamoiseau, *Eloge de la créolité* (Paris: Gallimard, 1989), 27 and esp. 34–39. "In Praise of Creoleness," trans. Mohamed B. Taleb Khyar, *Callaloo* 13 (1990), 892 and 895–98. The manifesto of these Caribbean writers describes a reality shared by Creole peoples but also a predica-

narrative becomes the site of a mediation and subversion of the visual representations that assign Shérazade her place in the discourses held by European cultures on the subject of the Oriental woman. The dialogue sparked between Shérazade and this order of representations becomes the driving force of a story that allows her to question and unravel the Orientalist myths in order to weave a new tale, one better suited to her own discoveries.

Like the eighteenth-century heroine *Manon Lescaut*, Shérazade is an itinerant, fugitive, picaresque character and something of a social parasite,[3] whose role is indispensable to the cultural redescriptions performed by the text. The classic novel by Abbé Antoine-François Prévost, often linked to the origins of the French novel, is also a story about the origins of French colonialism. The adventures of the Chevalier des Grieux and his lover Manon are inscribed in one of the "grand narratives" of the Enlightenment: stories of the great migrations of settlement and conquest of the New World by Europeans. Manon's transatlantic passage to America, however, ends in failure, and she dies in Louisiana. Like many Romantic heroines, Manon is defeated.[4] Unlike her, Shérazade succeeds in mapping out a new geography, not on the margins of the colonial empire but on the very territory of the former colonial power.

I begin by reformulating the question of the relations that obtain between different models of fiction and a postmodern conception of history and representation. Sebbar's *Les Carnets de Shérazade*, the second volume of the trilogy, is a useful text for analyzing both the common ground shared by postmodern and postcolonial writers and the divergent narrative solutions they propose to the problem of cultural fragmentation. *Les Carnets* presents a fictional itinerary marked by the contact and conflict of cultures, and it therefore raises the question of the relations between métissage and postcolonial identity, autonomy and interdependence, philosophical rel-

---

ment common to Maghrebian peoples, as well as immigrants and *beurs* living in France. See Carmen Bernard and Serge Gruzinski, *Histoire du Nouveau Monde: Les Métissages* (Paris: Fayard, 1993), for a comprehensive historical approach.

[3] I use this term in the sense made familiar by Michel Serres, *Le Parasite* (Paris: Grasset, 1980).

[4] The term "defeat" alludes to Catherine Clément's *L'Opéra ou la défaite des femmes* (Paris: Grasset, 1979), whose argument, though it deals neither with Prévost nor with Massenet's opera, applies perfectly to Manon.

ativism and critical humanism, deconstructionist ideology and multiculturalism. It is important to emphasize that deconstruction *qua* epistemology has emerged simultaneously with decolonization and has therefore been inextricably bound with a new vision of postcolonial realities and solidarities.

My approach is positioned in relation to current disciplinary controversies concerning the critical domain covered by the expression "Francophone literature." There has long been talk of replacing the term "Francophone" with one that would better reflect the diverse and heterogeneous realities of the discipline. The term "national literatures of French expression" has been used; others prefer "emergent literatures," especially since the University of Minnesota Press launched a series under that title in the 1980s. The series publishes translations of various contemporary novels, including *Amour bilingue* (*Love in Two Languages*) by the Moroccan writer Abdelkebir Khatibi, whose critical and theoretical essays serve as an important point of reference in this discussion.[5]

The attempt to redefine an increasingly protean discipline in light of the diverse geographic areas it covers—all of them marginal in relation to a canon and a center, "Franco-French" literature—has certainly become necessary. It is in the wake of deconstructive theoretical reflections upon what is the "center" with respect to the "margins" that this redefinition continues and that my current contribution is situated. The point, simply put, is to reject any reductive opposition between French literature and "Francophone" literatures, and to rethink the very idea of literature. After all, as Khatibi says, "Qui se réclame encore . . . de l'unité de la langue française? Qui parle encore aujourd'hui de LA littérature française? [Who still appeals to . . . the unity of the French language? Who today still speaks of THE French literature?]"[6] There has been at least since

---

[5] Abdelkebir Khatibi, *Amour bilingue* (Paris: Fata Morgana, 1983); *Love in Two Languages*, trans. Richard Howard (Minneapolis: University of Minnesota Press, 1990). See also Khatibi, *Figures de l'étranger dans la littérature francaise* (Paris: Denoël, 1987), and *MP*. I am not promoting the "emergent literatures" expression here, since it strikes me as ideologically suspect, suggesting an implicit opposition between canonical works and texts that innovate in opposition to them. I simply want to contextualize the debate. In my view, there has always been an interdependence between traditions, but this relation has often been obscured in the interests of rigid nationalism.

[6] Khatibi, *Figures*, 15.

Montaigne a network of influences and relations between the systems of representation of the "metropole" and the subjects or objects represented, whether in sixteenth-century texts on "cannibals," eighteenth-century literature on Persians, or the Africanist discourse of poets and novelists of the nineteenth century.[7] If these real or imaginary cultural contacts gave Montaigne the material for some of his essays, today they provide for Khatibi and Sebbar a language in which to narrate and reconstruct their *histoire raturée* (crossed-out history).[8] As a number of critics and anthropologists have noted, cultural exchanges on a global scale, far from creating strongly homogenized societies, tend to facilitate the evolution of a system of interdependencies and interrelations, a *métis* life-world where disparate traditions cross over and interrogate one another in the complex diachronic and synchronic field of discourse.[9]

The conflict that opposes the center to the margin is, according to Michel Foucault, the same ideological conflict that separates those who conceive of History as an uninterrupted continuity and those who understand contemporary societies through models of heterogeneity and heterotopy.[10] As Foucault explains in his *Archaeology of Knowledge*, the vision of uninterrupted history is tied to a certain conception of the subject:

Continuous history is the indispensable correlative of the founding function of the subject: the guarantee that everything that has eluded

[7]See Malek Alloula, *Le Harem colonial* (Geneva: Slatkine, 1981); *The Colonial Harem* trans. Myrna Godzich and Wlad Godzich (Minneapolis: University of Minnesota Press, 1986); Edward Said, *Orientalism* (New York: Vintage Books, 1979); Chandra T. Mohanty, "Under Western Eyes: Feminist Scholarship and Colonial Discourses," *boundary 2* 12/13 (Spring–Fall 1984); Christopher Miller, *Blank Darkness: Africanist Discourse in French* (Chicago: University of Chicago Press, 1985); V. Y. Mudimbe, *The Invention of Africa: Gnosis, Philosophy, and the Order of Knowledge* (Bloomington: Indiana University Press, 1988); and Tzvetan Todorov, *Nous et les autres* (Paris: Seuil, 1989); *On Human Diversity: Nationalism, Racism, and Exoticism in French Thought*, trans. Catherine Porter (Cambridge: Harvard University Press, 1993).

[8]To use Edouard Glissant's expression in *Le Discours antillais* (Paris: Seuil, 1984), 133; *CD*, 64.

[9]See Jean-Loup Amselle, *Logiques métisses: Anthropologie de l'identité en Afrique et ailleurs* (Paris: Payot, 1990), 9–10; Ulf Hannerz, "The World System of Culture: The International Flow of Meaning and Its Local Management," quoted in James Clifford, *The Predicament of Culture: Twentieth Century Ethnography, Literature, and Art* (Cambridge: Harvard University Press, 1988), 17n; and this book's introduction.

[10]Michel Foucault, "Of Other Spaces" *Diacritics* 16 (Spring 1989): 22–23.

him may be restored to him; the certainty that time will dispense nothing without restoring it in a reconstituted unity; the promise that one day the subject—in the form of historical consciousness—will once again be able to appropriate, to bring back under his sway, all those things that are kept at a distance by difference, and find in them what might be called his abode. Making historical analysis the discourse of the continuous and making human consciousness the original subject of historical development and all action are the two sides of the same system of thought.[11]

Against this totalizing and teleological vision of time, Foucault opposes a continuously changing network of nodes, a system of relations binding together a diversity of sites as well as subjectivities that are always in process.

For the colonial or postcolonial writer, caught in this unstable landscape despite herself and subjected to a system of thought that consigns her to the margins while necessarily implicating her in the system whose language she uses, the question of historical change has always been a primordial one. After all, how does one reconcile a vision of history whose "function is to ensure the infinite continuity of discourse" with the linguistic, spatial, and temporal dispersion of a once colonized subject? How does this subject reconcile the rêve d'habiter (dream of belonging and inhabiting),[12] the quest for a home, and the fate of being constantly torn between the metropole and its satellites, between the center that defines her and that she carries within and the margin where she must try to live and work—when her only tools are the same representational system that paralyzes her by negating her? No doubt this subject must try to conceive her relation to the other in a nonhierarchical and egalitarian fashion, without accepting the binary opposition between the societies "without history" and the European societies that claim to manifest a "historical destiny."[13] The massive dis-

---

[11] Michel Foucault, *The Archaeology of Knowledge and the Discourse on Language*, trans. Alan M. Sheridan Smith (New York: Pantheon, 1972) 12.

[12] Ibid., 25. See the excellent special issue of the Haitian journal, *Chemins Critiques* 1 (December 1989), titled, "Le Rêve d'habiter," especially the articles by Maryse Condé, "Habiter ce pays, la Guadeloupe"; Michèle D. Pierre-Louis, "La Quête de l'ailleurs"; Laënnec Hurbon, "Le Rêve d'habiter"; and Yannick Lahens, "L'Exil: Entre écrire et habiter."

[13] I thank Jean-François Fourny for having drawn my attention to the Heideggerian expression "historical destiny." See Martin Heidegger, "The Question Concern-

placements of population from the former colonies to the metropoles of the center have today reversed the patterns begun in the Renaissance and described in *Manon Lescaut*. This reversal has transformed the entire situation, along with the concepts of tradition, linearity, and referential illusion, which Western critics have learned to suspect through the works of Foucault and Derrida and which postcolonial writers have been deconstructing for two generations.

As Khatibi has noted, "*deconstruction,* as an overcoming of Western metaphysics, and as it has been developed in Derrida's singular style, has accompanied *decolonization* as an historical event. . . . This coincidence is not accidental." The *dé-constitution du savoir* (deconstitution of knowledge) has allowed a new generation of writers to avoid being duped by a "simplified Hegelianism" (in the style of Sartre or Fanon) and thus feeling "tenaillés par les affres de [la] conscience malheureuse [crushed by the torments of bad conscience]." According to Khatibi: "That is why, as we converse with Western reflections on difference (those of Nietzsche, Heidegger, and, among our close contemporaries, Maurice Blanchot and Jacques Derrida), we take into account not only their style of thinking but also their strategy and their weapons, in order to press them into the service of our struggle, which is necessarily another exorcism of the mind, demanding an effective decolonization, a concrete thinking of difference [une pensée concrète de la différence]."[14]

If it is true that we find this "pensée de la différence" put into practice in the project of demystification launched by various contemporary authors—from Samuel Beckett to V. S. Naipaul, Maurice Blanchot to Thomas Pynchon—this project remains negative with them, a vehicle of nihilism. These authors do not go beyond highlighting the failure of every form of transcendence, the conceptual impasse reached by all belief in absolute truth (whether it be political or humanitarian, religious or philosophical), and the concomitant fragmentation of the postmodern subject. But for authors such

---

ing Technology," in *Basic Writings,* trans. William Lovitt (New York: Harper & Row, 1977); and "Über 'die linie,' " in *The Question of Being,* trans. William Kluback and Jean T. Wilde (New Haven, Conn: College & University Press, 1958). See also Fourny, "Un conteur du Caire," *Yale French Studies* 82 (1993): 158–71.

[14]Khatibi, *MP,* 47–48, 50, 15, 20. See also Mary Ellen Wolf, "Rethinking the Radical West; Khatibi and Deconstruction," *L'Esprit Créateur* 34 (Summer 1994): 58-68.

as Maryse Condé and Leïla Sebbar, this fragmentation is not necessarily a fatal breakdown and dispersion; for them, the attempt to
deconstruct tradition is oriented toward a moment of insight, a *prise
de conscience*, that leads to renewal and affirmation. Its objective is
a practice of difference that targets not only the fictional domain,
the telling of a story and the narration of history—what Tzvetan
Todorov calls *l'histoire racontante* and Linda Hutcheon, "historiographic metafiction"—but also the cultural context of the narrative,
the broad domain of everyday practices, the symbolic realms of our
pluralistic, polyphonic, and intertwined societies.[15] Sebbar and Khatibi, like Salman Rushdie or Assia Djebar, create dispersed images
that reflect the contingencies of multiculturalism, whose social relations are constantly in a state of renegotiation. It is therefore not
surprising that these fictional postcolonial texts find resonance with
many contemporary readers: marginalized, exiled subjects and cultural nomads. Although such readers must invest themselves in the
work in order to make sense of it, they can discover there linguistic
forms and an eclecticism that parallel their daily experience.

It is in the fictional narration of the quotidian that writing becomes permeated by orality and that the oscillation between the
written and the spoken word reveals the essential preoccupation of
these postcolonial writers: namely, to let the silenced migrants and
cultural minorities speak in their own voices. Through their use of
linguistic particularisms the writers transform the dominant language, rendering it porous and open to what was once its other.
Such an approach, as we have already seen, is frequent among
Caribbean writers whose goal is either to creolize the French language (Condé, Chamoiseau) or to subvert it through the creation
of arresting neologisms (Césaire), neologisms that transform, in an
unexpected way, the relation between French and Creole (which is
increasingly being conceived of as a linguistic continuum rather
than a simple diglossia; see Chapters 2 and 3). This invention of a
protean hybrid language is the common denominator of many writers from the third world, as Khatibi defines the term: "What I call
the third world is that formidable power of survival and transfor-

mation, that plural thinking of survival which must live in its unspoken liberty, a liberty without a final solution.... Whoever maintained that new civilizations are not already at work in the place where everything appears to be inert, dead, inconsistent, and absurd?" (*MP*, 17).

Since there are no more "grand narratives" to legitimate knowledge, the crumbled past of the postcolonial subject can now be narrated only in stories and *histories* that convey the fundamental heterogeneity of her experience. The reader is therefore forced to situate each text in relation to a historical context whose function is not to make the novel more "authentic" but to highlight the symbolic interpenetrability of history and fiction, of the real and the mythic. A discursive space suspended between different yet often inseparable, cultural spaces, the postcolonial novel exhibits the mixture of cultures and the métissage of forms that also defines the "postmodern condition."

The métissage of forms is distinguished in the Caribbean and African Francophone context by a set of complex relations to official History. History is experienced and conceptualized by Francophone writers in three distinct modalities, deployed either simultaneously or sequentially, depending upon the requirements of their project. Understanding the originality of such authors as Devi, Condé, Cliff, and Sebbar requires an awareness of these three modes.

On the one hand, history can simply be *suffered*. This is the case for Véronica in Condé's *Heremakhonon*. Véronica represents the colonized subject who has come to an awareness of her situation but, as a result of her search for unavailable certainties, becomes mired in disdainful self-mockery. Caught in a vicious circle, she cannot escape her need for origins, even when these turn out to be illusory. Because she considers her own legitimacy uncertain, Véronica falls into the impasse of exile. The weight of her "yearning for history"[16] is the mark and sign of a lack of being which can never be made good.

On the other hand, for Aimé Césaire, Léopold Sédar Senghor,

---

[16]"The yearning for history is in the harking back to a history so often relived, the negation of history as encounter and transcendence, but the assumption of history as passion" (*CD*, 81).

and the negritude poets, history is a discourse to be *taken on*: one takes back the discourse of the colonizer in order to invert it, placing a positive value on everything previously considered negative. One reclaims the cultural values and spirituality of the black world and opposes them to European rationalism and what Condé has called "la technicité desséchante du monde blanc [the desiccating technicity of the white world]."[17] One puts down roots in a mythic Africa, Fanon's "great black hole," where a rediscovered chronology and point of origin foster the emergence of a self-awareness that was previously lacking.[18] But this myth of the origin is, in the end, nothing but an inverted image of the other, as both Frantz Fanon and Maryse Condé have emphasized.[19]

In both these modes, the writer remains dependent upon a system of representation created by European discourse and thus imposed by the other. The quest for origins and the search for antecedents remain central, whether they succeed or fail.

The third modality, shared by the texts whose postcolonial strategies interest me here, consists of a radical and subversive *appropriation* of the cultural codes by a subject who constructs herself through her discourse. Underlining the ruptures of the historical perspective, this subject projects herself in the fictitious and the fabulous, thereby authorizing herself to assume her own destiny through utterances that allow her to construct her own symbolic context. The past is neither *suffered* nor *taken on*. It is re-presented and redefined according to criteria that correspond roughly to the decentering of the subject effected by contemporary philosophy. There is no longer any synthetic activity by a subject of history, real or fictional—just an endless reproblematization of time and space with respect to a relational, hybrid context, always fluid and mobile. Movement becomes at once interior and discursive. It does not lead to a point of origin (geographic or mythic) but allows one to reconnect the severed ties of the colonial diaspora, following a model and a logic that deal in fruitful pluralities rather than sterile

[17]Maryse Condé, "Négritude césairienne, négritude senghorienne," *Revue de Littérature Comparée* 3–4 (July–December 1974): 418.

[18]Frantz Fanon, *Toward the African Revolution*, trans. Haakon Chevalier (New York: Grove Press, 1969), 27.

[19]See also Fanon, *Black Skin, White Masks* (London: Pluto Press, 1986), and Condé, "Négritude."

particularisms. As Michel Serres notes, in this ideological context "the essential thing is never the image and its fullness of meaning, nor representation and its smoke and mirrors; the essential thing remains the system of relations."[20] These relations undergo constant redefinition through the redeployment of narrative and enunciative agencies.

Edouard Glissant names this aesthetics a "poétique de la Relation,"[21] which he defines as follows:

> This practice of cultural Creolization [métissage] is not part of some vague humanism, which makes it permissible for us to become one with the next person. It establishes a Relation, in an egalitarian and unprecedented way, between histories that we know today . . . are interrelated. . . . The aesthetic we have come up with is that of a nonuniversalizing diversity, the kind that seemed to me to emerge from global Relation. . . . A nonessentialist aesthetic, linked to what I call the emergence of orality: not to the extent that the latter dominates the audio-visual but because it summarizes and emphasizes the gesture and the speech of new peoples. (CD, 249, 253)

For Leïla Sebbar too, "colonialism has given rise to phenomenal historical displacements." She adds, "I am not sure that these displacements have always been negative; they have overturned archaic and oppressive traditions, and have given rise to progress through the contact of cultures."[22] These critics are echoed by sociologists such as Dominique Schnapper, who stresses that the phenomenon of migrant acculturation produces identities that "can only be defined as an ongoing creation."[23] The work of postcolonial authors remains the privileged locus for this "ongoing creation" of plural identities. The encounter between the other and the same, presented from the perspective of this "other," promotes "cultural

---

[20]Serres, Parasite, 15.

[21]Glissant's translator renders "Relation" in this context as "cross-cultural relationship"; I have followed Glissant in identifying this special sense by capitalizing the R and have modified the quotation accordingly.

[22]Leïla Sebbar, in her exchange of letters with Nancy Huston, Lettres parisiennes: Autopsie de l'exil (Paris: Barrault, 1986), 119.

[23]Dominique Schnapper, "Modernité et acculturations," Communications 43 (1986): 151.

reinterpretations" which, in turn, influence the network of representation and signification to which the literature belongs.

Two general tendencies can be traced in the novels of Sebbar, as in those of Condé and Cliff: deconstruction of the myth of stability surrounding the dominant culture, its myth of sameness; and positive valuation of the diversity and heterogeneity of the other. The goal is to demonstrate the possibility of opting out of the discourse of sameness without thereby falling into the trap of symmetry—a trap that the essentialism of negritude was not able to avoid. That is why, in Cliff, Condé, and Sebbar, the appropriation of narrative is a process of incorporating a number of linguistic and visual coordinates that produce what I would term a combined reality check and reality effect. Condé and Cliff reconstruct the Caribbean imaginary, introducing in the colonial language a vocabulary that describes the unspoken experience of their people. This vocabulary allows access to a symbolic structure that changes as the narratives progress. The narratives thus articulate real and dynamic relations of "ongoing creation" in connection with the diverse cultures sustaining them.

Similarly, Sebbar's novels, which belong to what has been called the "Maghrebian literature from France," allow us to hear the voices and expressions of Maghrebian immigrants, and her narrative integrates these oral patterns. It thus flaunts its own dispossession, since it knows itself to be, in Derrida's phrase, *parole soufflée*: hybrid speech, impure speech, always already borrowed from others and retransmitted by textual means.[24] Sebbar invents a new France, tailored to the migrants working their way across it. Her novels are examples of texts that are "unclassifiable" according to the traditional criteria that oppose "French" and "Francophone" literatures, since the standard opposition between the center and the margin is rendered inoperable. Neither "Francophone" nor exactly French, Leïla Sebbar herself is the type of the postcolonial writer whose (certainly metropolitan) works force us to rethink our pedagogical and ideological categories.[25] Her use of the themes of

[24]See Jacques Derrida, "La Parole soufflée," in *L'Ecriture et la différence* (Paris: Seuil, 1967), 253–92.

[25]See Michel Laronde, "Leïla Sebbar et le roman 'croisé': Histoire, mémoire et identité," *Celfan* 7 (1987–88); Mildred Mortimer, *Journeys through the French African Novel* (Portsmouth, N.H.: Heinemann Educational Books, 1990); and Winifred Wood-

exile, deracination, loss of memory, silence, and revolt places her among the Francophone writers who have risen up against the "civilizing mission" of France in Africa and elsewhere. But her original contribution is to have made immigrant women—doubly marginalized by their womanhood and their Arab identity—the very center of a work that problematizes the entire visual and discursive tradition of European Orientalism.

Born in Algeria of an Algerian father and a French mother, Sebbar chooses to write about what Michel Laronde calls "the *beur* indenture" while distancing herself from her fictional subjects.[26] Often denounced by Maghrebian intellectuals who consider her work suspect, given that she does not speak Arabic and is not herself an immigrant, Sebbar explains her position in letters to Nancy Huston:

> Every time I have to talk about my writing I must situate myself in my métissage, repeat that French is my mother tongue, and explain in what way I am neither an immigrant nor a *beure*, but simply an exile. Although I am certainly a gilded exile, I am from a land that is the land of my father and that haunts my memory, and I am living in a land that is the land of my mother, my language, my work, my children, but where I do not really find my home. . . .
>
> I am not an immigrant, nor the child of immigrants. I am not a Maghrebian writer "of French expression." . . . Now I know that I must find a way to speak, declare, affirm without ambiguity, without guilt, while saving myself the time to develop the subtleties of this singular position of mine: I am French, a French writer born of a French mother and Algerian father . . . and the subject matter of my books is not my identity. . . .
>
> My books . . . are the sign, the signs of my history, the history of a *croisée* [mixed-race person], of a *métisse* obsessed by her path and the intersecting roads, obsessed by the surrealist encounter of the Other and the Same, by the unnatural but lyrical crossing of the country and the city, . . . of tradition and modernity, of East and West. . . .
>
> I am there, at the crossing . . . in my place, after all, since I am a *croisée*, one who searches for a filiation, who writes in a lineage, always

hull, "Exile," *Yale French Studies* 82 (1993): 7–24, and *Transfigurations of the Maghreb: Feminism, Decolonization, and Literatures* (Minneapolis: University of Minnesota Press, 1993).

[26]Michel Laronde, "La 'Mouvance beure': Emergence médiatique," *French Review* 161 (April 1988).

the same, tied to history, memory, identity, tradition, transmission—
I mean to the quest for an ascendance and a descendance, a place in
the history of a family, a community, a people, with respect to History
and the universe. It is in fiction that I feel like a free subject (free from
father, mother, clan, dogma . . .) and strengthened by the responsibility and the burden of exile [*la charge de l'exil*]. Only there do I pull
myself together, body and soul, and build a bridge between the two
shores, upstream and down.[27]

Sebbar writes fiction in order to build herself a past and a future.
She plays on the historical foundations of discourse in order to
transform reality, putting into practice a *pensée nomade* (in Gilles
Deleuze's sense),[28] characterized by a play of overlapping and intertwining narrative voices. In *Les Carnets* we move from Shérazade's interior monologue to free direct and indirect discourses that
disregard the passage of time, moving upstream to blend stories
from sixteenth-century Arab Spain with the contemporary adventures of Jeanne and Saïd. These narratives reflect the ties that bind
the trucker (symbolically named Gilles Rivière) and Shérazade
(who can also go by the very French name Camille). Shérazade is
following the trail of North African immigrants and *beurs* out of
Marseille, while Gilles, born on the island of Ré, dreams only of
becoming a sailor and heading for the tropical isles, "from Pacific
to Pacific, passing through the Indian Ocean and the Caribbean
Sea" (*CS*, 21).

Representing the cultural itineraries and models of fiction that
develop according to a *logique métisse*, Sebbar's narrative progresses
through a set of relations that always postpone and defer the moment of conclusion. The activities of writing and reading come to
mirror each other, and a *mise en abyme* of the reading process is
activated from the very beginning of the narrative journey, since
Shérazade is writing in a notebook with the same title as that of
the book, *Les Carnets de Shérazade*. The notebook carries the number
seven, a symbolic number for Shérazade as well as the author, who
uses it in the organization of the book: Shérazade's journey through
France lasts seven days. Narrators and narratees interact in ways
that also mirror the writer-reader relation. It is not always easy to

[27]Sebbar and Huston, *Lettres parisiennes*, 125, 126, 138.
[28]Gilles Deleuze, "La Pensée nomade," in *Nietzsche aujourd'hui* (Paris: UGE, 1973).

identify the exact moment when the narrative perspective changes; the continual movement from the thoughts of one character to those of another obscures the trail. As the free direct or indirect discourse floats from one person to the other to communicate different points of view, the interest seems to lie not in the distinct individuality of each one but in the imperceptible slide from one identity to the other. While Shérazade is the nomadic fugitive, she also becomes all the historical and fictional characters whose adventures she recounts. Instead of erecting an artificial partition between the self and the other, the narrative shows how the narrator is transformed, step by step, with every story told, at every new stage of the voyage. She is at once the subject who speaks and the one whose story is reconstituted and absorbed in the text. Intertextuality thereby points toward a nomadism that is, in the end, only a problematization or *mise en abyme* of the very process of interpreting and decoding cultural ideologies. Reading the book thereby becomes a cultural itinerary that forces us to transpose the familiar and the foreign: the center-margin hierarchy is replaced by a more complex network or grid of interconnections.

Whereas the fictions of Condé and Cliff produce defamiliarization and estrangement on the level of *language*, Sebbar uses *visual* and literary associations to deconstruct the European tradition. Cliff and Condé travel to the interior of a European language, which becomes "other" while remaining an integral part of their imagination as "bilingual" writers and thus places them in an ambiguous relation to this code. Similarly, Sebbar takes up certain cultural myths in order to identify the source of their attraction and the fascination they still exert, thereby establishing a dialogue between the past and the present. Her approach is what Khatibi calls a "voyage dans l'inactuel et le mémorial [voyage into history and remembrance]": that is, a return to and dialogue with the past.[29] It is through this dialogue that her characters manage to construct a postcolonial identity that is emphatically not the internalization of the exotic desires projected on them by the dominant culture.

The narrative creates a space in which Sebbar can begin to rebuild an entire cultural memory, a mythic core into which she can then braid images of ancient traditions as well as new explorations

[29]Khatibi, *Figures*, 10.

undertaken in the course of her textual and visual journey. The journey becomes essential to her *appropriation* of time and space, history and geography. Shérazade brings along with her Flora Tristan's *Le Tour de France* and Rimbaud's letters, which serve as a constant frame of reference. Sebbar thus makes Khatibi's remarks her own and adopts his advice: "Let us walk with the travelers: they alone have guided me, in this literary map of time and space, in every metaphor of displacement, marginality, exile. To get near these figures of the stranger, I had to borrow their journeys, their crossroads, their wanderings, and their return to a paradoxical France."[30] This "paradoxical France" Sebbar calls *"la mythologie FRANCE."*[31] She does so in order to demystify the very concept of *"francité"*; her purpose, however, is to piece together a new symbolic space, hybrid and *métis*, in which difference and paradox show up precisely where one might have thought to find the *France profonde* of quiet pastures and authentic images. Under the guise of a simple linear narrative unfolding over a seven-day period, Sebbar completely destabilizes the cultural reality of the Hexagon.[32]

A traveler, Shérazade reinvents the travelogue as it was originally conceived by eighteenth-century writers (Gautier, Nerval, Flaubert, Fromentin, and others). A picaresque heroine, she is in motion. But this movement does not lead her from the margins to the center, as it does the heroes of Balzac and Stendhal who come to Paris from the provinces in search of happiness and fortune. As she looks for images in museums and libraries, Shérazade discovers herself through the Orientalist painters and their representation of odalisques. Her relation to the past, as to herself, passes through the medium of these historical associations. Through this medium, Sebbar shows us the process whereby women come to identify themselves with the images projected onto them by society, a process described by the critic John Berger:

To be born a woman has been to be born within an allotted and confined space, into the keeping of men. The social presence of women

---

[30]Ibid., 13.

[31]Sebbar and Huston, *Lettres parisiennes*, 40.

[32]The "Hexagon" is mainland France (the geographic region can be inscribed in a hexagon). This term is learned early by French schoolchildren and is synonymous with the idea of a well-ordered France.

has developed as a result of their ingenuity in living under such tu-
telage within such a limited space. But this has been at the cost of a
woman's self being split into two. . . .

And so [a woman] comes to consider the *surveyor* and the *surveyed*
within her as the two constituent yet always distinct elements of her
identity as a woman. . . . Men look at women. Women watch themselves being looked at. This determines not only most relations between men and women but also the relation of women to themselves.[33]

Because Shérazade is aware of the way she is viewed by the
dominant culture, her self-image is inscribed within the framework
supplied by this culture. But because the text presents and disman-
tles the mechanisms through which she became aware of the conventions that surround the representation of odalisques, she can
engage this dominant culture in a dialogue and take an active role
in decoding these images. She thereby introduces another discourse
into the very heart of the cultural conventions that only *described*
her as a passive, *watched* woman. As she invests herself in this code,
it is with the goal of *reinscribing* the images of odalisques in the
context of immigrant culture. As readers, we are therefore forced
to superimpose the two contexts, the two traditions, both of which
turn out to be plurivocal. Thus, when Gilles discovers Shérazade
asleep in his truck, we see him watch her as if she were a sleeping
odalisque:

Dans son camion, à Marseille dans les docks, il y a une fille endormie,
une inconnue. . . . On voit mal sa bouche renflée à cause de la position
du visage sur le skaï du siège molletonné. Elle a de longues paupières
bistres, orientales. . . . Il a regardé une moitié de fille, un demi-visage,
un corps . . . coupé en deux, exposé du côté droit. Il s'arrête à nouveau
aux mains nues croisées sur l'extrême bord du siège, dans la même
position, offertes et fragiles. [In his truck, on the docks in Marseille,
there is a woman asleep, a stranger. . . . Her mouth is barely visible,
bulging from the position of her face against the stuffed vinyl seat.
She has long eyelids, bister, Oriental. . . . He watched half of a girl, a
half face, a body . . . cut in two, exposed on the right side. His glance
stops anew at the bare hands crossed at the far end of the seat, in the
same position, open and fragile.] (*CS*, 13–15)

[33]John Berger, *Ways of Seeing* (London: Penguin, 1972), 46–47.

One need only think of Ingres's *Odalisque endormie* or *Odalisque à l'esclave* to recognize these artistic figures in the description of the young fugitive stretched out on the front seat, her face and body half concealed, half offered to the gaze of the observer. Here, Gilles's male gaze creates a *lieu commun*, a topos, of Orientalist paintings, situating the woman inside a specific cultural matrix that defines her as "strange" and "exotic." But Shérazade resists the efforts of these men who would like to assimilate her to this static image of passive womanhood. Touched by these images, she uses them to develop her own relation to colonial history, to construct her own ties to Algeria *and* France. Matisse's *L'Odalisque à la culotte rouge* hypnotizes her and forces her to leave (*Sh* 245). No longer a spectator but a reader—in the way Michel Tournier understands this in *La Goutte d'or*: one must learn to read in order to free oneself from the enslaving power of the image—Shérazade frees herself from both the weight of this tradition and the need for origins. The return to Algeria is never realized; it is constantly postponed as Shérazade continues to explore the paths of immigrants across France. All in all, we see her choosing a *beure*—therefore, *métisse*— identity, and not a univocal point of origin. It is the voyage that defines her, not the origin or the destination.[34]

When Shérazade, at the Louvre with her friend Julien, discovers Delacroix's *Femmes d'Alger dans leur appartement*, a dialogue is established (*Sh*, 98, 158). The canvas gives Julien an image of the Arab woman that influences the way he perceives and examines Shérazade. But for her, Delacroix's representation of this patriarchal imprisonment is the key that allows her to enter a previously unknown historical dimension: this canvas is her first visual contact with harem women. These women are "moins sultanes soudain que prisonnières. N'entretenant avec nous, spectateurs, aucun rapport. Ne s'abandonnant ni ne se refusant au regard. Etrangères mais présentes terriblement dans cette atmosphère raréfiée de la claustration [suddenly less sultanas than prisoners. They have no relationship with us, the spectators. They neither abandon nor refuse themselves to our gaze. Foreign but terribly present in this rarefied atmosphere

---

[34]See Michel Tournier, *La Goutte d'or* (Paris: Gallimard, 1986); *The Golden Droplet*, trans. Barbara Wright (New York: Doubleday, 1987).

of confinement]''; [35] Shérazade compares them to the North African women living in small apartments in the French suburbs like the one she had fled. She learns to read the current reality of Arabs in France in the light of this artistic context.

> The boy left her at the door of the apartment. . . . She rang. . . . The hallway was dark, the entrance minuscule. Shérazade remained standing at the door. . . . She had hesitated, alone on the landing, as if she were going to see her mother, her sister, the grown ones and little ones. . . .
>
> (Here) with Farid's mother, Shérazade remembered . . . the Oriental women of French painting, the white harem slaves, beautiful and idle among luxurious perfumes and silks, languid, as if asleep. . . . They were loved. But what about the Oriental women in France, in the districts at the outskirts of capitals, her mother, Farid's mother, . . . all of them cold among the gray and black bricks. (CS, 150–52)

These images build up a contrast between the small, dark apartments in the cold suburbs and the interiors depicted by Delacroix. Shérazade's position at the entrance of the apartment is the same as that of the painter, whose gaze invades the closed space of the harem. She takes over the painter's position but does so in order to denounce the stifling world of Arab women, their status as "Oriental women," displaced, dislocated, and shipwrecked in France.

Wandering across France, Shérazade discovers that diversion and diversity have always already been present in the Hexagon. From one library to another (one of them recalling Montaigne's very famous library), she forges a new vision of history, her purpose being to attempt a *re*construction of the past by using the disparate elements that are at her disposal:

> One evening, late at night, Shérazade was reading in the library. As if it was known that Shérazade would come to this house, there were rows upon rows of the books she sought. . . . There she found, available day and night, books that she read with the passion of one possessed. They told an ancient story, the story of her fragmented

---

[35] Assia Djebar, "Regard interdit, son coupé," in *Femmes d'Alger dans leur appartement* (Paris: des femmes, 1980), 171; trans. Marjolijn de Jager as *Women of Algiers in Their Apartment* (Charlottesville: University Press of Virginia, 1992), 136.

memory, and a new story, modern, where continents and civilizations crossed, *a history that would be her own.* (CS, 129; my emphasis)

One of the postulates of Orientalist discourse is to make the woman and the "Exote" into the very figure of absence.[36] Here the variables of the equation are transformed by a narrative that presents a revision of both the eighteenth-century novel and the nineteenth-century pictorial tradition. If at the end of her journey Manon Lescaut found silence and death in what Prévost describes as the vast sandy wilderness of the New World, Shérazade, by contrast, acquires the right to move freely across a land that she appropriates through the spoken and written word.[37] The history she reconstructs allows her to plant new stakes about her territory, a territory that expands in the course of a *récit* whose narrative economy is founded on the principle of exchange and barter—a principle as ancient as the one used by "the real Sheherazade" (CS, 141) in *A Thousand and One Nights.*

Like her namesake, Shérazade is a storyteller and a narrator who exchanges words for the possibility of going on. She trades her stories for Gilles's offer of transportation. She is the typical parasite. As Michel Serres puts it: "The parasite innovates. . . . It evades, it dodges exchange. It does not make an even trade, but makes change. It tries to exchange words for material substance, air for solid."[38] Through her mastery of speech, Shérazade succeeds in "making an exchange," thus transforming the symbolic economies of the culture. She constructs a parallel, inverted universe for herself, subjects it to continuous reorganization through the tactics and strategies of resistance that force her reader to rethink history, art, and literature in light of new paradigms. As Michel de Certeau noted, "immigrants are the pioneers of a civilization based on the blending of cultures."[39]

---

[36]I use the term "Exote" following Victor Segalen in *Essai sur l'exotisme: Une Esthétique du divers* (Paris: Fata Morgana, 1978).

[37]Abbé Prévost, *Manon Lescaut* (Paris: Garnier-Flammarion, 1967), 184–85.

[38]Serres, *Parasite*, 50.

[39]Michel Certeau, "Idéologie et diversité culturelle," in *Diversité culturelle, société industrielle, état national* (Paris: L'Harmattan, 1984), 232; and see de Certeau, *The Practice of Everyday Life* (Berkeley: University of California Press, 1984) for his distinction between a tactic and a strategy. See also Woodhull's careful interpretation of de Certeau's position in *Transfigurations*, 101–2. Woodhull is uneasy with the

Sebbar shares with all the postcolonial writers I have discussed in this book the goal of deconstructing European history and the cultural stereotypes it has served to transmit since the beginning of the colonial era. In *Les Carnets* this deconstruction of the representations and clichés of the dominant culture is accomplished through travel and the use of orality. Like the Caribbean writers, Sebbar tries to make orality intervene in the written, thereby infusing the narrative with the everydayness of the spoken, with an idiolect that is more or less recognizable to the reader, depending on the latter's position with respect to the microculture that is thus being brought forth: African, Indian, Caribbean, or regional French. This hybridization of the literary text in contact with its other—an oral otherness, internal to the text, from which emerges a muted and obscured cultural context—maps out a narrative strategy that establishes a dialogue between "high" and "low" culture, between the written record and popular experience, bringing together disparate, often antagonistic traditions and thus proposing a creative alternative to the polarizing and exclusionary approaches of dialectical thinking.

---

ambiguities of Sebbar's statements about her identity. I prefer to see this ambiguity as a source of both lucidity and agency.

Conclusion
Whither Feminist Criticism?

I began this study by asking whether a truly comparative and multidisciplinary feminist criticism can help us articulate a common ground for constituencies that appear to have become hopelessly polarized during the past decade or so of feminist academic practice. I have discussed the work of writers who search for forms of "universality" that do not negate the specificities of their own experiences. I have focused on literary texts and cultural problems, rather than on the vast field of theoretical feminisms. My reasons for doing so consist primarily in the fact that fictional works make concretely visible the networks of influence and the questions of identity that are central to the debates over authenticity and postcolonial culture. The ambiguities and indeterminacies inherent in the literary text prevent the articulation of rigid or universalizing theoretical conclusions.

I hope, however, that the investigations conducted in this book have shown that a feminist critical practice remains one of the most important intellectual tools for interrogating the production and circulation of both academic knowledge and symbolic economies. Feminist scholars in history, sociology, anthropology, psychology, psychoanalysis, philosophy, and literary theory have provided paradigms that have broadened our understanding of the politics of representation—and, more specifically, the representation of women as the *object* of patriarchal knowledge—across time and place, across disciplinary and cultural boundaries. What *literature* in particular (and critics who work on narratives by women) have contributed to this field of inquiry is the analysis and representation of the *subjective* experience of muted groups within social structures that rarely allow them to speak as subjects and agents of knowledge—except perhaps on the rare occasion when, having acquired a real or metaphoric "room of her own," a woman writer can finally narrate the real from a different perspective, and construct alternative scenarios. All the writers studied here have just such a contribution to make. Many of them have also written about their creative practices, and I have found it useful to let their comments guide my critical interventions.

Having encouraged cross-fertilization among different disciplines, feminism has been instrumental in interrogating the nineteenth-century model of the university organized around disciplines and periods. As Naomi Schor and Elizabeth Weed put it in an issue of *differences* titled "Feminism and the Institution," to question the traditional model of the university is "not only to critique and resist disciplinarization within the university, but to struggle against the split between inside and outside." It is of course true, as Elaine Marks affirms in the same journal, that one of the most surprising developments in women's studies and feminist theory in general has been "the reproduction of familiar discourses and paradigms that existed—whether in the United States, or France, or England, or Italy—within other political, intellectual, and pedagogical fields, as if the 'feminist' inquiry were imprisoned in national, sometimes chauvinist modes of thinking and writing." And Marks goes on to say: "'Feminist studies' worst enemies have been those who have treated 'feminism' like a new religion with dogmas that can allow for only one possible interpretation."[1]

I think the only way out of that fundamentalist feminist impasse is, and will continue to be, through the awareness of the multicultural, multiracial dimensions of various strands of feminism inside and outside the academy—and that is where working between disciplines has become imperative today. I hope my book will contribute to this continuing dialogue.

---

[1]Naomi Schor and Elizabeth Weed, editors' preface to "Notes from the Beehive: Feminism and the Institution," *differences* 2 (Fall 1990): vi; and Elaine Marks in Barbara Christian, Ann duCille, Sharon Marcus, Elaine Marks, Nancy K. Miller, Sylvia Schaffer and Joan W. Scott, "Conference Call," *differences* 2 (Fall 1990): 72–73.

Index

Reading Women Writing

A SERIES EDITED BY

Shari Benstock and Celeste Schenck

Printed in the USA
CPSIA information can be obtained
at www.ICGtesting.com
LVHW041533080823
754621LV00003B/209